1955

Happy Birthday

Paul Pearlman

The "Non Parent"

TYRANT *from* ILLINOIS

"While government by the deliberation of legislative bodies is not so prompt, and sometimes not so efficient, as the government of one or a few, yet it is not so liable to make the capital mistakes and the irrevocable blunders that have condemned absolutisms in the eyes of civilization."

—J. G. Cannon to the Sixty-first Congress.

JOSEPH GURNEY CANNON

TYRANT
from ILLINOIS

UNCLE JOE CANNON'S
EXPERIMENT
WITH PERSONAL POWER

by BLAIR BOLLES

NEW YORK

W · W · NORTON & COMPANY · INC ·

T O

MONA

Contents

TYRANT *from* ILLINOIS

The Noblest Roman

"UNCLE JOE" CANNON had an extraordinary number of friends. He survives in fame as a tyrant, bursting with mean stratagems, but until his sunset years, he was tolerant, benign, and fair. Those qualities won him the popularity which he exploited so curiously after three score ten for unexpected political ends. Even when he is recalled as the despot who made his whim fiat in Washington, his attractiveness dilates with each passing day for Americans of this mid-century era—considering that we live in disordered uncertainty whether life has any meaning and, if it has, in confusion whether it means that individual men should submerge their personal aspirations in order to assist their fellows to realize the combined mass wish of all. Cannon had serene conviction. He lived in the blessed state of knowing without doubting what he wanted for himself and his country. Yet oddly, Cannon can be thanked, or blamed, as much as any man for the sense of confusion that now bewilders us.

The evidence of the friendly feeling he aroused in his contemporaries is abundant. On his seventieth birthday his admirers at the Capitol gave him a party in the ballroom of the Arlington Hotel. Everybody who counted in politics in Washington was present. More to the point, the guests showed up because they liked him as a person, not merely because they respected or feared his position as Speaker of the House of Representatives (except a few like President Theodore Roosevelt, who forced himself to bow to Cannon from a sense of discretion). By midnight, when the sandwiches were curling and the whiskey was gone, Cannon had shaken 1,000 hands. Cannon was a Republican, but Democrats crowded the ballroom. By the old man's side in the receiving line stood Albert Sydney Burleson, a Democrat from Texas, who later joined Woodrow Wilson's Cabinet as Postmaster General. The room was decorated plainly, to suit Cannon's simple taste, but the atmosphere danced with good spirit. Cannon stood under red, white, and blue silk streamers which, fluttering in the breeze of an electric fan, bore this legend in gold letters: THE NOBLEST ROMAN OF THEM ALL. The guests applauded the sentiment.

In those days, in 1906, the Congressmen were so fond of John Joseph Gurney Cannon that they dared to express their goodwill in burlesque. Cannon was presiding over the House on a soggy June day about eight weeks after the birthday reception. He lolled in a high-backed chair, the homely seat of authority for the Speaker, as he fingered his gavel and gazed heavy-lidded at the streaks of sunlight pouring through the ochre-tinted glass roof of the chamber. At his elbow stood the invaluable Asher Crosby Hinds, his parliamentarian, who advised him on the precedents for any knotty situation on the floor. The galleries were full, and an air of expectancy hung over the hall. The last hours of the Congressional session had come. The day's meeting would end in adjournment *sine die*. A dozen whispered conversations filled the room with a kind of soft noisiness. They ceased suddenly when, without warning, the entire Democratic membership rose to their feet. Cannon hit the desk with the gavel to demand order, but the sound was overwhelmed by a screech of song from the standing members. Looking at Cannon, they shouted some homemade verses:

> Everybody works but Cannon,
> And he loafs around all day,
> Presiding in his office
> In a fascinating way.
>
> He's supposed to be the Speaker
> But Hinds is the whole show.

Everybody works in our House
But Uncle Joe.

When the song was over, Cannon joined the Republicans and
the visitors in the gallery in laughing with the Democratic glee-
men. The joke pleased the Speaker, who, everybody knew, spent
long hours at work in his office across the hall from the House
Chamber while various substitutes held the chair. The verses
underscored his high standing in a community where friendship
sometimes showed itself in teasing humor.

He valued friendship. Sometimes he was a little tart, and he
gave a sharp tongue to what and whom he did not like. He irked
or enraged a great many persons, but he was a sociable man and
always good company, especially for those who could easily bear
the habits of swearing and spitting which he had kept from his
frontier days along Sugar Creek in the Wabash country. In those
days many an old man had a sandbox by his chair. President
Roosevelt advised his daughter Alice never to stand between Cannon and cuspidor. She played poker with him one evening, and
it revolted her to hear him ask his host to place an umbrella stand
by his chair, since there was no spittoon. But for every man and
woman who shuddered at such coarseness, there was another who
laughed and cheered him for keeping alive the strong mannerisms
of the heroic age of pioneers.

The old man attracted goodwill by his comic qualities. He
was both humorous and witty. "With the possible exception of
John Quincy Adams, no one ever entertained the House better,"
an historian of Congress, de Alva Stanwood Alexander, wrote
long after Cannon's era of greatness. His natural appearance at
seventy was serious and intelligent. He was a roughly handsome
man of middle height, lean as a greyhound. He had a well-shaped
narrow face, dominated by a gaunt aquiline nose set between
shrewd, alert blue eyes above ruddy cheeks fringed with a short
white beard, which was stained brown at the edges by 10,000
cigars. He could be graceful in manner, but despite the many years
he had spent among cultivated men and women in Washington,
he still dressed and behaved a good deal like a Wabash rube. That
enlarged his comic reputation.

On his head he kept a disreputable-looking smashed black or

gray felt hat, turning greenish with age along the brim where it tilted down over his high sloping forehead. He wore it at his desk as well as on the street. His rumpled black suits actually were well cut and cost money, but he dared not admit it. His tailor sewed him a new outfit each autumn from cloth made by hand on looms in Aiken, South Carolina, where he bought the goods for sentimental reasons, because some of his Quaker ancestors had lived near there about the time of the Battle of King's Mountain. He consciously strove to give the appearance of untidiness because he feared his farmer constituents would not send him back to Congress if he strutted among them in well-brushed clothes that fit him nicely. Long ago he had read a sartorial lesson in the fate of President Chester A. Arthur. Although Arthur served competently in the White House after the murder of Garfield, the Republican Party in 1884 refused to nominate him for a full term as President. Thus they ended his political career. He was a dude. "Arthur was defeated by his trousers," Cannon said. Of course, it was not wholly true. Arthur lost out to stronger rivals in a contest for power. But Cannon let his own trousers sag about the gaiter tops like a showboat clown's.

The newspapers exaggerated Cannon's mannerisms and made them famous everywhere. It was in keeping with his reputation that he cooled himself in the midst of a campaign speech on a hot day by dousing his head and back with the ice water from a gallon pitcher. Tales about his profanity excited laughter, and storytellers often chose Cannon arbitrarily as the hero for their blasphemous anecdotes. The New York *World* assured its readers that the Speaker said, "Hell," to a clergyman in 1906 under the following circumstances:

For the two hundredth time Cannon opened a session of the House by stating: "The hour of noon having arrived, the Chaplain will offer prayer." Henry N. Couden, the blind Chaplain, who had lost his sight at Shiloh, prayed for the customary thirty seconds while Cannon thought of other things far away. After Couden's "Amen," Cannon said: "The hour of noon having arrived, the Chaplain will offer prayer." Hinds, the parliamentarian, nudged the Speaker and reminded him that Couden had just performed his duty. Thereupon Cannon turned to Couden and said, "Oh, hell, Chaplain, the joke's on me."

Cannon tickled a nation which still found amusement in the cracker-barrel writings and weird orthography of Josh Billings and Petroleum V. Nasby. Like the heroes of the fables spun by those two, the Speaker was a smart freshwater man who could take the count of the city slicker every time. He had no use for urban rhetoric. "There is no information in declamation," he once said. Plain, unvarnished, sincere, he was among orators what the primitive is among painters. He favored brevity. To a ninety-minute talk he gave a ninety-second reply. He put over his points by roughly skillful ridicule. Representative John Wesley Gaines, an orotund declaimer from Tennessee, protested bitterly to the House because President Roosevelt did not know what had become of a sideboard which some anti-alcohol women of Tennessee had given Mrs. Rutherford B. Hayes almost thirty years earlier in gratitude for her teetotal sentiments. She had left it in the White House for her husband's successors. "My God, Mr. Speaker, where is that sideboard now?" cried Gaines. The issue died when Cannon said: "Mr. Speaker, we are told that in the early days of the Republic, Abigail Adams hung out her washing in the East Room of the White House. My God, Mr. Speaker, where is that clothesline now?"

Whenever he addressed the House before he became Speaker, he commonly gave most of his talk in shirtsleeves, even in winter, because the heat of his exertions in debate drove him to tear off his coat and even his collar before he was fairly started. In the excitement of speaking he would beat the air with his left fist. Once when Cannon asked Representative Sunset Cox to yield to him during a debate in the House, Cox agreed with the provision that Cannon must keep his hands in his pockets. For two minutes Cannon met the requirement. Then out flashed his left hand, Cox called, "Time," while the other members laughed and called to Cox to let Cannon go on. He habitually threw himself about the chamber as he ground out the words in his thin, tireless voice. Pirouetting on his small feet with the jerky movements of an arthritic dancer, he capered along the aisles of the House with a series of wild gestures. He invariably marked his climax by locking together the little fingers of his left and right hands. He would bend and struggle to free them while his face reddened and the sentences flowed on without interruption. The account of the wrestling match of Cannon's fingers became legendary and was told in the lobbies from Congress to Congress. Some years after Cannon's election as Speaker, Peter Johnston Otey, a land buyer from Lynchburg, Virginia, with a gift for imitation, made himself a favored entertainer of the House by putting on Cannon's dance of the fingers. Otey amused Cannon as well as Cannon's colleagues.

But comedy was not the heart of Cannon. While his humor attracted people, what held them was his frankness and fairness. He faced reality openly. In 1890, a month after his constituents voted him temporarily out of Congress, he met two defeated colleagues at the bar of the Grand Pacific Hotel in Chicago, Major William McKinley of Ohio (President a few years later) and Senator Thomas Carter of Montana. Cannon's friends shrugged off their loss. Carter said it suited him to get out of Congress at last. McKinley said he was glad it had happened that way. Cannon stuck a pin in those gassy balloons. "That's what I am saying to everyone else," he said, "but, boys, don't let's lie to one another."

Democrats trusted him because he lacked pretense. "He is nearly always wrong, but there is no sham in him," John Sharp Williams, the Democratic leader in the House, said. "I believe in consultin' the boys, findin' out what most of 'em want, and then goin' ahead and doin' it," Cannon told an interviewer for *Review of Reviews* soon after he was first elected Speaker in 1903, because "the Speaker is the servant, not the master, of the House." He expatiated on his attitude to John Sharp Williams. With delphic obtuseness, Williams said, "Mr. Speaker, I will always think you are as fair as I believe you will be." Cannon replied, "John, I am going to be as fair as I can consistent with the exigencies of American politics."

The members who were not entertained by Cannon's humor or stirred by his honesty had a special reason for honoring him. He was the champion of the Congressmen. By one passionate address, delivered with noontime fire at three o'clock in the morning, he had liberated the House from its old bondage to the Senate, and the Representatives did not forget.

This declaration of independence arose from a difference between Cannon and Senator Benjamin Ryan Tillman of South Carolina. Tillman said that the Federal Government owed South Carolina $47,245.77 for expenditures made by the State on behalf of the Nation during the war of 1812. Cannon placed the debt at thirty-four cents. On March 1, 1903, Tillman, an irascible farmer who once had promised his constituents that he would stick his pitchfork into the ribs of President Grover Cleveland, promised to filibuster against every bill before Congress if South Carolina's claims were not allowed in the Sundry Civil Service Bill. The threat was ominous. The Fifty-seventh Congress would end automatically on March 4. Appropriations bills had to be passed before adjournment or the executive branch of the government could not operate. The House refused to grant Pitchfork Ben his $47,000. The Senators, however, surrendered to him because their rules, requiring the unanimous consent of all members for the consideration of a measure, did permit one Senator to halt the proceedings.

When the news reached the House early in the morning of March 4 that the Senate had passed Tillman's bill, Cannon took the floor. The light of the moon, almost ready to set, seeped thinly into the House Chamber. The Representatives slouched sleepily at their desks, but Cannon brought them awake in a hurry. Red-faced, thrusting his left hand at the air like a wobbly swordsman, he poured forth his resentment of the Senate, which, he warned, "must change its method of procedure, or our body, backed up by the people, will compel this change."

I am getting to be a somewhat aged man. I pray God that my life may be spared until an intelligent and a righteous sentiment, north and south, pervading both of the great parties, will lash anybody into obedience to the right of the majority to rule.

The speech did not save the Treasury from Tillman's raid. But it led to a change in the relationship of House and Senate. During the summer recess a few months afterward William Boyd Allison of Iowa, one of the Republican leaders in the Senate, went out to Illinois to ask Cannon what sort of legislative program he thought the Republican Party ought to lay before the next Congress. Until then Senators had been instructing, not asking, Representatives what to do. Allison's visit meant the triumph was complete. The effects of Cannon's rebellion slowly spread far beyond the Capitol. Uncle Joe put his colleagues at ease in their home communities. By elevating them from their roles as Washington lackeys to the Senators, he gave them what he himself already enjoyed, some independence of their State machines, which usually were managed by the Senators or the men for whom the Senators fronted. It was not so easy thereafter as it had been previously for a Senator to tell a man when he could or could not run for Congress. Before the Representatives could foresee that happy development, in the dim hour between midnight and dawn on March 4 Cannon's colleagues clapped thunderously for him, and they elected him Speaker when the next Congress opened. After that only President Roosevelt outranked him among the Republicans, as a result of the decline of the Senate, but until he was seventy Cannon used his authority gently. J. Adam Bede, a Representative from Minnesota, wrote in those days that the Speaker was "unique and kindly." His fairness drew tears from John Sharp Williams, a sentimental Mississippian who rejoiced at signs of decency in men.

It was for Cannon the humorist, Cannon the shameless, Cannon the liberator that the Democrats sang on adjournment day more than three years after the fracas with Tillman. The thought of the demonstration still warmed him when, the day after adjournment, he boarded the steam cars for the West at the dingy old B Street station where Guiteau had shot Garfield during Cannon's fifth term in Congress. He headed for his home town, Danville, Illinois, where he intended to take it easy on Independence Day setting off devil-chasers and four-inchers with his two little granddaughters. He was a widower, but he was not neglected and alone.

His admirers extended far beyond Congress. In his back pocket he carried a letter from a citizen in St. Louis. "Say, Uncle Joe, the fellows down here are hollering for you for President," it said. And he relished these sweet words from E. B. Chapin, a newspaper editor in Champaign, Illinois: "The country owes you a term in the White House, and I want to see you have it." By his personality he had gained a strong political following, at the very moment his political opinions were going out of fashion. As he prepared for his departure from Washington, the thought that he was a man of stature affected him deeply. The friends who took him to the train expected to see him again in the autumn, but never again did they meet precisely that Cannon. The Uncle Joe of adjournment day was still a modest man, and the Cannon who came back took conspicuous advantage of his own importance and paraded it.

Heroes and Villains

THE SEEDS of the new Cannon had already begun to sprout, invisibly, before the birthday party. The Washington he was leaving after adjournment had been filled with a complaining clamor, and Cannon disliked the din. From the Speaker's chair it had grown clear that 1906 was a year of discontent. People were pushing their troubles off on Washington. The Capitol appeared to have been moved to a valley like the bottom of a cup, with all of America rising around it and cascades tumbling down from every height—cascades not of water but of half-baked and full-fledged reform ideas, statements of personal problems, suggestions for improvement, fulmination against lack of improvement, pleas by consumers, criticisms of the state of the nation, denunciations of the great men of the nation, requests for soft jobs, petitions for funds, and above all calls for new laws to get rid of old injustices. This outpouring of dissatisfaction with the economic customs of the day was planting in some people a sense of desperate impatience with the special conception of a perfect America which Cannon had come to cherish. The cure prescribed by the malcontents was extension of the powers of the federal government to control the economic affairs of individuals. Cannon thought the government reached far enough already. "I am god-damned tired of listening to all this babble for reform," he said. The state of the nation suited him. "America is a hell of a success," he said. Why tinker with it?

11

The inundation raining on Washington angered him, and he meant to halt it.

Cannon and the reformers sought the same goal. They both wanted to preserve the American opportunity system. But Cannon thought that opportunity flowed from self-reliance. He was the politician of Paul Bunyan's America, a bountiful, boastful land, the scene of gigantic feats and accomplishments by men who went about their affairs without much restraint from public officials. Nobody told Paul Bunyan where to get off, and nobody helped him along. It had not been the custom to cry, "Help!" to Congress in every difficulty when the citizens of eastern Illinois thirty-three years earlier had sent Cannon, then a red-whiskered hick "with hay in his hair," as he himself recalled it, to the Capitol as Representative for the first time. He abided still by what he had said thirty years earlier, that the function of the federal government "is to afford protection to life, liberty, and property under the Constitution, and when that is done by a wise legislature, then let every tub stand on its own bottom, let every citizen root hog or die."

In those thirty years the United States had left the Age of Great Expectations and entered the Age of Uncertainty. Cannon at seventy was witnessing the climax to the era of economic expansion inaugurated by the surrender at Appomattox. After the Civil War, industry grew and flourished. Invention speeded the wheels in the factories, eased the work of the farmers, and put new comforts into the home. The visible aspects of the American way of life changed so swiftly that Uncle Joe had remarked, "in a life of some three score years, living in a period when you measure time by events instead of years, I have lived one thousand years." Yet the wonderful process of development was itself the creator of discontent. The country in 1906 was paying dearly for the fact that the rewards for acumen and ruthlessness in business had grown to exceed the rewards known to the Western world in any period since the Italian traders of the Renaissance were making the fortunes that glorified Venice and Florence. The price was class consciousness. The gulf between those who succeeded in business and those who did not make a living at business had become so wide that the millions on the poor man's side of the gulf could see clearly that they had a life distinct and apart from the money-makers. From their distinct life flowed distinct interests, and the satisfaction of those interests they sought from Washington. Their discontent was the social fee which the nation paid for economic improvement.

The gulf was still widening in 1906. Business was strengthening itself by fortifying the trusts. Speeches in the *Congressional Record*, Cannon's favorite reading matter, reported that the common run of manufacturers owed fealty to the railway trust, and that tobacco growers and small retailers and small and big consumers were the vassals of the tobacco trust. The sugar trust and the steel trust gripped home, farm, and factory. Disturbed by the power of those monopoly corporations, indignant men were suffering a sort of delirium, in which they could see the walls of a room closing in upon them. The attempt which Theodore Roosevelt had made to talk big business into behaving nicely was failing. At his recommendation, Congress in 1903 created the Bureau of Corporations, which had the authority to collect and to publish information about American business. But a year later John Moody's book, *Truth About the Trusts,* a sober statistical analysis of American economic phenomena, concluded that the restraints which the government then could legally apply to business would no more halt the growth of monopoly than the shout of a sea captain could turn aside the northwest wind. The hour seemed near when no space would be left in America for individuals outside the trust system to make a decent living and to get ahead and hope for contentment. It looked to some as though America was losing its wonderful flexibility, which made it easy for a man to move from one economic and social stratum to another, and which, under the general label of "opportunity," accounted for the development of the U.S.A. from a sparse society scattered through a few isolated settlements on the Atlantic coast to a mighty nation filling half a continent.

Senator Robert M. LaFollette of Wisconsin said that the trusts would murder the American ideal of "equal opportunity for all in industrial development." He and his followers from the farming states in the Western plains and forest region felt the power of monopoly in the railroads, which, like a storm that waters the crops at the same time it blows away the barn, both blessed and harmed the men of the plains and far prairies. The tangled financial connections of the railroads' owners gave the train lines themselves the character of monopolies, and the policies of the lines stimulated the trend toward monopoly in other businesses. Railroads supported the meat monopoly by limiting the number of refrigerator cars available for carrying the packers' produce from the stockyards to butcher shops in distant cities. One railroad man in Wall Street, E. R. Harriman, managed a considerable segment of trans-Mississippi America by his majority ownership of the Union Pacific and his minority control of the Santa Fe, the Alton, the Southern Pacific, and the Baltimore and Ohio. The scope of that empire increased in 1906 when President Stuyvesant Fish of the Illinois Central surrendered to Harriman full control of his line, which competed with Harriman's Alton and, like a steel spine for America, joined the Great Lakes to the Gulf of Mexico. President Roosevelt informed Congress on May 4, 1906, that many railroads were giving Standard Oil a preferential rate for the hauling of tank cars which enabled that petroleum monopoly to profit heavily at the expense of its rivals and the public. "There is not an independent oil company in the United States . . . that does not fear the Standard Oil monopoly," LaFollette announced to the Senate a month after Cannon's birthday party. Standard controlled the pipelines through which its competitors moved their oil from refinery to market. Appalled by such conditions, LaFollette in the spring of 1906 summed up the case for change:

Against the natural laws of trade and commerce is set the arbitrary will of a few masters of special privilege. Between railroads and other monopolies controlling great natural resources and most of the necessaries of life there exists a "community of interests" in all cases and an identity of ownership in many. We have observed that these great combinations are closely associated in business for business reasons; that they are also closely associated in politics for business reasons; that together they constitute a complete system; that they encroach upon the public rights, defeat legislation for the public good, and secure laws to promote private interests.

LaFollette had old memories of business interests' calling the tune for politicians. Twenty-five years earlier he had been criticizing lumbermen in Wisconsin for grabbing land, abusing the forests, and giving orders to officials of the state. The lumbermen retaliated. They could not prevent his election to the House of Representatives in 1886. But their agent in Washington, Senator Philetus Sawyer, persuaded Speaker John G. Carlisle to keep La-Follette off the Public Lands Committee when he took his seat in Congress. Now the malcontents of 1906 saw bigger Sawyers on every hand. The political power of the corporations "is acknowledged in every county and manifest in every lawmaking body," LaFollette told the Senate. "It is idle to ignore it. There exists all over the country a distrust of Congress, a fear that monopoly wealth holds the balance of power in legislation." The shameless attitude of the monopolists supported the complaint. During the hearings ordered by the New York State Senate early in 1906 into the practices of insurance companies, Charles Evans Hughes asked E. R. Harriman: "It has been charged that through your relations with Mr. Odell [Benjamin B. Odell, governor of New York, 1903–1905], you have political influence. What have you to say to that?" Harriman replied: "Well, I should think that Mr. Odell had political influence because of his relations with me."

The courts put flesh on the phantasms in the nightmares of the reformers. It was a tradition of the bench to weaken the Sherman Anti-Trust Act. Hardly had it become law when the business-minded justices who dominated the courts during the second administration of Grover Cleveland actually encouraged the process of business combination by their decisions. On March 21, 1906, Judge J. Otis Humphries, in Federal District Court in Chicago, decided that four meat packers, Swift and Company, Armour and Company, the Cudahy Packing Company, and the Fairbanks Canning Company, had violated the Sherman Act. He added, however, that the individual officers responsible for the conduct of those companies were immune from prosecution under the criminal provisions of the Act. The strange judicial logic angered President Roosevelt, whose Department of Justice had entered the suit against the meat men. In vexation he sent a special message to Congress which stated that the "beef-packing cases offered one of the instances where there was not only the moral certainty that the accused men were guilty, but what seemed, and now seems, legal evidence of the fact." He said that Judge Humphries' decision was a "miscarriage of justice." The decision had a double effect. It strengthened the confidence of the officers of corporations that they were greater than Sherman's law, but at the same time it nourished the public indignation against the trusts and wealth.

The growth of the power of the great companies and their owners put the employees of the companies at a disadvantage in bargaining and threatened to kill their hopes for better working conditions. Even in small industries which competed for labor and for markets, most of the workers were afraid to join trade unions. The monopoly trend accentuated the independence of the employers. They paid poor wages. Two-thirds of the laborers took home $600 apiece a year. So the rise of the trusts prompted Samuel Gompers, the little English cigar-maker who was president of the American Federation of Labor, to petition Washington for help. He requested Congress to enact laws to outlaw the use of the injunction in labor disputes; to require immigrants to pass an education test before they could move inland from Ellis Island (employers encouraged the importation of illiterate foreign workers who would accept low pay); to limit the work day to eight hours, and to require employers operating in interstate commerce to pay liability to their workers who suffered injury on the job. A considerable segment of the population that had no direct interest in labor conditions appreciated Gompers' problems because a new kind of writer, appalled by abuses in society, was creating dissatisfaction among persons who otherwise might have remained contented.

The publication in the spring of 1906 of Upton Sinclair's *The Jungle,* an exposure of the filthy slaughtering methods in the Chicago stockyards, goaded President Roosevelt to appoint investigators, but the inquiry did not hurt the economic position of the swine kings in Packingtown as long as they had Judge Humphries to lean on. The best-seller lists of the year in which the House first elected Cannon to the Speakership, 1903, included two novels which damned the evils running in the train of monopoly—*The Pit* (83,000 copies sold by November 1903) and *The Octopus* (27,-000). David Graham Phillips condemned the influence of business in government in *Treason in the Senate.*

Even the conservative periodicals that had no real concern for reform took to contemplating, for their readers, how the increasing size of individual businesses and fortunes would ultimately affect the country. The New York *Herald* early in 1906 estimated that seventy Americans each owned estates of $35,000,000 or more, and that 5,000 men possessed an average of $15,000,000,000, or one-sixteenth of the entire wealth of the United States, and forecast that by mid-century the millionaires would accumulate $50,000,000,000 or $100,000,000,000 unless barriers were put in their way. Charles Evans Hughes, the conservative Republican who became Chief Justice of the United States, recommended a ceiling for the wealth of insurance companies—$2,500,000,000 in net assets and no more. By February 1906 the moral implications of wealth had become so intriguing that the *Cosmopolitan Magazine* asked a number of leading Americans: "Does the possession of $1,000,000,000 by one man constitute a menace to the Republic?" Three answered, "No"—Charles Eliot, president of Harvard; E. Benjamin Andrews, chancellor of the University of Nebraska, and John Wanamaker, who had made more than $1,000,000 by his enterprise as storekeeper. But others were willing to say, "Yes"— Ernest Crosby and the Reverend Washington Gladden, well-known social reformers, and Jack London. Many Americans reflected about such opinions, and their reflections encouraged the unrest.

Strange intellectual support for the belief that great wealth might beget social immorality, by reducing millions to dependence on a few, came from some of the beneficiaries of the monopoly system. They allied themselves in the National Civic Federation. The Federation had an honest purpose. Improvement of society was really its goal when Mark Hanna, the wealthy, wise, and tolerant friend of Cannon's late friend, President William McKinley, encouraged its founding at the commencement of the twentieth century. It grew on the assumption that bettering of society is not the job of any political party or the members of any social or economic class, but of everybody. The Federation members had come by 1906, however, to include hypocrites, who privately repudiated its published sentiments, and cynics, who distracted attention from their business methods by their participation in the works of the Federation. But it supplied the reformers with a numerous claque of best people who removed the blemish of "unfashionable" from their activities.

A revulsion in the universities against the common political interpretations of the theories of Charles Darwin about natural selection buoyed the discontent. The great biologist had engendered belief for fifty years that social progress was natural and automatic, and the belief fathered the assumption that the state blocked progress when it interfered in the economic and social affairs of the nation. "The struggle for life, with all its attendant consequences of inequality and poverty, is the mainspring of civilization. . . . All the blessings of life are the direct outcome of that struggle, and there is no substitution for it," an English political Darwinian, E. B. Müller, wrote in 1893 in the London *Fortnightly* at a time when government was self-effacing in both England and the United States. Among intellectuals one preacher of that harsh code survived in the United States in 1906. He was William Graham Sumner, professor of social and political science at Yale, who contributed the following statement to the controversy about the concentration of wealth:

The millionaires are a product of natural selection, acting on the whole body of men to pick out those who can meet the requirements of certain work to be done. . . . It is because they are thus selected that wealth—both their own and that entrusted to them—aggregates under their hands. Let one of them make a mistake and see how quickly the concentration gives way to dispersion. They may fairly be regarded as the naturally selected agents of society for certain work.

But re-examination of Darwin by sociologists was isolating Sumner, who was an academic counterpart of "Uncle Joe" Cannon. In 1906 Erville Bartlett Woods wrote an article (published in the *American Journal of Sociology* in May 1907) in which he overturned the belief that Darwin the natural scientist was a guide to government and political science. He denied that Darwin had discovered a basic truth about the relations of men in society when he made his strictly biological observations. Darwin, he said, did not try to derive from biological processes the sole criterion of moral or physical well-being. "From the very outset the mission of mind was to grapple with the law of competition and as far as possible to overcome and destroy it," wrote another sociologist, Lester Ward. "This iron law [of competition], as it may be called, is found everywhere to lie athwart the path of human progress." These and similar writings encouraged the reformers to seek through government what yet another sociologist, Sidney Low, called the "scientific control of the social forces by the collective mind of society for its advantage."

Despite the Civic Federation and the sympathy engendered by the popular and academic writers, and the laws they provoked Congress to enact, the malcontents were seriously handicapped. They suffered from disunity. They were a heterogeneous lot. Besides agrarian reformers, leaders of organized labor, and the intellectuals exposing social, economic, and political sore spots in the nation, they included a few convinced socialists. Jack London, the he-man author, was describing the works of Karl Marx to crowds in parks in New York City. Governor Hill of New York wanted to nationalize the coal mines. William Randolph Hearst, in editorials written in capital letters, was plugging for halfway socialism: the nationalization of the railways. But to their consciousness of their class distinction from the big-business men, the factions among the discontented added consciousness of their further distinction from one another—or rather each faction was unconscious of the fact that it had natural allies for the fight against business in all the other factions. The farmer, the laborer, the small shopkeeper, the socialist, and even the writer who seemed to represent all, separately attacked the common foe in aloof loneliness. Moreover, the national landscape in 1906 did not seem to justify the lamentations they raised in Washington.

The year smiled in a golden age of dazzling prosperity which had continued almost uninterrupted, broken only by the brief depression of 1903–1904, since the enactment of the Dingley Tariff in 1897, during President McKinley's first term. Cannon wondered whether LaFollette and the others were inventing the problems which they called upon the federal government to solve. He found that jobs were going begging because there was more work than there were workers, that farming had never in its history been such a sure-fire money-maker as it was then in the U.S.A. (1906 was the best American crop year up to that time), and that the wage-earner ambitious to become his own boss could borrow capital in America at the world's lowest interest rate. In the little pocket of his trousers Cannon carried proof of the economic soundness of America as it then operated. The talisman was a watch. As he told an audience of voters in Shawneetown, Illinois, it had been manufactured by men whose high wages attracted laborers to America from all over the world, and he had bought it for only 74 cents. Why experiment with a system that meant low prices

and high pay? Cannon's confidence that all was well had a powerful hold on the country, and it endowed him with many supporters
who found no fun in his comedy.

Muffled by the continued blessing of good times, the cry for
change was bringing few results until Cannon took alarm at it.
The persistence of the reformers dismayed him. The agrarians in
the early months of 1906 had tried to crowd the calendar with
hateful bills. They wanted the federal government to prohibit by
statute the inclusion of watered stock in railroad evaluation; to
forbid judges to take part in decisions on corporation cases in
which they had a personal interest; to prohibit corporations from
making financial contributions to political parties. To save the
nation's timber resources for the generations to come and to check
the gluttony of the lumber kings, they proposed that the federal
government manage forest areas in the White Mountains and the
southern Appalachians. They sought an elastic currency to break
the eastern banks' hold (as they saw it) on the national monetary
system, which in their mind enabled New York and a few other
seaboard cities to dominate the economy of the West as completely
as London dominated the Barbadoes. They called for the direct
primary and the direct election of Senators, in order to remove a
barrier between the public and their officials—the barrier of election of Senators by legislatures—which made it easier for the representatives of corporations to manage political affairs to please
them. Neither those nor Gompers' proposals became law then.
But between the reception at the Arlington and the adjournment
fiesta, Congress did approve bills authorizing the federal government to determine fair railway rates and to set up a system of meat
inspection at federal expense. After the Senate passed the inspection bill, Roosevelt had to send a special message to the House
in order to goad it, too, to act, despite Cannon's dislike for the
measure.

Above all, the Speaker took alarm from the reformers' cry for
downward revision of the high protective duties in the Dingley
Tariff. Nelson Dingley, the author of that tariff act, was a kind
of perambulating calculating machine from Maine. "He'd rather
have a pad and pencil on his knee than a pretty girl," said another
Down Easter, Tom Reed. LaFollette condemned protection as the

chief prop of the trusts. Cannon looked upon the Dingley Law as the foundation of the boom times he saw all around him.

Politically the protective tariff was a contradictory issue. In 1906 it was supported mainly by opponents of interference by government in private economic matters, but protection meant interference. Nobody in the nation escaped the consequences of high duties. It was supported also by opponents of the political program of the labor unions, but all advocates of protection justified it on the grounds that it created jobs. Its strongest friends were the most conservative Republicans who objected to "class legislation," but the most conservative Democrats fought protection because, they said, it benefited one class of Americans, labor, at the expense of the other classes. Free trade is an "aristocratical idea" and "the free traders of America seem to have a deep-seated enmity toward the people who work," William Culbertson, a Kentucky protectionist, told Congress during the plush days of the late nineteenth century. Protection was supported by advocates of rugged individualism and competition, but it limited competition between American and foreign products and, according to LaFollette and others who thought like him, it limited competition within America. Cannon passed over the contradictions. The protective tariff made work, encouraged industry, and enriched the farmers. "Since the enactment of the first revenue under Washington to the present time," he said, "the periods of prosperity have been under protection, and the periods of adversity have been under the policy of free trade or tariff for revenue only."

He aimed a lesson from Scripture at the malcontents. "The devil was the first smasher of precedents," he said. Cannon gloried in his changelessness by describing his attitude with a special word. He was a "standpatter." The American language took the word from the game of poker, which Cannon had been playing three times a week since Judge David Davis of the Illinois bench taught it to him in chambers during Buchanan's presidency. The player who "stands pat" declines to change his hand after the deal by discarding on the chance that he will be dealt a better card. The label so blatantly advertised Cannon's indisposition to change the American scene by changing America's laws that Theodore Roosevelt requested him to discard it. "The voters do not under-

stand the expression 'stand pat' and do not like it," said Roosevelt.
Cannon continued to flaunt his label.

When he left the chair at the end of the Congressional session
in June 1906, Cannon concluded that only by crushing the reformers could he save his America. In order to accomplish that
aim, he began to exploit his genial nature and honest name. He
thoroughly understood the American penchant for identifying
great questions with the personalities of admirable and sinful
persons. He knew that at heart we accept the legend of St. George
and the dragon. We relish combat between good and evil, and we
lionize the political protagonists who can reduce complex problems to simple matters of a choice between right and wrong, with
one protagonist standing for right and the other for wrong. In
our own era Franklin D. Roosevelt implanted in millions a feeling
of positive fervor about public finance, which usually leaves most
people cold. He did not treat it like an accountant facing a hole
in the books. Instead, he swooped down dramatically like Sir
Galahad, brandishing the sword of goodness, upon the financial
sinner, the Economic Royalist. He thrilled his following by elevating a dispute over political theory into a conflict of morals. He
seemed to realize that it was not enough for him to have right on
his side. He had to create an ogre on the other side.

Men make issues. The raw materials of political battle are always with us, but it takes two geniuses, the complementary bad
and good, to mold the materials into form, and the bad is
perhaps more necessary than the good. From the birth of the
Republic we have treated government as a holy battleground
from which a virtuous Gabriel is bound to drive some defiling
Lucifer and his evil companions. About the time of Cannon's
birth, Andrew Jackson was strengthening his cause by holding
up Nicholas Biddle as a bad man and exposing him. Soon after
Cannon's first election to Congress, Samuel J. Tilden won the
leadership of the Democratic Party by laying bare the wickedness of the members of the Tweed Ring, and he so clearly embodied trueness and right that his countrymen cast more votes for
him in the presidential election of 1876 than they gave Rutherford B. Hayes, the victor. Cannon from experience, then, had
reason to expect that the public would support his ideas out of

affection for his person, that as long as he symbolized weak government the voters would rout the friends of strong government.

Cannon's experiment in heroism led to an ironic end. The four years he gave to the experiment proved the truth of the assumption that the electorate sees issues as personalities, but he proved it in a way he could not forecast. He began as the hero and ended as the villain.

At the beginning he tried to choose his own villain, President Roosevelt, who, he grumbled, had "discovered the Ten Commandments." From a distance Roosevelt looked like the ideal villain for Cannon. The Speaker's interest in heroism swelled with his ambition to win the Republican presidential nomination in 1908, and he assumed that his chances of winning the honor from whomever Roosevelt might support would improve from his drawing a dramatic distinction between himself and the President. Disagreement was natural to the two men. Roosevelt had lodged his first complaint against Cannon in 1891. Roosevelt then was Civil Service Commissioner, and Cannon was chairman of the House Appropriations Committee. Exasperated by Cannon's eagerness to save the taxpayer by limiting the appropriation for the Civil Service Commission, Roosevelt said: "We cannot escape from the fact that it was no credit to the Republican party of the House that Mr. Cannon of Illinois should be one of its leaders."

Roosevelt was one of those men who draw back from the consequences of their own thoughts. Intellectually he was a reformer. But his social and political instincts kept him from following the bent of his thought very far. He had too much respect for respectability. This made him conscious of bad taste in other reformers. He teetered between admiration and scorn for those hard-working authors who were writing revelations about business and politics for the magazines. Certainly, the articles created a public opinion favorable to reform. But they lacked uplifting quality and they ignored the good in America. So, at a dinner in Uncle Joe's honor, he disparaged the authors as the modern equivalent of John Bunyan's "man with a muckrake." As the commander of a poor man's movement (and the drive for reform came essentially from the poor), he suffered from his admiration for what in his day was called "good breeding." In his life of Gouverneur Morris he noted that Morris "had about him that 'touch of the purple' which is always so strongly attractive."

He frustrated himself also by a romantic belief in party solidarity. His refusal to precipitate quarrels within the party after he became President prevented him from having it out with Cannon—even when Cannon tried him most sorely. Who can forget that Theodore Roosevelt brightened the presidency with dramatic bravado after many drab decades? Or that he had the courage to press the railroad rate bill and the bureau of corporations bill and the pure food bill and the meat inspection bill through Congress? But who can blink the fact that he foundered in action? Here was a modern Hamlet of indecision. Mr. Dooley paraphrased the President's attitude toward the trusts: "On wan hand I wud stamp thim underfut; on the other hand, not so fast." For Cannon such a man was an exasperatingly elusive enemy, intangible as the fading Cheshire cat, a softly-stuffed opponent, like a pillow. Roosevelt almost feared Cannon. "You must lay down on Uncle Joe," Roosevelt was advised. "It will be a good deal like laying down on a hedgehog," he rejoined.

Cannon served Roosevelt faithfully during his first two years in the Speakership, from 1903 to 1905, because the young President was following the conservative policies of Cannon's friend, the late President McKinley. But Roosevelt grew independent just when Cannon began his second term in the chair, in December 1905, and it was then that the harmony began to sour. The President's message to the new Congress that month uncovered his change of policy. "Experience has shown conclusively that it is useless to try to get any adequate regulation and supervision of . . . great corporations by state action," Roosevelt said in the message. "Such regulation and supervision can only be effectively exercised by a government whose jurisdiction is co-extensive with the field of work of the corporations—that is, the national government." After that Cannon could not regard Roosevelt as the leading source of Republican thought.

Cannon slowly discovered that he was precipitating a serious conflict not with Roosevelt but with LaFollette. Unlike the President, LaFollette followed his opinions to their ultimate conclusions. His actions supported his words. He had the faith of the evangels in his own rightness. So the Speaker and the Senator made exciting opponents, each powerful and pertinacious. The substitution of villains led to Cannon's undoing.

LaFollette was not, of course, the only one to oppose Uncle Joe, nor was he the leader of those who did. Many men, some of them hating LaFollette even more than they did Cannon, closed in on the Speaker. But LaFollette was the rock in the center of the snowball that flattened him, and the two men most dramatically typified the conflict of their times.

CHAPTER —•— 3

The Antagonists

LaFollette was a pupil of the school which teaches that individuals take their political philosophy from the personal economic circumstances of their early lives. In reviewing his personal history, he traced his own interest in the working classes to the fact that as a child and young man he had labored on the farm and worked meanly at the university to provide for his mother and sister and younger brothers. To his death, he identified himself with those who derive their livelihoods from their own muscular efforts and other people who ordinarily possess no capital, unless it be a farm, to subsist on beyond the day when they can work no more.

If LaFollette's own conception of the origin of his leanings had been true, Cannon would have out-shouted LaFollette for reform. Their early lives were strikingly similar. Both men grew up in poverty on the frontier because both lost their fathers in mid-childhood, both sacrificed adolescent hours of play and sleep to perform as family breadwinners, LaFollette plowing and planting and tending the stock on a wind-bitten farm in Dane County, Wisconsin, Cannon selling calico and plow-shares in the general store and keeping his mother's house and lot in good trim in Parke County, Indiana. LaFollette studied law at the University of Wisconsin, in the same county as his mother's farm, while Cannon went more than a day's journey by horse to learn his law in an office in an unfamiliar town, Terre Haute, Indiana. He slept on a wooden bench in the office of his sponsor, John P. Usher, and he walked 150 miles to Cincinnati to polish his legal education at the college there for six months.

LaFollette's career opened in the congenial surroundings of Madison, the town where he had been studying for five years. Looking for success in new country, Cannon went to live among strangers in Shelbyville, Illinois, where he began to apply the knowledge he had gained from Usher and in Cincinnati. His board and lodging cost one dollar a week, and he often had to borrow the sum. Forever afterward he associated Shelbyville with disappointment and grinding poverty. Out of hunger for the salary that went with it, LaFollette and Cannon, each before he was thirty, ran successfully for the office of district attorney, Cannon in Coles County, Illinois, where he prosecuted the instigators of the Charleston Riots during the Civil War, and LaFollette in his native Dane County. In other words, as young men both lived a kind of life common in the Middle West in the second half of the nineteenth century. Each proved for himself that the United States was indeed the land of opportunity. Yet their parallel origins and similar ordeals led eventually to dramatically conflicting attitudes toward life, society, and politics.

A sense of justice, grounded in his country's egalitarian tradition, started LaFollette on a slow journey toward leadership of those restless westerners who saw the clouds filling the sky when Cannon knew it was sunny and unstreaked. LaFollette had serene confidence that fair play guided life in the United States when he decided to run for the district attorneyship in Dane County. The district attorney was paid $800 a year, and he was sending money to his mother, he had a fiancée whom he longed to marry, but he was in debt. Although he was only twenty-five and had been a lawyer only a year, he understood that the race for the office was open to all. Let the voters make their choice. Any American could reach for any American prize.

To his astonishment, he learned that this was not so. The Republican Party in Dane County had a boss in E. W. Keyes, the postmaster in Madison, and the boss picked the candidates for office. The boss told LaFollette not to run.

LaFollette's alarm at losing his chance to make the $800 broadened into indignation over the realization that one man was trying to deprive all men in Dane County of the right to vote for whom they pleased. It was unjust to deny Americans freedom of choice and the opportunity to try to advance. It damaged the precious idea of equal treatment for all. He defied Keyes and ran. He won by ninety-three votes. Thus he weakened the power of one boss. When he ran again two years later, Keyes did not oppose him.

LaFollette took years to develop his instinct for egalitarianism into a system of political thought. But each day added to him another bit of his final nature. The star that pulled LaFollette onward was belief that the perfection of real justice was attainable, not in the courts alone but in all existence. To one of such faith, the sight of evil, no matter how many times experienced, was an everlasting goad. Men disposed to live and let live might in time have lost their fervor and accepted the world as they found it. But as long as he breathed LaFollette could never accommodate himself to situations which aroused his conscience.

He discovered that political corruption supported economic corruption. The federal government had given to the railroads grants of land in Wisconsin, through which the roads agreed to lay rail. But the roads often exploited the land without crossing it with steel. The managers of the roads thus were building themselves into a privileged class by operating small dukedoms at public expense. In Wisconsin they grew rich by selling timber from their land grants, which actually belonged to the nation, not to them. Few Persian grandees ever gained so much for so little. Yet as they themselves benefited from public generosity, they preached to those whom they served the gospel that man must pay for what he gets. The Norwegian farmers in Dane County were among the many who suffered from this code of the railroads. The rails charged the farmers high rates for hauling their corn and wheat to the cities, where the buyers dictated the prices to the farmers. The same rails charged high rates for carrying to the country the city-made goods which the farmers bought, at the prices set by the sellers. As a result, the farmers suffered coming and going. They had to absorb the transportation charges for what they sold and in effect pay the charges for what they bought. The story was thirty years old when LaFollette canvassed the

farmers over the protest of Keyes and was still a source of fury
and indignation.

To save themselves from being forced to devote every last acre
of their land grants to the purpose for which they received it and
from being forced to charge fair freight rates, the railroad men
posted allies in the federal government and paid them to nullify
the effect of the farmers' clamor for economic liberty. Upon com-
prehending that, District Attorney LaFollette resolved to become
a part of the federal government himself in order to defend the
farmers and forests and democratic institutions of Wisconsin.
Wherever in the United States there were railroads and farmers,
you could hear the story of discrimination in charges. It was not
a problem that Wisconsin could solve alone. So the plight of his
rural constituents, helplessly trying to wriggle loose from the economic vise which the railroads screwed up tight, widened La-
Follette's political interests. He needed more authority than the
District Attorney's if he was going to safeguard justice.

The voters in Dane County and in the neighboring counties
elected him their Representative in Congress in 1884. The victory
widened the gulf between LaFollette and the bosses. If he had
not been a flouter of custom, he would have cleared his candidacy
with Philip and John Spooner before offering himself to the electorate. The Spooner brothers, who were the leaders of the Republican machine in Madison, passed on the candidates for national
office, just as Postmaster Keyes censored the nominations for local
office. LaFollette ignored them and ran without their permission,
not only because the unfairness of bossism revolted him but because he suspected the bosses of helping the masters of the dukedoms. John Spooner afterward represented the Wisconsin railroads in the Senate. Winning in spite of the Spooners, LaFollette
departed for Washington in the autumn of 1884, a full year before the Congress to which he had been elected would meet. He
wanted time to prepare himself for the fight against the agents of
the spoilers.

The principal agent, Senator Philetus Sawyer, friend of the rail-
roaders and timbermen, greeted him pleasantly. But when Sawyer
learned that the young Congressman, then twenty-nine, intended
to press Congress to withdraw land grants from railroads which

had not fulfilled their end of the bargain, he arranged for La-Follette to become a member of the House of Representatives' Committee on Indian Affairs, where the idealist from Dane County would have little to say about the railroads and their timber-cutting. So the bosses defeated his purpose in going to Washington. He sat in Congress three terms without ever surmounting the barrier that Sawyer put in his way. In one respect, the six years in Washington meant only an interlude in his life. Yet the frustration in each of those six years strengthened his determination to enrich America by instituting fairness, balance, and equality in the distribution of political authority and economic opportunity.

In Washington, LaFollette found Cannon, who had been in the House eleven years when the Forty-eighth Congress convened in December 1884 for its final session, from the gallery where he was scrutinizing the assembly in which he was to sit. The symbols in the future struggle to define the nature of America became friends. Neither of them had yet lost that attitude toward life which their early years had given them. Their first bond was their common interest in farmers. Like LaFollette Cannon represented a rural constituency, and, contrary to his economizing tendencies later, he believed then that the Republic owed his farmers help in making a living. He encouraged his fellow Congressmen to appropriate money generously for the Department of Agriculture. The sums over which Congress haggled then seem skimpy now, but an annual budget of $200,000,000 was something to whistle about when Cannon arrived in Washington.

In their formative years, the two men agreed on so many things that they could not possibly regard one another as hero and villain. In spite of thinking that the railroads and the bosses twisted his country's ideal of equality of opportunity, LaFollette then accepted the common belief that each American held the key to his future within himself. "In the United States," he assured Congress, "limitations upon the intellectual development, the social place, and the financial success and triumph of each person are fixed by his own character and power alone. Whatever his condition at birth, he will win wealth and power and fame if he is capable, honest, industrious, plucky, and courageous." He and Cannon went after one another in the arena two decades later because Cannon never ceased to approve those words of LaFollette's, but LaFollette changed his mind. Cannon himself in the 1880's had no fixed ideas about government and society. He had not turned into such an inflexible opponent of change that people could say of him, as they did later, that if he had attended the caucus on Creation, he would have voted to keep chaos. He had one crusading interest in fairness which brought him close to the heart of many who afterward cursed him. Remembering that his father had moved his family from the sweet fields of western North Carolina to the pioneer wilderness of Indiana in order to get away from slave country, remembering that an uncle he visited in Cincinnati during his law school days had run a station on the Underground Railway, and remembering that he himself had become a Republican immediately after the Jackson conference out of opposition to slavery, Cannon strongly objected to segregation of Negroes from white people. To show his sentiment, he voted against the first version of the Interstate Commerce Commission Bill because it encouraged segregation.

As LaFollette remained in the background at the Capitol, Cannon steadily rose in stature. He was always on the lookout for new friends among the new Congressmen, because he had an uncomfortable sort of notoriety outside the immediate circle of his colleagues at the Capitol. He occasionally cut loose in public with the coarse language which he later reserved for private conversations. Once ladies left the gallery in blushes when he spoke on the floor. He was called "Foul-Mouth Joe" before he became "Uncle Joe." Yet his colleagues appreciated him for his candor, his thoroughness, and his brightness. He was a leader among the Republican Representatives whom LaFollette joined. When the voters in the election of 1888 gave his party the majority of seats in the House, after a long period of supremacy for the Democrats, Thomas B. Reed, the stiletto-witted Speaker, assigned him to the Rules Committee. The appointment was a mark of esteem, for the committee, or rather the majority members of it, governed the business of the House. The majority members numbered only three—Cannon, Reed, and Major William McKinley, the President-to-be. They agitated the United States with the political sensation of 1890, during LaFollette's last term in the House.

The excitement occurred because the House consisted of almost equal numbers of Republicans and Democrats. When Con-

gress convened in December 1889, the Republicans had a majority
of only eight—so dangerously small that they spent the first six
weeks of the Session in raising their number to twenty-four, by
ruling against the Democrats in eight contested election cases.
The Democrats grew sullen as the majority added to its strength,
and then showed their spirit by refusing to vote on roll calls.
John Quincy Adams had been the first member of the House to
stay silent when the clerk called his name and he was present.
Until his day the House rules required all present to answer the
call, but by the time Reed became Speaker many followed the
silence custom, hallowed by the passage of almost sixty years
since Adams had initiated it. Such abstentions immobilized the
House, when those members who did answer did not comprise a
quorum. With the House inert, the federal government could not
function. Reed asked Cannon to find him an avenue of escape from
the parliamentary trap.

Cannon obliged with a report, which Reed and McKinley approved as the recommendation of the Committee on Rules. The
document lay on Reed's desk one day late in January when he
submitted another contested election case to the House. A Democrat demanded a roll call. When the clerk read the names for the
ayes and nays, only one hundred and sixty-three members spoke.
They did not make up a quorum. The very Democrat who had
asked for the roll call and one hundred and sixty-four of his colleagues remained silent. To the astonishment of the House, Reed,
following the suggestion contained in Cannon's report, with which
few members were yet familiar, instructed the clerk to record the
names of those present and not voting and to count them in the
quorum. At once the Democrats arose from their desks and shouted
"Despotism." They swarmed to the well of the House and climbed
toward Reed's chair. The sergeant-at-arms waved the mace aloft
in a vain effort to restore order quickly. One Democrat, determined not to be counted, knocked a hole through a door with two
good kicks and fled from the chamber through the splintered
panels. Reed, a large and imposing man, said nothing during the
turmoil. He stood easily at his desk, his hand resting on the head
of his gavel. When quiet returned, he announced in his authori-
tative drawl that a quorum was indeed present. Within a week
Cannon formally presented to the House his report on the rules.

It justified the quorum count by citing precedents from the New York State Legislature, city councils in Indiana and Illinois, and the British House of Commons. The House approved the report. Thereafter the Speaker continued his practice of counting silent men. The House of Representatives could legislate once more.

The adoption of the rules report is the beginning of the road which led to Cannon's Speakership and his nation-shaking power, although his best years seemed to be behind him when Reed put him on the Rules Committee. His highest ambition had been thwarted. Twice he had sought election to the Senate, and twice the legislature at Springfield had turned him down. At fifty-four he had no goals; he simply worked from day to day. But life can be an autumn flower. Any man of middle years who stares at his socks in discouragement because he has not made his mark can cheer up by contemplating Cannon. Those rebuffs at Springfield made possible subsequent glory, because the source of Grandfather Cannon's strength as dictator flowed from his position in the House. The quorum fight attracted national attention to Uncle Joe for worthy reasons which put into the shadow his reputation for vulgarity of language and which enhanced his standing with his fellows in Congress.

In ignorance of what manner of man he himself was about to become, LaFollette voted for Cannon's rules, which fortified Speaker Cannon when he turned into the political giant. In after years Senator LaFollette could not condone the legislative policies of Representative LaFollette. Representative LaFollette praised the protective tariff as the source in American life of a unique equilibrium which, after the completion of his intellectual evolution, he said the tariff was eliminating from American life. Cannon enormously admired LaFollette's ability to justify protection. He arranged for LaFollette to be made a member of the Ways and Means Committee, which wrote the tariff bills. There LaFollette helped to compose the McKinley Bill, a high-tariff masterpiece. The McKinley Bill strangely affected LaFollette's life. In casting his vote for it in the House, he ended his career as a protectionist. The bill, which became law in the spring of 1890, displeased the country, and in the autumn the voters replaced both Cannon and LaFollette with free-trading Democrats. Cannon was back in the

House in two years, in a position to rise gradually above the mark he had attained in his Rules Committee work for Tom Reed, but LaFollette never returned to that branch of Congress. Nine years he spent in a kind of Garden of Olives, and when he emerged his thoughts about America were clear and comprehensive.

Back in Madison, LaFollette brooded about the one surpassing question which overwhelmed his interest in his personal affairs. Was it possible to bring the influence of wealthy men over the economic and political life of the country into line with the influence of the poor and weak? His determination to answer the question affirmatively took command of him one afternoon in the Plankinton House in Milwaukee.

He called at the Plankinton at the request of Philetus Sawyer. The old lumber Senator greeted him cheerily and sat down beside him. It was 1891. LaFollette no longer had any political standing. But he was kin by marriage to Judge Robert G. Siebacker, of the Wisconsin Superior Court, and Siebacker had before him a number of cases which interested Sawyer. The defendants in the cases were five former state treasurers. Each of them had invested the state funds under his control and had pocketed the interest. Sawyer assured LaFollette that they were innocent of wrong. They had merely been following custom. The state had not been robbed of any funds. It would be unjust should the five lose the suit. They would be branded as dishonest when they had been as honest as others. Sawyer leaned closer to LaFollette. His voice fell to a whisper. Would it be possible for LaFollette to see Judge Siebacker in order to serve the ends of justice? If he would only ask the Judge to decide in favor of the treasurers! Sawyer could not ask him. It was a task for a lawyer. And since lawyers lived by fees, LaFollette should receive $1,000 for his intervention.

Bribery—the cancerous word leaped to LaFollette's mind. He fled from the hotel. He said nothing to Sawyer, then or ever afterward. He had been offered a bribe to influence his relative. The men he had been fighting were not only unfair in denying equal political voice to the people under their economic domination, but they were also immoral. It was a gruesome discovery for a man who had trusted all men before he met Postmaster Keyes. Injustice and immorality went together. Not only did politics need reformation, evil needed repression. And reform and repression could be accomplished by the same stroke. The revelation in the Plankinton ignited LaFollette into a crusader. He saw himself anew—he had been ordained to break the power forever of such as Sawyer and the Spooners.

Before he could obey the impulse born in the Plankinton, La-Follette had to make a practical decision. Should he make Washington or Wisconsin his base from which to crimp the powers of the railroads and lumbermen? Mainly because the Republican Party refused to nominate him again for the House of Representatives, he decided that his crusade should begin in Wisconsin and end in Washington. But in Wisconsin it was not enough to be a district attorney. He must control the governorship. At first he sought to preserve his personal independence by playing the role of king-maker. In 1894 he worked for the nomination of Nils P. Haugen as the Republican candidate for governor. Haugen was an equalitarian. Alone among Republican Representatives from Wisconsin he had kept his seat in Congress in the avalanche of 1890. But Haugen lost the governorship nomination, and LaFollette lost when he sought it himself in 1896 and 1898. The powers he yearned to wreck were strong enough to prevent him from getting in position to wreck them.

LaFollette sought the governorship again in 1900, and at last he won it. To the residents of Wisconsin LaFollette had become as familiar as their white pine forests when he succeeded at last in his quest for the governorship. Canvassing the whole state, he had spoken to thousands, in speeches from the hustings and in conversations at the roadside and in kitchens and parlors and church halls from Presque Isle to Beloit. People thronged to hear him as though he were a show, because he was the great orator of the northwest.

It took two glances and a few minutes of listening for a man to catch the attractions of Robert Marion LaFollette. He looked like a jockey. He stood five feet four—shorter than the little public figures of our day, Harry Truman, Winston Churchill, Joseph Stalin. His thin straight nose and the lines in his cheeks made his visage stern. His head was too large for the rest of him. His red hair was so thick it rose straight up from his scalp, like a flame blown by bellows, before it fell back toward his collar. His speaking performance was austere. He had no elocutionary tricks, no gestures. He usually signalled "Finis" simply by crossing his arms across his chest.

In the country areas people swarmed about LaFollette because the issues he dealt with oppressed them. The urban people listened because they knew he had so much influence among the farmers that he might win power over the cities. The goal he held out to city and country in 1900 was the revival of "representative government." To reach that goal, he advocated introduction of the primary, state regulation of railway rates, and taxation of the railways on the same basis that governed taxation of other enterprises doing business in Wisconsin. The officials in Madison knew neither the real value of the railways' Wisconsin property nor how much revenue those railways, which operated also in other states, derived from Wisconsin. Tax money might be escaping. A new revenue law was needed. Illinois and Iowa regulated rail rates, and in those two states freight charges on commodities used or sold by farmers were 39 per cent lower than in Wisconsin.

LaFollette was an indomitable man. It was a good thing, because disappointment, delay, and frustration were his lot. The legislature elected with him in 1900 defeated his bills for the primary and fair taxation of the railways. Agents of the railways were thick in Madison on LaFollette's inauguration day and thereafter. They entertained the members of the legislature in ways that smacked of delightful luxury to gentlemen used to the rugged life of Wisconsin. Even the governor's supporters sometimes were absent during crucial roll calls—drunk on the enemy's whiskey. LaFollette was re-elected governor in 1902, and again the legislature turned down his "representative government" program. "The contest must go on and on, till it is settled and settled right," he said.

LaFollette defied the tradition of his state in 1904 by seeking a third term as governor. The conservative Republicans rubbed their hands in joy. They thought that the combination of his record of failure with two legislatures and the picture he gave of overweening ambition in trying to monopolize the highest office in Wisconsin would ruin him. The railroads halted trains to enable engineers and conductors, firemen and brakemen to vote for anti-LaFollette delegates to the Republican nominating convention.

Station agents organized campaigns in towns and villages against the governor. But the convention chose LaFollette, and the state sent him to Madison for a third term. To cover more ground, this innovator campaigned by automobile, which still resembled a buggy without shafts. In Norwegian, which he had spoken from childhood, he described to serious dairymen the impertinence of the lobbyists in Madison as he beseeched Wisconsin to elect a legislature that would accept his program. The appeal struck home. The new legislature enacted the primary law, created a Wisconsin State Railway Commission, authorized the state government to regulate rail rates, and passed the fair taxation law. It did more, because by 1904 LaFollette, coached by his wife and by counsellors in the political science department of the University of Wisconsin, had begun to notice injustice in the city as well as on the farm. He presented the legislature with an urban reform program, and the responsive members enacted laws directing factories to provide sanitary working conditions for their employees, establishing public employment offices, requiring private employers to compensate workmen for their injuries, and forbidding child labor.

In victory LaFollette remained discontented. At the Republican State Convention in Iowa in 1902 Governor Albert B. Cummins condemned the protective tariff as the "mother of trusts." The speech impressed LaFollette. The defender of the McKinley Act was beginning to see protection as an evil. There had been a time when he thought the tariff brought prosperity to the farmer. Behind its protective wall manufacturers could develop such wide markets for their products that the prices of those products actually fell far below the level of protective duties. Representative LaFollette himself had told Congress how protection reduced the price of horseshoe nails, which were necessary for farming in Wisconsin. Now he gathered from Cummins that the tariff strengthened business monopoly by saving it from competition and thereby raised prices. He saw a direct link between the tariff and the economic power of the railways in Wisconsin. The Standard Oil Company was a trust, and H. H. Rogers, first vice president of Standard, was not only a director of the Chicago, Milwaukee and St. Paul Railway but the "real power" of that line, according to the Milwaukee *Journal.* The tariff schedule on petroleum products kept high the price of kerosene with which the farmers lit their homes.

The Milwaukee road and the Chicago, Northwestern were the two railways LaFollette had in the front of his mind when he signed the rate control bills which the legislature passed up to him. Their corporate tie-ins with businesses that admittedly were trusts gave the rails a trust flavor of their own—a flavor which could not be totally expunged by a governor and legislature in Madison. H. H. Rogers' base was New York. The tariff which strengthened Standard Oil and through it strengthened the Chicago, Milwaukee and St. Paul was a federal law. And the governor soon realized that a Wisconsin alone could not control the Milwaukee and the Northwestern. Those railway companies were at home in Illinois, Iowa, Michigan, Minnesota, North Dakota, South Dakota, and Nebraska as well as Wisconsin. The state commission needed the buttress of a new federal rate law. To put himself into a position to reform the tariff and to strengthen the federal control over the railways, LaFollette ran for the United States Senate. He won. In January 1906 he took his seat in the Capitol, where Cannon's authority was already supreme, although not yet absolute.

By then the transition in relationship between LaFollette and Cannon from their mutual sympathy of 1890 to a kind of Hindu-Moslem hostility was complete.

Cannon played into the hands of LaFollette and the other advocates of the statism that he hated by descending to tyranny. His zealous determination to kill the agitation for stronger government provoked him to seek and attain absolute mastery over the House by perverting the rules from which he drew his powers as Speaker. In contact with this autocracy, the affability of the Arlington reception curdled. Two years after the birthday party the friendly Burleson was complaining, "The House of Representatives has ceased to be a legislative body." It enacted only the laws that Cannon deigned to have enacted. Men who cried, "Put 'er there," when they greeted Uncle Joe under the silken streamers came to damn their friend as "Czar" and "Iron Duke." Having established a personal hegemony over the House, he extended it to the Senate, and then took control of the President and the Republican Party and thus at length over the Union it-self. "The whole country lies, practically, in Papa Cannon's hands," the magazine *Independent* said at the period of his supreme power.

Cannon was the emery wheel against which Americans sharpened their understanding of their own political problems. The educative process was slow, however, because like every epic event, the struggle developed gradually. Cannon's abilities gave him strength enough to stave off the reformers at the out-set of conflict. He supported his dictatorship by shrewd use of his wit, ingenuity, and temperament. He was determined, sagacious, and confident that right was with him.

The gaining and keeping of great power in the United States by one person, following the man-made rules that govern the conduct of the House, calls for talent and skill in human relation-ships and for political knowledge and aptitude far greater than that required in fascistic or communistic dictators. The latter have guns and police and discriminatory laws and edicts and usually a muffled press and suborned lawyers and docile courts to keep them in authority. Cannon had but two weapons; his own talents and Jefferson's *Manual of Parliamentary Practice*. They served him until LaFollette's supporters in the House re-vised the rules in Jefferson's *Manual* when Cannon no longer could summon a majority in the House to defend them.

When Cannon's heroics failed him, his idea crashed. In over-turning the Speaker, the public invited America to begin the creation of the modern welfare state, which horrified him. Can-non's fall opened the way for bigger government, for Wilson and New Freedom, leading in time to the New Deal and Fair Deal of Franklin Roosevelt and Harry Truman. The fall also planted the seed for the puzzling confusion that besets us in the ques-tion whether by empowering the state to save us, we are putting the state in a position eventually to swallow us. In other words, Uncle Joe's experiment in heroism ushered the United States politically and intellectually into the twentieth century.

CHAPTER ——•—— 4

Vermilion Street

ARRIVING in Danville—a railroad town in the midst of farming country, laden with the sweet odors of green corn and smoke from the engines—Cannon went straight to the roomy house of maroon brick at 418 North Vermilion Street, where his grandchildren lived. Uncle Joe could catch a glimpse of it from well down the street as the shiny yellow trolley from the depot turned up Vermilion at the Public Square in the middle of town. The mansard steeple rose above the great oak tree in the front yard, and in the late afternoon in summer threw a shadow on the house across the street. A few years ago modernizers tore down the house and put up a Piggly-Wiggly store. In 1906 it was a landmark. It was comfortable outside and in. Five sets of fat columns placed two by two held up the roof of the wide front porch, a cool retreat in the evening, for it faced east. Within was living space for the children and their nurse; for Uncle Joe's younger daughter Mabel and her husband, Ernest X. LeSeure; for Uncle Joe's maiden daughter Helen, who mostly stayed with him in Washington; for Joe himself, when he was there; a music room, dining room, parlor, sun parlor, upstairs sitting room, quarters for the servants, and a study for Uncle Joe. Altogether, 418 looked like good money for a small city. It was a symbol of his progress in the land of opportunity from the poverty of his young manhood, when he had sometimes walked as far as twenty miles

40

along the dusty Illinois roads to plead a law case for a fee of $5. The house was a monument to a career. It commemorated clear-cut victory in the God-helps-those-that-help-themselves battle to get ahead. It represented the kind of world and life he was out to save by standing off LaFollette and Gompers and Roosevelt and the whole tribe of reformers.

Cannon had bought the house with profits from the money which his albino brother, the late William P. Cannon, had invested for him in farms in New York and Indiana and Nebraska and in traction companies in the Middle West. This brother had spent a forlorn boyhood. The neighbors in Parke County, Indiana, near where Sugar Creek runs into the Wabash, had teased him for his squinting pink eyes, and Mrs. Cannon taught him at home rather than send him down the lane to school, where children and teachers alike thought that under pale hair lay a weak brain. But Bill had a talent for making money, and he began to show it as soon as he left the backwoods of Indiana. He settled in Tolono, Illinois, in 1860, and founded a bank in the rear room on the second floor of a pine clapboard building, where in a small roller safe he kept the deposits of the merchants and the corn farmers. When the Civil War ended, Albino Bill lent money at 2 per cent a month. When fire burned down the building and charred the currency on deposit, he borrowed money out of town, repaid his customers, and kept the bank going and put half the ownership in Joe's name. He moved to Danville in 1880 and set up the Second National, and continued to his death with fine shrewdness and decency to make money. The city gave him a perpetual franchise to make and sell illuminating gas. Joe had a direct hand in the business only occasionally. While Bill laid the foundation for two small prairie fortunes, his own and his brother's, Joe worked in Washington year after year from 1873 onward, with a two-year lapse, for a government salary that never exceeded $5,000 a year.

Had fate not made him a widower, perhaps Uncle Joe's interest in accumulating money would have died before his treasure grew large enough to affect his political attitudes. When he neared his fiftieth birthday, he told his wife Molly that they had $25,000. "Father, that is enough," she said. But in a few years she died. Joe had been a tender husband in that frontier tradition which called upon men to look up to their wives as a bit above human-kind. For his wife he abandoned the church he had been born in. He was a Quaker, and Mary Reed was a Methodist, and a Methodist parson married them without a Quaker by-your-leave. When a Friend directed him to express regret in public at having married out of meeting, he returned: "If you mean that I am to get up in meeting and say that I am sorry I married Mary, I won't do it. I'm damned if I'm sorry and I'm damned if I will say I am." He worshiped thereafter by the rules of John Wesley, but he remained on good terms with the Quakers.

His parents named him John Joseph Gurney for a great English Quaker, and it was said—but not corroborated—that Gurney visited Dr. Cannon's house in New Garden and looked at young Joseph in his cradle. Uncle Joe was a Republican because he had been a Quaker whose relatives made a crusade against slavery, and they paid dear in loss of personal comfort for that crusade. His father harbored fugitive slaves, and in Indiana he was fined because he defied the law and prejudices of his non-Quaker neighbors by letting young Joseph work in a field with a freed Negro. Joseph's Quaker cousins in Cincinnati helped operate a station on the Underground Railway. The history of his forebears in the United States was the history of Quakers fleeing from persecution and restraint. He could trace the wanderings of those ancestors with other followers of Fox from England to Nantucket to South Carolina to North Carolina to Richmond, Indiana, to Annapolis, Indiana. Cannon's collision with Quaker marital precepts could not destroy that heritage.

The old man saw a reflection of Molly in his elder daughter, Helen. A statuesque woman, she had lost her father's rough simplicity on an educational passage through Wellesley, Paris, Stuttgart, and Dresden. Unmarried, she kept house for the Speaker in his Washington residence, a three-story, twenty-room stone-front on Vermont Avenue. "Half way between wealth and poverty," Uncle Joe located it, although its dining room, large enough to seat thirty, suggested that the balance was on the side of wealth. Helen spent many an afternoon in fine weather and rain leaving cards on her father's behalf at the homes of the long succession of officials whose wives and daughters, through the magic of calling cards, managed year after year to exchange visits, in full satisfaction of protocol, without ever actually seeing one another. She gave many a lunch, and almost nightly she played bridge, instead of the poker beloved by "Papa," as she called the Speaker. She judged her father's friends with less charity than he and pointed out to him the ones she mistrusted. In all she was a precise and overpowering woman, but she pleased her father.

He once refused to attend a dinner at the White House, to which President Roosevelt had invited him and Helen, because she objected that the man assigned to escort her to the dining room had no rank in official society. Like Renaissance ambassadors, who resented any slight done them as a slur on the kings they served, Helen Cannon held that it would signify that her father, the Speaker, was unimportant if she accepted an escort from far down the list. The President staved off that kind of embarrassment in the future by giving a dinner each year for the Speaker; and there was no doubt on those occasions that Cannon and his daughter were the ranking guests.

Except on Vermont Avenue and in Danville, the men's world monopolized Cannon. But women pleased him. He respected their minds and instincts, and he favored women's suffrage when it was a wild idea. "Women have to take care of themselves and take care of the men at the same time," he once said.

The house on Vermilion Street no longer belonged to Cannon in 1906. He had given it to LeSeure, his son-in-law. Seldom did present come deeper from the heart. Joe loved him for loving his daughter Mabel, and he admired him for his financial talents. LeSeure, the young vice president of the First National Bank, looked out for Uncle Joe's investments after his brother Bill's death. Bill had made money for himself and added to Cannon's wealth by operating the gas company, the Danville street railway, and the Danville electric light company. The two men had owned the enterprises jointly until 1903, when LeSeure sold them for a substantial gain.

Having given the house to LeSeure as a gesture of profound friendship, Cannon retained absolute sovereignty only over the few square feet of the first floor that his study took up. This room nicely suited the old man, who always mixed the homely with the elegant. He drank champagne from a kitchen tumbler. A large brass cuspidor sat on the oriental rug. The centerpiece was a mahogany desk, handsome but marred by deep scratches in the wood, dug by the nails in Cannon's shoes which he rested on the edge. He liked to read with his feet higher than his head, while wearing his old hat, and he read the same words over and over. He kept a Bible on the desk, and the shelves along the walls of the study were filled with bound copies of the Congressional Record. Once upon a time he had soaked himself in Aesop and Plutarch and Josephus, but with age his reading tastes became more and more select. Now the recorded words of God and Congress were enough for him, and he knew them almost by heart.

The study, the house, Danville, and the five rural counties roundabout that made up the Eighteenth Congressional District (which Cannon represented in the House) comprised the old man's heartland. Cannon would mean nothing in Washington unless he remained the favorite in Danville. Before he could spread his influence over all America, his district had to accept his influence as supreme. So the future was uncertain in the early summer of 1906, because it was an election year, and he must persuade his constituents once more to choose him to speak for them in Congress.

The deep-planted political habits of his constituency favored him. He was the Republican representative of a Republican district in a Republican state. Except in the southernmost counties, it was as much a tradition for the voters in Cannon's prairie domain to mark their ballots under the eagle each election day as it was to plant new seed each spring. For half a century (excepting the two years from 1893 to 1895) his party had controlled the government of Illinois, by electing either the governor or a majority of the members of the legislature at Springfield. No Democrat had beaten Cannon since 1890. The presence of the Soldiers Home at the edge of Danville gave him a running start over any other candidate. The federal government had built the home in Vermilion County because Congress in 1898 passed Uncle Joe's bill authorizing it, and most of the 2,500 old warriors living there voted the straight Cannon ticket. The men his own age who had fought him in politics until the turn of the century had given up the ghost or abandoned the struggle, and his younger constituents supported him automatically in deference to his age and honors. In the Eighteenth District he had become almost a natural feature of life, like sunshine and snow.

A compulsion to prove that he was younger than his years fed his desire to return to Washington for the joust with reform. He feared a do-nothing old age. He had suffered in watching his mother's helpless agony in her last years, when she had to sit immobile in a chair while wishing vainly she could go down to the Quaker meeting of a Sunday or stir around in the kitchen in the morning or step out into the garden to trowel the flowers on good days. He preferred to give up the ghost in the manner of his dim-sighted brother William, of whom a walk to the Public Square always reminded him. William's bank, the Second National, faced the Square. In it William had been busy almost to the moment when he died, five years earlier, in the prime of health, from a skull fracture. Taking a breather from the ledgers, he had climbed one day to a narrow window sill in the bank and had balanced himself there to hang a curtain. He fell head first to the marble floor and was gone within the day. That departure matched his father's end. Dr. Horace Cannon, too, died in harness. He was swept to death one afternoon in the spring torrent of Sugar Creek, which was rushing like the limited toward the Wabash River, while going on horseback with quinine in his pill-bag to soothe a neighbor ridden by the ague.

Cannon had always gagged at the thought of doing make-believe work. In 1904 Governor Odell offered hm the vice presidential nomination on the Republican ticket. Cannon laughed. "I'd rather go back to hoeing potatoes," he said. The vice president had a sinecure, and Cannon meant to be in the thick of things. "We have motormen on my street-car system who have more influence with me than the governor of New York has," said Cannon. He had the last word on the subject with his friend Julius Caesar Burrows: "You will see me an archangel before I am vice president."

Fear that age would put him on the shelf chilled Cannon. He stooped a bit as he walked in his hitching way—"like a mate ashore," a friend described it. His red whiskers had turned white, and he drank whiskey for his health instead of for fun. But he liked to show off his vigor. He learned to ride a bicycle at sixty-five. On a steamboat trip he took to the West Indies, as he neared seventy, he danced jigs and hornpipes on a heaving deck while the other passengers slumped in their chairs in oyster-eyed discomfort. When he returned to the U.S., he walked the legs off young Senator James R. Hemenway on a hunting trip in Indiana, where Cannon brought down five quail with thirty-five shots.

"I have more work in me than any three men in Congress," he told a newspaper interviewer. "I can sit up more hours than any man in the House and accomplish more in quantity and quality than any three of the hardest working members twisted and doubled together. I can do with less sleep than any man of 25. I can do these things, and do them year in and year out, and when Congress adjourns I am fresh as a daisy. Yet when I go out on the stump . . . and talk night and day for a week without rest, something not one man in a hundred half my age can do, I find myself referred to in the newspapers as 'that venerable statesman from Illinois who was a contemporary of Lyman J. Trumbull and Stephen A. Douglas and Abraham Lincoln.' It is a damned outrage to put me into the 'venerable statesman' class, and I don't like it."

He kept stepping lively almost because he seemed to want to outwit death itself. Death was lonely, and he was a gregarious man. Since the Spanish-American War he had eaten no lunch, from a conviction that, after sixty, short rations meant long life, but daily he accompanied his cronies to lunch sheerly out of love for company and talk. He liked to know that his friends were thinking about him. "Ah, when we cross over, how soon we are forgotten," he lamented, with a glance at himself, when his friend John Ketcham, the deaf Congressman from New York who had served thirty-four years in the House, died in 1906. At three score and ten Cannon pictured himself as just a beginner in life. He was frail, but he told the Doorkeeper of the House that he would reach 100. In his Vermilion Street study he copied down an epitaph he had seen on a three-year-old's grave in Cheltenham, England.

> It is so soon that I am done for,
> I wonder what I was begun for.

ran the words on the headstone, and Cannon implied that they would be appropriate for a man of seventy.

That determination to conquer age put energy into Cannon's campaign for re-election. From the beginning of the contest in August, Uncle Joe was relieved to find that Samuel Gompers and his American Federation of Labor was the only faction of the mal-

contents that intended to oppose him. He was poison, indeed, to
a few sharp-eyed improvers and hungry seekers after special favors. Cannon opposed the legislation authorizing the federal government to subsidize the Merchant Marine, and the New York
Commercial, in reprisal, called him "our un-American Speaker."
To a storekeeper in Indian Territory he became "the most con-
temptible tyrant in all history," when he held up the bill for ad-
mitting Oklahoma Territory and Indian Territory to the Union as
a single state. The merchants of the territories resolved to punish
Illinois by boycotting all goods from that state as long as it kept
Cannon in office, but the Speaker stuck to his guns. In the summer of 1906 Benjamin Orange Flower, who in his lifetime edited
six magazines devoted to social betterment, denounced Cannon
in *The Arena* (fourth in his line) and wrote about him:

During the past winter he perhaps more than any other man in
public life has stood between the people and the trusts and monopolies;
preventing the relief which the former sought from oppression, extor-
tion, and corrupt practices. He was distinctly the friend of the criminal
rich and the oppressor of labor.

Most of the laboring men in the Eighteenth, however, saw
Cannon differently. The district was a stronghold of the railway
brotherhoods, not affiliated with Gompers' Federation. The rail-
roaders in Illinois supported Uncle Joe, against the advice of their
leaders. "Mr. Cannon has been Speaker of the House during the
last three sessions of Congress, and many cases can be cited to
show where he has used the great power and influence of that
office to defeat the legislation which ours and other organizations
of labor have sought," H. R. Fuller, legislative representative of
the Brotherhood of Railway Trainmen, wrote to his brothers in
Danville during the 1906 campaign. But on his home grounds
Uncle Joe pulled more weight than Fuller. The Wabash had shops
out near Danville Junction, and the Speaker knew how to please
the engineers and firemen and conductors and brakemen. When
the Chicago and Eastern Illinois blacklisted their striking employees after the great walkout in 1894, Cannon found jobs with
other roads for most of them who came from Danville, and the
memory of that bold assistance was still warm in 1906. He was
solid with the railway mail men. The superintendent of the railway mail service raised the pay of Oscar Cooper, a clerk on the

Chicago-Carbondale run, from $800 to $900 a year because Cannon asked for it. Clyde Acree, another constituent, a mail clerk on the Wabash, applied for a transfer from the Danville-Thebes run to the main line into St. Louis. Second Assistant Postmaster General Joseph A. Stewart in Washington turned him down. But when Cannon put on the heat, Acree got his transfer.

Against such practical evidence to the contrary, the assertion of Gompers that Uncle Joe was the enemy of labor lost the punch it would have carried in some factory districts. The one labor group in Vermilion County which set out to drub him was the United Mine Workers, whose members worked in the coal shafts not far from Danville. The Socialists nominated John A. Walker, a U.M.W. member, with the backing of John Mitchell, the Mine Workers' president, and of Gompers. The Walker candidacy pleased Cannon because it prevented the voters who would vote against Cannon from giving united backing to the Democratic nominee, Charles G. Taylor.

The issue in the Eighteenth turned on the injunction, which judges were issuing to employers under the aegis of the Sherman Anti-Trust Act, on the ground that strikers restrained trade. Walker said it was unjust and unfair for the courts to enjoin unions from striking. "I will at all times be opposed to this legislation," Cannon told his constituents when he spoke on the anti-injunction bill. Disunity in the Federation weakened Gompers and Walker. After the executive committee of the Gompers organization voted in September to take an active part in politics, principally in order to retire Cannon for good to Vermilion Street, E. H. Nockels, secretary of the Chicago Federation of Labor, arranged a mass meeting on November 1 at the Bradley Plow Works in Kankakee, and invited a number of labor bigwigs from Chicago to attend. To greet the strangers fittingly at the station, he asked the musicians' union of Chicago to send a band, but the union wanted more money than Nockels would pay and refused to go to Kankakee. Nockels had to hire a local pickup band. Cannon took this division of interest as a good omen.

By soliciting re-election on the ground that he could save the Eighteenth District and America from such as Gompers, Cannon worried President Roosevelt, who gave him the following advice by letter:

I want very much that our people shall quit attacking Gompers. . . . If the attack is continually made, the average labor man grows to believe that the head of the Federation of Labor is being attacked as such; in other words, that he is attacked as the representative of the working man, and that the working men must all band together to resent it.

Cannon replied:

There are enough members of the Federation of Labor in my district, if they vote solidly against me, to defeat me. . . . When it is once understood what Mr. Gompers is demanding, I am satisfied there is a considerable number of Republicans affiliated with the Federation of Labor who will not follow him to the extent of casting their ballots in accordance with his dictates. So that, if it becomes necessary, in my district I must strike him, or rather what he demands, from the shoulder and let the blow land in the solar plexus.

In September Senator Albert Beveridge of Indiana wrote the President:

Mr. Cannon in his speech at Danville has utterly missed the meaning of the times. He entirely fails to comprehend the great movement of the American millions which you are leading; he is utterly ignorant of the spirit that is now spreading over this nation.

But Mr. Roosevelt sent his handsome son-in-law, Nicholas Longworth, to Danville to speak up for Cannon after Richard Yates, a Republican, former governor of Illinois and son of the state's Civil War governor, had embarrassed the President by telling a crowd in the Public Square at the end of North Vermilion Street that Roosevelt and William Jennings Bryan stood side by side as "champions of the people against the greed and avarice of the moneyed tyrants." Yates cited Cannon as the agent of the avaricious and recommended that the district replace him with Walker or Charles Taylor. It was not politic for Roosevelt to let his opinions be identified with those of Bryan, the leader of the Democratic Party, who had lost to the McKinley-Roosevelt ticket when he ran for the presidency in 1900. Had Dick Yates kept his mouth shut, the President might have been satisfied to ignore the contest in the Eighteenth Illinois. Instead, he instructed Longworth to say: "The President has done his greatest work in the last five years, during which time his right hand and helper has been

Speaker Joseph G. Cannon, your own distinguished citizen, whom you should return to the White House."

Cannon's outlook had grown bright by the time the corn was in the cribs. The banks and saloons did not open on November 6, and the enfranchised citizens went to the polls. The voters followed Longworth's advice. The final tally showed that Vermilion, Kankakee, Edgar, Douglas, and Coles Counties had cast enough ballots for Cannon to give him a majority of 10,027 over Walker and Taylor combined. He won by a larger margin than he had in 1904. Those prairie votes were all Joe needed to launch his continental struggle between heroes and villains.

CHAPTER — — 5

Uncle Joe's Court

THE ELECTION campaign made Cannon everybody's symbol of the old-fashioned ideas. In trying to thrust Uncle Joe from office into obscurity, Gompers had raised him to a prominence which few men in the United States ever enjoyed. After the votes had been counted, people no longer thought that Cannon just stood for the 1800's. In his person he actually embodied the 1800's in the struggle to fend off the novelties of the new century. The campaign, his own speeches, the speeches against him, and his final triumph dispersed the fog which formerly had hid his nature and his intentions from all but a few and exposed him as the great defender of the glories of the past, or the perpetuator of the abuses inherited from the past, depending on the point of view.

Earlier he had seemed, as far as most observers were concerned, to be but one among many men banded together in the House equally, none more important than the other, against the promoters of reform. When Uncle Joe returned to Washington for the opening of the Lame Duck session of the Fifty-ninth Congress on December 3, 1906, however, the relationship between Cannon and his fellow standpatters in the band was clear. Cannon was supreme and the others were the loyal friends who did the Speaker's bidding. Those special friends made up a kind of court circle, which was Cannon's instrument for applying the rules with strong discipline. It existed because he created it. It had power because he inspired its members to be loyal not only to him but to one another, and they were not divided by jealous quarrels and rival ambitions.

As courtiers, Cannon chose men who were professionally congenial. In the main they were businessmen or lawyers who had grown up on the farm. Cannon liked that kind. "The men who are efficient and industrious are those who have their feet in the soil," he said. Since many of them were self-made, and, by climbing Horatio Alger's ladder, had satisfied themselves that self-reliance does lead to success, every one appeared to himself and to his fellows to be a breathing refutation of LaFollette's opinion that the federal government and the state governments must reshape the American social structure by statute if the country was to remain the land of opportunity.

The leader in Cannon's court was Sereno Elisha Payne, the chairman of the Ways and Means Committee. On him Cannon counted more than any other. Payne was adept, in the role of a tree fallen across the road, in barring the passage from his committee to the House floor of bills that would weaken the tariff, that keystone in the fortress of the past. He had sat upon the committee since 1889, and he praised protection. He had written five tariff acts of his own, all monuments to the tradition of high duties. He was an aloof man, disliked by most of his colleagues except the very few Congressmen in the first rank of Cannon's friends. The knowledge that he suffered from a short temper provoked some mischievous Representatives to goad him occasionally with impish remarks in debate, so that they could enjoy the sight of the dignified chairman blushing brightly, even to his ears, beneath the snowy crown of his thick hair and around the trim edges of his pure white mustache. To save himself from embarrassment, he seldom appeared upon the floor, and then he hardly ever spoke, except to say, "I object," or, "I move that this House do now adjourn." He loved baseball, and when he had to sit through the debates in spring and summer, he paid a messenger to report to him at half-hour intervals with the score of the game Washington was playing that day. He was a tall man, and as large as Tweedledee beneath his vest. When he walked down an aisle of the House, his abdomen sometimes brushed the ends of the benches. He spent most of his working hours behind the high oaken double

doors of his committee rooms, across the corridor from the House
chamber, where he laid plans by which Cannon could circumvent
the pressures from the White House and the reformers. He was
a lawyer by profession, but he had held public office during most
of his adult life, beginning as city attorney for Auburn, New York.
He had been a member of Congress since 1883. He was sixty-
three years old on June 26, 1906—the most elderly of the indispensable friends.

Joseph Albertus Tawney was chairman of the Appropriations
Committee, where he could keep the federal government cut down
close to the size satisfactory to Cannon by limiting the amount
of money it spent from year to year. Tawney was a blacksmith,
born in Gettysburg, Pennsylvania, seven years before the battle.
Like Cannon, he was a mover. He went West at twenty-two to
seek his fortune. For a while he continued to forge horseshoes,
and he became a master mechanic. He settled in Winona, Minnesota, and studied law at LaFollette's old school, the University of
Wisconsin. He went to Washington as a Representative in the
1890's. He spoke well, he thought clearly, and his colleagues respected him. He was a handsome man, dark-haired and luxuri-
ously mustached, and the years of pounding metal with the sledge
hammer had given him a strong, athletic physique. He was a conservative man, but he could not escape exposure to the reform
wind blowing across the plains from Wisconsin into Minnesota.
So his thoughts did not always match those of Cannon's other
friends. He had an independent streak that sometimes alarmed
the Speaker. For a long time he was a member of Ways and Means,
until in 1905 Payne reported to Cannon that Tawney, affected by
the sentiment of his region, was talking tariff reform. Cannon removed him from the committee before he could do any damage.
But the Speaker admired Tawney. He worked hard, and he was
at home with figures. The Speaker appointed him chairman of his
own old committee, Appropriations, in hopes that realization that
government costs money would sober him. In Cannon an uneasy
fear survived that Tawney might sometime try again to play his
own hand in his own way, yet at the same time Cannon realized
that Tawney's interest in protecting the sugar-beet growers in his
district made him a high-tariff man at heart. On his new committee
Tawney devoted himself to buttressing his power as chairman in

order to strengthen the position of the Speaker. He put aside—at least, he certainly seemed to put aside—his discontent with the tariff, and he comforted the Speaker with his ideas for maintaining the supremacy of the standpatters.

The discontented might still have defeated Cannon after their repulse by Payne or Tawney at the committee doors, had it not been for John Dalzell, a shy and gentle man of iron. The tariff reviser or advocate of heavy spending could pursue his goal on the floor of the House of Representatives itself, where all the members of all the committees gathered each day at noon. There a Representative could beseech his colleagues to pass the bills which had strangled in committee, or to change bills which suited the Speaker by adding amendments which satisfied the opponents. A Representative could have done such things, that is, had Cannon not possessed means to balk him. The most important means was the Rules Committee, which since the day Cannon had revised the rules to strengthen Reed, had been deciding the length of time, if any, the House might give to the debate of a bill important to the whole country, and determining how many and what kind of amendments the members might offer to the bill. The Rules Committee was a Congressional Thermopylae Pass. In command of that narrow entranceway into the House, Cannon could almost command the House itself.

A triumvirate on the committee dictated to the multitude in the House. The committee formally consisted of five Representatives, three Republicans and two Democrats, but the Republicans did not let the latter discuss business before them. "I am invited to the seances but I am never consulted about the spiritualistic appearances," John Sharp Williams, the ranking Democratic member, once remarked. Cannon himself was the chairman. His party colleagues were Charles Grosvenor, who was serving his last term in Congress, and Dalzell. Upon the latter Cannon relied to speak up for the Rules Committee on the House floor and there to deliver those ukases, disguised as resolutions, which prevented the freely chosen Representatives of the people from attempting to translate the people's wishes into legislation.

Dalzell was the only bore among the Speaker's special friends. He made long speeches in the House in a tinny voice, and he filled the speeches with long quotations from dull documents and read long tables of statistics. Hs appearance was far from formidable. He had a small head and a thin, sad face, decorated with a silky mustache that was too large for its setting. Outwardly he looked like Mr. Pipp—Charles Dana Gibson's symbol of the henpecked legion. He was hard of hearing, and during exchanges in debate he stood bent forward at the waist and his hand cupped to his right ear in order to catch the flow of words. Yet nothing escaped him. His exterior misled the casual. He was sharp of brain and firm of manner. Cannon had grasped his real worth soon after he arrived in Congress in 1887 as a Representative from a Pittsburgh (Pittsburg in those days) district. He was a graduate of Yale and a lawyer, sixty-two years old in 1906. He had the talents of a field marshal. He could organize a plan of action to be carried out in Congress in defense of the position which the Speaker had taken in committee meeting. This perfect second man had no desire to be chief. He never sought a committee chairmanship. So Cannon appointed him number two not only on Rules but also on Ways and Means. In the House he spoke for Payne as well as for the triumvirate, and off the House floor, except when committee business separated them, he spent his time with Payne. How often the lesser members saw huge Payne and spidery Dalzell walking together through the corridors of the Capitol, the former taking long lumbering strides and the latter almost skipping to keep up, and both of them working over the plans to fortify their Speaker.

James Eli Watson, a gay-witted lawyer from Rushville, Indiana, and James Robert Mann, a bitter-tongued lawyer from Chicago, reinforced Dalzell in upholding the cause of tradition on the floor. The Speaker, whose only children were his two daughters, treated the Jameses as tenderly and as proudly as though they were his sons. Uncle Joe appointed himself mentor to Watson soon after the latter entered the House of Representatives in 1895. He was young enough (forty-two in 1906) to be Cannon's child, and his Indiana origin further disposed Cannon to like him. Remembering his own boyhood near the Wabash, Cannon thought the best of almost all Hoosiers. The Hoosier country was so pleasant that even Dr. Cannon, the Speaker's father, once admitted that he liked it, although he had moved his family there as reluctantly as a soul setting out for Limbo. "Good-bye, God," he shouted at the sky as he left his home in North Carolina, "I am going to Indiana."

Watson had a good-humored, joshing manner, mixed with re-
spectful deference, which kept Cannon at ease. Above all he was
a talented peacemaker. That faculty helped Cannon win the
Speakership, for Watson dissolved a quarrel which had been
smoldering for two years between Cannon and Colonel William
Peter Hepburn, a Representative from Iowa. They fell out during
the House debate over the inter-oceanic canal. Hepburn said the
canal should cross Nicaragua. Cannon preferred a crossing at Panama. In the heat of their disagreement, the two men wounded
one another's feelings with savage personal jibes. It was a wonder
to the onlookers that they did not strike each other in the face.
The memory smarted so that they stopped speaking to each other.
That was still the situation when Uncle Joe announced his candidacy for the Speaker's office. Since Hepburn carried weight in
the Iowa delegation to Congress and since the attitude of the Iowa
delegation toward the candidates would affect the result of the
contest for the Speakership, Watson feared that the sour sulki-
ness of the two men might bring unhappy consequences. So he
persuaded Cannon to seek out Hepburn and apologize for having
imputed insincerity and deviousness to him, during the canal debate, by comparing him with the ink-squirting cuttlefish. Hepburn thereupon put Iowa behind Cannon's ambition and ended
all doubt about Cannon's chances.

The Speakership having been gained, Watson aided Cannon
once more by his instinct for fomenting good relations between
men. He persuaded the Speaker to give John Sharp Williams the
privilege of naming the Democratic members of the committees,
even though the Speaker, by the rules, had the privilege of naming all the members from all the parties. Sympathy between Democrat Williams and Republican Cannon was natural. They held
the same opinion about the relation of the state to society. Great
government meant great danger to Williams. "Every govern-
mental abuse is based upon some plea or pretext, and the usurpa-
tion of power by government is generally based upon 'necessity,'
the tyrants' plea," he said. His new power over committee appointments turned Williams into the autocrat of his party in the
House. Out of gratitude for this elevation, Williams often
obligingly withheld from his list of candidates for committee
posts the name of any Democrat whom Cannon found especially

objectionable, although William Randolph Hearst, with his Socialist notions, slipped into the Labor Committee. On the House floor Minority Leader Williams opposed the Speaker's program only perfunctorily, and, in this atmosphere of goodwill, it was easy for him to laugh at his exclusion from the serious meetings of the Committee on Rules.

Mann was more formidable than Watson, because his profound knowledge of parliamentary practice and his thorough preparation for discussing whatever legislative matter was at hand made him the superior of all Representatives in debate. No wonder Cannon encouraged him to stay in the House Chamber, where he spent more time than any other member of the court. He spoke there so often that he seemed to dwell on the floor, where his fierce scowl and sharp sarcasm made him really a fearsome creature to many of his colleagues. He was a tall, serious, black-bearded man of fifty-one, who had dedicated his life to civic duty. Hardly had he been graduated from the University of Illinois when he became successively attorney for Hyde Park (then the largest village in the United States, now a part of Chicago), Chicago city councilman, a director of the South Side Park Board, and a director of the Chicago Board of Education. The path led at last to the House of Representatives in 1898. There he was known as a city man, but he had grown up on his father's farm within sight of Bloomington, Illinois. That cinched his standing with Cannon, who wrote to George B. Van Norman, of the Chicago stockyards, that Mann was the "peer, as a legislator, of any man in the House."

Mann had an extraordinary ability for ruining the work of the opposition by accepting their proposals and then draining out their substance. By that means he had saved the trusts from effective restrictions during the early years of Roosevelt's presidency. In his capacity of chairman of a sub-committee of the House Interstate and Foreign Commerce Committee, he had repeated the arguments of the trust-busters as he pressed upon the House a bill which granted to the Department of Commerce and Labor the authority, through the Bureau of Corporations, to gather and publish statistics about business combinations. The bill, said Mann, would fix the clock of monopoly, and Roosevelt was on his side. In truth, as Mann expected, the bill left the trusts as strong and the trust-busters as weak as they had been before.

Because he was a man of conscience, however, Mann sometimes met the reformers half way, especially with respect to
reforms pressed for the sake of decency in human relationships
rather than for the purpose of working economic revolution. He
sponsored the pure food and drug bill which Congress enacted
in June 1906. In those days people risked death whenever they
ate dinner or took medicine. Benzoic acid was used to preserve
food, but it often poisoned the food it preserved. Opium-
addiction and alcoholism could be traced to the taking of cheap
patent remedies for illness, which contained habit-forming drugs
without its being so announced on the label. There was enough
morphine in "Kopp's Babies' Friend" to kill baby after baby whose
trusting parents had administered the tonic to relieve the child
of the pain of colic. The Senate passed a bill which permitted
patent-medicine makers to omit the information about drugs
and alcohol from the labels. Mann insisted that the information
appear, and, in keeping with the custom established during Cannon's Speakership, the Senate gave way to the House.

Another leader in the Speaker's select society, James Schoolcraft Sherman, of Utica, New York, sat like a clam in the House.
He made one speech there in almost twenty years. His duties
distracted his attention from the floor. It was up to him to see
that the nation was persuaded that the matters for which he himself and Cannon stood made good sense. He had to anticipate the
drift of opinion outside the House, so that the Speaker's court
could be ready to frustrate the opinion when it threatened to do
harm and to exploit it when it promised to help. Cannon never
forgot that the roots of his power, like the roots of the discontent,
lay far, far from Washington. Mann, Watson, Dalzell, Tawney,
and Payne could function only as long as the nation tolerated
them. The House and its committees no more created American
opinion than Niagara Falls creates the water which it spendidly
glorifies. So the Speaker allotted an important place in his court
to a small group of Representatives who acted as his privy council-
lors, advising him on political affairs with which the managers
of the House calendar had no immediate concern, laying plans
for dealing with the electorate whose articulated opinions made
and unmade Presidents, Senators, and Representatives, and

could make or unmake the Speaker. Sherman's political antennae were so sensitive and his recommendations for action seemed to be so wise that Cannon had chosen him chairman of the Republican Congressional Campaign Committee. The Committee had the responsibility of preserving the Republican majority in the House.

Sherman was a city man who came from families of glassmakers and Lake Champlain steamship captains. Cannon valued him too much to bother about the fact that he could not tell a plow from a harrow. In urban ways he was an educated man, a graduate of Hamilton College, which a century ago was strong in Greek, mathematics, and sports. Sherman excelled in all. He was a member of the New York State bar, but he never practiced law. Business and politics were his lines. He was president of the Utica Trust and Deposit Company, president of the New Hartford Canning Company, director of the Union Can Company, and director of the Dana Hardware Company, all of Utica. He had been mayor of Utica at twenty-nine and a member of Congress at thirty-two (he was fifty-one in 1906). He was so congenial that people called him Sunny Jim, but he was more than merely congenial. He had a rare friendly concern for his fellow beings. His letters disclose the great amount of time he spent in soliciting funds from his Congressional colleagues for the widows of Senators and Representatives whom he had known and who had left only small estates and to whose relicts Sherman owed nothing except a measure of man's humanity to man. He had a benign round face and a baldish head. His ruddy cheeks and his full figure, padding a short frame, falsely advertised that he was a man in perfect health. He suffered devilishly from gallstones, which often kept him in bed in pain, absent from his political duties. But even when illness laid him low, his thoughts centered on the Old Man, as he called Uncle Joe, and he spent a few hours of each agonized week writing letters which suggested actions for others to execute on behalf of the Speaker.

Sherman addressed most of this correspondence to Representative Henry Clay Loudenslager, secretary of the Republican Congressional Campaign Committee and a member of the court. Loudy was a self-made farm boy from Gloucester County, New Jersey, whom Americans scarcely knew about at all. His appearance lacked distinction. He parted his hair in the middle, which was the common style. He let his mustache grow over his cheeks three inches beyond each corner of his mouth, which was the common style. He dressed no more nattily than his colleagues. He was silent on the floor, and in committees his name was not connected with legislative issues that drew the attention of many Americans. Those who did have a few scraps of information about him were puzzled that Cannon admitted him to the circle. The two men disagreed completely on one question, the navy. Cannon took no stock in the contention that the United States should build up its sea power. It was expensive. He often opposed President Roosevelt's strenuous recommendations to this end. But Loudenslager, who lived across the Delaware River from the Philadelphia Navy Yard, championed Roosevelt in the House every time he requested the addition of a new dreadnaught or cruiser to the puny American fleet.

In the hidden recesses of Washington where the engines of the House of Representatives operated, Loudy's individuality and worth gleamed so clearly that Cannon overlooked his naval eccentricity. The particular advantage which Loudenslager brought to the circle was that he could describe the standpat position in terms that at least seemed profound at a time when, on the whole, the changers were analyzing the natures of society and government with more depth than the conservatives. In the election just passed he had proved the strength of his arguments in direct competition with the arguments of LaFollette, who toured New Jersey in September 1906 to damn Republicans friendly to big business. He spoke within ten miles of Loudy's home. His chief purpose was to persuade the Jersey voters to defeat Senator John F. Dryden, who was running for re-election as the candidate of the established Republican organization, and to elect in his place George L. Record, the candidate of the New Idea Republicans. But he also marked for banishment from public office all other candidates who did not sympathize with the New Idea, which was the LaFollette idea, as it had been translated into the laws of Wisconsin. "Democracy is on trial for its life in this country," LaFollette said in New Jersey. "A certain enemy is working against the wishes of the masses of the people which is described as a gathering together of those who are rich as against those who are not rich." Loudy was rich. He had prospered in the great blooming of America that followed the Civil War. But his constituents either did not regard him as a plutocrat or did not mind his being one. His arguments for the old way satisfied his district. LaFollette's invasion failed. The election confirmed Loudenslager in his office, but Dryden retired to private life. That result persuaded Uncle Joe that by careful preparation he could deaden the influence of LaFollette and other restless men in the majority of the Republican Congressional districts.

The two friends who completed Cannon's circle had a wistful quality that distinguished them from their insouciant associates. In their lack of self-confidence, they needed a hero to whom they could attach themselves as to a kind of balloon in order to raise their personalities from the dust where they drooped, and the hero that filled the bill was Cannon.

Cannon gave Joseph Crocker Sibley a sense of political as well as psychological stability that he had missed before he made Cannon's acquaintance. He had experimentally sought serenity by joining a succession of parties. In the early 1890's he was a Populist. He then let the Prohibitionists nominate him for office. He served two terms in Congress as a Democrat. At the turn of the century, when he was fifty years old, he became a Republican, and his constituents in northwestern Pennsylvania sent him back to the House of Representatives under that banner. In his new party he had access to Cannon, whose resolution impressed and steadied him. Sibley the Republican turned toward extreme conservatism. The railway rate bill of 1906 gave him such a fright that he pleaded with Congress to veer, before too late, from the road "that must, if followed, lead on to the commune, to the abolition of the individual and of competition." He was a substantial man in the business world, where he had grown rich manufacturing oil-pumping machinery and therefore had something to lose to a government of swelling power. He had witnessed the conduct of political affairs from the vantage points of so many parties that he considered himself a cosmopolite in such matters. Cannon agreed with him, and admitted him to the court as an adviser to Sherman.

William McKinley of Champaign, Illinois (no kin to the late

President), was consumed by political ambition, but his illusion that he himself lacked political competence caused him to transpose his ambition to Uncle Joe. His wife, a sort of poet, had destroyed his self-confidence by demonstrating, through conversation and deeds, the superiority of her intellect and tastes to his, and then by going off to Paris to live alone. His friends who did not know the sad story that he hid in his breast thought that he was a widower or even a bachelor. The bashful little man spent money for companionship. He took ten colleagues at a time on cruises through the Caribbean Sea, and he gave the most extravagant hotel dinners in Washington, at tables decorated with a pastry cook's map of the United States and with Capitols constructed of meringue. Yet little Mac was a man of the world. Once a drug clerk at $4.50 a week, he had become a millionaire long before his fiftieth birthday in 1906 from the profits of his street-car line in Bay City, Michigan, his gas and light plant in Defiance, Ohio, his electric plant in Champaign, and his Illinois Traction Company, which criss-crossed his state with interurban sleeper lines and joined it to St. Louis by the McKinley Bridge. He entered the House in 1905 as Representative of the Illinois district next to Cannon's. The Speaker joshed him for his methodical effort to master the rudiments of politics. "McKinley keeps his ear so close to the ground that he gets it full of grasshoppers most of the time," said Cannon. Mac laughed off the remark. He admired the Speaker for his shrewdness and his loyalty to principles of government to which Mac attributed the strength of his country. Hardly had he reached Washington when he decided that Cannon should be elected President in 1908, and he set himself to planning, by the business-efficiency methods which had made him a public utilities leader, the course which would assure his project of success. He gave a loud "Aye" when he heard the unmetrical lines read by Representative David J. Foster of Vermont, another admirer of the Speaker:

> Cannon, youngest of his peers,
> Conquers time at seventy years!
> I, plain citizen, may stand
> For the voters of our land:
> Since he bears no sign of age,
> But the white hairs of the sage,

Ready are we and intent,
To make the young man President.

None of the members of the court directly represented any of the great corporations or famous personal fortunes which bothered the economic reformers. Cannon's friends in the House had no venal interest in saving the trusts. The impression is common that from the Civil War to World War I the great business enterprises owed the continuation of their ability to exploit the government and the safeguarding of their privileges to hirelings and sycophants in Congress, especially in the Senate. The history of Cannon weakens that impression as far as this century is concerned. It was Cannon, not any group of Senators, who protected the great enterprises in the turbulent years when he was Speaker.

Cannon and his court were the allies of the giant capitalists only by accident (although the steel companies were said to have easy access to Pittsburg Dalzell). They took their stand to defend the culture in which they had grown up and developed into manhood, not to help the "princes of privilege." Cannon's record brings to light no contact between him and the entrepreneurs and millionaires whom Roosevelt dubbed "the malefactors of great wealth." Their center was New York City. Cannon's metropolis was Chicago. The Cannonites were mostly small town men, and many of them were midwesterners. They devoted themselves to protecting private enterprise, but they never went out of their way to help New York and New Yorkers. Their political attitude flowed from their similar personal experiences with existence in America. The attitude developed independently of pressure from the railroads, the investment bankers, the oil companies, and the other monopolists that benefited from the policies furthered by the members of the Speaker's court. The friends believed in natural progress. They feared that official interference with big business would mean official interference with their businesses.

The common conception of America which held the court together did not permit the degeneration of the circle into a ring of dishonest bargainers. The friends stole nothing and sold nothing in the public domain. Their morals were uncorrupted. Their fastidious circle had none of the scaly flavor of the crude gangs that often hold the city hall or the county headquarters in their clutches. But they believed in government by dictation of the wise to the innocent, provided the dictation occurred legally within American institutions. In deciding on their policies as Congressmen they represented not their constituents but their Speaker. Louis XIV would have understood the purpose of the court, although its setting might have confused him. The business-minded courtiers established in the Speaker's Rooms a small Versailles on a constitutional foundation.

In their zeal to perpetuate the kind of America in which they themselves had flourished, the members of the court usually carried out the Speaker's wishes without insisting that he honor theirs. The one reward for loyal service which Cannon had to give them was a committee chairmanship. The House was divided in those days into sixty-two standing committees (nineteen in 1951). Most of them, like the Committee on Ventilation and Acoustics, existed only to provide chairmanships for deserving members. Mann was chairman of the Committee on Elections Number One, Sherman of the Committee on Indian Affairs, Loudenslager of the Committee on Pensions, Sibley of Manufactures. Like Dalzell, Watson had no chairmanship, but Cannon assigned him to Ways and Means in order to add to the reliable standpat majority backing up chairman Payne.

Chairmanships were valuable to the chairmen. Before the House Office Building opened in 1908, chairmen alone had offices provided at public expense. The corridors of the Capitol were lined with chambers, some of them magnificent with huge chandeliers and ornamented walls and ceilings, but most of them small, often walled in tile, many of them crazily shaped, a few of them in the basement—all reserved for chairmen. Representatives who were not chairmen had to work at home or pay from their personal incomes for the rent of space for their desks in office buildings or hotels. They met with visiting constituents in the lobby of the House or on sidewalks or in bars. Furthermore, chairmen received free stationery from the House and were paid $125 a month above their salaries to enable them to hire clerks and stenographers. Chairmanships meant far more than convenience and added income. Chairmen had special privileges in the conduct of the business of the House. The attainment of a chairmanship improved a member's standing with his constituents.

In awarding chairmanships Cannon could demand—and usually obtain—the fealty of a sixth of the House, of almost one-third of the Republican members. Recognition of this fealty was so common that even Democrats, customarily helpless in their minority position, supported the tyranny which the fealty stood for. In writing his *Autobiography*, George Norris recalled that, when he was a young member of the House Public Lands and Buildings Committee, a "discussion arose whether the Committee could draft a public building bill, and it seemed to be taken for granted that the decision was to be made by the Speaker. The senior Democratic member of the Committee, Representative Bankhead of Alabama, actually made a motion that the chairman of the Committee should seek a conference with the Speaker and ascertain whether or not we should be allowed to have a public building bill at that session. . . . Bankhead's motion carried unanimously."

CHAPTER ——•—— 6

Broiling the Lame Duck

<hr/>

IN THE late autumn of 1906 Cannon could have wondered whether the elections had weakened the court too much to enable it to go on stifling the opposition. Not all his followers had fared as well as he. Tariff reformers had turned out three Cannon standpatters— Joseph Weeks Babcock in Wisconsin, James T. McCleary in Minnesota, and Colonel John F. Lacey in Iowa. Ohio decided that it had had enough of Charles Grosvenor, the Santa-Claus-faced "Sage of Athens," who was one of Cannon's two Republican colleagues on the Rules Committee. Even the satisfied easterners lashed out against a Cannon man. Representative James Wadsworth, of Geneseo, New York, taking the side of the packers, had opposed the meat inspection bill. His democratic rival for the 1906 election, Peter A. Porter, campaigned from the back of a cow, and won. The country as a whole reduced the Republican majority in the House from 56 to 32. It particularly grieved Cannon that he was losing also Representative Nathan Lucius Littauer, who was going back to private life of his own volition. The lone Harvard man in the Speaker's court, Littauer was the wealthiest and most urbane member of the circle. His father, a German immigrant, for nine years had peddled notions through the Adirondack country from a sack carried over his shoulder, until in 1855 he settled in Gloversville, New York, where he founded a drygoods business and established a glove factory. Both undertakings prospered. Representative Littauer inherited and expanded the businesses. He was president of Littauer Brothers, of the Fonda Glove Lining Company, and of the Gloversville Knitting Company. He ran for Congress in hopes that he could get the tariff on gloves increased, and succeeded in his mission so well that in 1906, after ten years in the House, at the age of forty-eight, he did not consider it necessary to seek re-election. Littauer was friendly with Roosevelt as well as with Cannon, and the welcome he enjoyed at the White House bolstered Uncle Joe's position. For Littauer planted in Roosevelt's mind the seed of the thought that Republican leaders ought not to attack one another openly by name lest they risk the loss of the party's pre-eminence in the nation. That opinion disarmed Roosevelt for the contest with Cannon.

Even before the election Cannon had not been strong enough to refuse all compromise with spokesmen for discontent. There were weak spots in some of the great committees. Wisdom was not implanted everywhere. Agriculture and Banking and Currency were unreliable. The existence of such chinks in his fortress had forced Cannon to temporize now and then. That rate bill of 1906, for example—he had let it go through as a blackmail payment for repression of a worse horror. Mr. Roosevelt had told the Speaker he wanted the tariff revised. As a sop, Cannon accepted the rate bill, and Roosevelt said no more about the tariff. In a House full of opposition, the Speaker might have to go along with any number of rate bills, unless he could find a new source of strength that meant more than the strength of numbers.

Cannon had a long time in which to find the answer to the question which vexed him. When he called the House to order in December 1906, four weeks after the elections, he saw on the benches before him the very men whose defunct political careers he was prepared to mourn. There sat Grosvenor, Littauer, Babcock, McCleary, Lacey, and Wadsworth. They were not shades. They were living men, every one of them ready to introduce bills, make motions, strike out the last word, and to behave generally like any Congressman who enjoyed the confidence of a majority of his constituents.

Washington in 1906 was not more than a six-day journey from every corner of the Republic. But the Constitution, written before the railroads came, still gave Representatives time enough to journey by ox team from their districts to the capital. The United States had not yet amended the provision in Article I, Section 4—"Congress shall assemble at least once in every year, and such meeting shall be on the first Monday in December, unless they shall by law appoint a different day." For the men newly elected to Congress in 1906 that meant the first meeting in which they would take part would probably begin in December 1907.

So Uncle Joe still had the use of his old friends to put Roosevelt, Gompers, and the followers of LaFollette more thoroughly in their places.

With the aid of his court, Uncle Joe used the Lame Duck session as a laboratory for tyranny. The experiment in absolutism which he conducted in the winter of 1906–1907 destroyed any lingering doubt that he could, by the methodical employment of his own rare abilities, control Congress when he willed it.

The issue of the moment was immigration. Having in June 1906 imposed on the House his wishes in the matter, Cannon now demonstrated once more that he could force the Senate to dance to his pipes and even that he could induce the President himself to help repress legislation which the President favored. People were growing so accustomed to the idea that, in his particular sphere, he could stop them at will that they let him stop them. He became a fascinator, like a cobra.

In 1906 more than one million immigrants entered the United States, and most of them came from southern and eastern Europe. It was the high tide of the great movement of peoples across the Atlantic to the land of opportunity. The earnest agents of steamship lines were busy urging oppressed and poverty-stricken men and women south of the Alps and east of Germany to seek a fortune in the free republic in the New World. The stream of newcomers who responded to those blandishments and to the urgings of cousins and uncles already on the ground disturbed many Americans who had been here long enough to feel like proprietors of the nation. One who saw dark menace in this immigration was Gompers, an immigrant himself. The newcomers from Italy, Hungary, Russia, and Poland worked for mean wages. They knew nothing about civil rights and labor's rights. Most of them accepted

mistreatment with docility. Most of of them could not read or
write at all in their own languages, much less make sense to one
who spoke English, and they had to surmount the language barrier by shrugs. Yet America attracted them. No pogroms fright-
ened the Jews in New York. A low level of living in Chicago was
better than a good level of living in Warsaw or Eboli. Since they
intended to stay in this good country, the immigrants competed
for jobs with American workmen. And they depressed the working
conditions which Gompers was trying to elevate.

Distinguished Americans who loathed trade unionism shared
Gompers' fear of the new immigrants on the ground that the Slavic
and Mediterranean peoples would derange the racial stock of the
American. These immigrants were flushing poisoned waters into
the American cultural river. American society had been founded
from the British Isles, and it had matured with the help of settlers
from Ireland, Germany, and Scandinavian countries, with a few
Frenchmen for flavor. The race-conscious Americans believed that
the genius which their compatriots had shown in developing the
Republic was the fruit of the Anglo-Saxon heritage, and they worried lest the fleeing subjects of Romanov, Habsburg, and Savoy
would put out the spark of genius and emasculate the "American
push." The State Immigration Convention held in Richmond in
1894 under the auspices of the Virginia Agricultural and Mechanical Society for the purpose of attracting new blood to Virginia
farms and industries heard the speakers say that the immigrants
must be selected for their ability to mix easily with the descendants of Englishmen and Scotsmen who were the lords and yeo-
men in Virginia society.

Racial consciousness was strongest in Boston, and no man in
Boston objected more strenuously to the new immigration than
General Francis Amesa Walker, president of the Massachusetts
Institute of Technology. For him the eastern and southern Europeans were "beaten men from beaten races," decanted into America from a "foul and stagnant pool of population . . . which no
breath of intellectual or industrial life has stirred for ages." The
strangers with olive-skin or hooked noses or broad Slavic faces
had aroused General Walker from the moment they began to arrive in the United States in numbers. In an address at Cornell
University on April 12, 1895, he said that the influx of immigrants

was menacing American peace and political safety because "in all the social and industrial orders of this country since 1877 the foreign elements have proved the ready tools of demagogues in defying the law, in destroying property, and in working violence." Boston was the home of the Immigration Restriction League, the secretary of which, Prescott F. Hall, coalesced the arguments of the race-conscious and the labor leaders. "The more enterprising and desirable emigrants are unwilling to go to a country where they are obliged to compete with the lowest grade of labor," he wrote.

A decade's reiteration of those arguments brought the United States in 1906 to the verge of closing the door against the new immigration. The recommended device for exclusion was simple —a statute forbidding admission to the United States to aliens over sixteen years of age who could not satisfy the harbor inspectors that they could read English or some other language or dialect. Most of the new immigrants were illiterate. Such a bill had almost become law in Walker's heyday under the sponsorship of another Yankee believer in racial purity, Senator Henry Cabot Lodge. Both the Senate and the House in 1896 had accepted Lodge's contention that the American wage-earner faced an "appalling danger" in the "flood of low, unskilled, ignorant foreign labor which has poured into the country for some years past, and which not only takes lower wages but accepts a standard of life and living so low that the American workingman cannot compete with it." But two days before he relinquished the White House to William McKinley, President Grover Cleveland vetoed Lodge's literacy test bill.

Lodge was President Roosevelt's closest friend in Congress, and Roosevelt favored the literacy test. He recommended enactment of it in his messages on the state of the Union in 1901 and 1902. The "race suicide" of native Americans, their failure to reproduce themselves through large families, distressed Roosevelt, who was a young man when General Walker made his statistical discovery that the birth rate of the natives had begun to fall when the number of arriving immigrants rose, for the first time since the Battle of Lexington, in the middle years of the nineteenth century, after the Irish famine and the failure of the liberal revolutions in central Europe. The size of the immigration—the old world every year pouring into this country almost a third as many persons as in-

habited the thirteen colonies during the war for independence—
was disturbing enough even without speculation about birth rates.
At its convention in Buffalo in 1905 the Brotherhood of Railway
Trainmen criticized the failure of the Republican Party to pass
a restrictive law during the monopoly of leadership it had exercised in the Senate, House, and presidency since the end of Grover
Cleveland's second term eight years earlier. The Farmers National
Congress passed a resolution favoring the literacy test when it
convened in Richmond in September 1905, and the delegates to
the 1906 convention of the American Federation of Labor in Nash-
ville voted 1,858 to 352 for the test.

That ferment encouraged Lodge. In 1906 he and Senator William P. Dillingham, of Woodbury, Vermont, once more persuaded
the Senate to restrict immigration by the literacy test, and Lodge's
son-in-law, Representative Augustus Peabody Gardner, introduced
a restriction bill in the House.

Cannon disagreed. He had no pride of race. Considering his
friendship for Littauer, the slurring observations about Jews which
debased the arguments of the racial purists angered him. Immigration control portended strong government. Secretary Hall of
the Restriction League exulted in his book *Immigration* that
"through our power to regulate immigration, we have a unique
opportunity to exercise artificial selection on an enormous scale."
Instead of economic statism he sought biological statism. Cannon
certainly did not want to ease the lot of the union leaders. It was
good news to him that the new immigrants increased the labor
supply too quickly to permit the unions to absorb them readily,
although in the past the unions had drawn most of their members
from the foreign-born. The Knights of Labor had been an organization of aliens. The mine owners in the Eighteenth District benefited from the new immigration. Before 1890 only 7 per cent of
the workers in Illinois coal mines came from countries whose
peoples did not speak English or a Teutonic language. Nine years
later 25 per cent of the miners were Italians, Frenchmen, Belgians,
Russians, and Slavs or Magyars from Austria-Hungary. By 1906
the number of Italians and eastern Europeans in the Illinois mines
had greatly increased. The newcomers could not understand what
Walker, the Mine Worker Socialist opponent of Cannon in the
1906 election campaign, was saying because they did not speak his

language. They lived to themselves, worked hard, and took low wages.

Their presence in the United States and the constant swelling of their numbers by new arrivals excited Cannon because he took them as proof that America was still the land of opportunity, whatever LaFollette and the other dissatisfied critics might say to the contrary. The immigrants listened to the steamship line agents only because the United States really was as prosperous as the agents said. Once here, the immigrants wrote home about the American wonderland, and new immigrants came—every one a witness in support of Uncle Joe. What if a few anarchists and socialists arrived with them? Cannon pitied such people, without fearing them, as he pitied idiots and homeless children—they were not half so dangerous as the reformers with roots in America. To Cannon's way of thinking, the immigration not only upheld his conclusion that "America was a hell of a success," but it was nec-essary to America's continued success. The flow of immigrants stimulated industrial expansion, and the expansion satisfied him anew that he was sound in his notion that the United States and all the industrious people in it would grow ever richer if (exclud-ing the tariff) the government would only let nature take its course.

So Cannon in 1906 set out to thwart the restrictionists. Never was he more adroit. He made full use of his court circle. At every critical point one of its members arose by his instructions to save the situation. It was a famous victory, and it cost him dearly when it had been forgotten by all but Gompers and Augustus Peabody Gardner.

In the first session of the Fifty-ninth Congress, after the Senate had approved Lodge's bill, the House Committee on Immigration and Naturalization recommended to the House that it follow the Senate's lead. For once the clouds lifted for Gompers and he looked upon the sun. But wait. Two members of the House Committee opposed Gardner's bill. They were a Republican, William Stiles Bennet, and a Democrat, Jacob Ruppert, Jr., who is remembered now as the man who bought Babe Ruth for the Yankees. Both represented districts in New York City, which benefited directly from the immigration. The steerage ships kept the port busy, and the immigrants provided labor for the merchants and the needle trades thriving in New York. Bennet and Ruppert explained in a special report why they could not support the literacy test. While those dissenters were but a minority of two on a committee of fourteen, Cannon knew it was possible that they could be made to outbalance Gardner and the other eleven.

Cannon had two objectives to overwhelm. The first was the Committee of Immigration and Naturalization. The second was the Senate. To take the first objective, he made his plans in the Rules Committee, which appointed June 25 as the day on which the House would debate the immigration bill. Shortly after noon the faithful Dalzell addressed his colleagues on behalf of Rules, to present its resolution governing debate. Only three hours would be allowed, and no more than one amendment could be offered to each section of the bill. The militant supporters of Gardner objected. They needed a longer time to state their case for the bill. But their comments were useless. The House approved Dalzell's resolution. The debate began. Cannon left the chair and retired to the Speaker's rooms. He handed the gavel to Jim Watson.

Gardner, speaking first for the bill, read a letter from Gompers and itemized the unionist and biological arguments that had been accumulating for a decade and more. The debate was perfunctory until the afternoon was far gone. Then arose Charles Grosvenor, of the Rules Committee triumvirate. His lovely white beard, ending in a stubby point over his diaphragm, glistened richly in the heat of the fresh summer. He was not an opponent of the bill. He had voted for it in 1896. But he had an amendment. In substitution for Gardner's section on the literacy test, he asked the House to adopt the following:

A Commission is hereby created, consisting of two Senators . . . and three members of the House of Representatives . . . and two citizen members. Said commission shall make full inquiry, examine and investigate into the subject of immigration.

Gardner started to his feet. The amendment expunged the test. On behalf of Cannon, Grosvenor was knifing the heart of the immigration bill while he pretended that he was strengthening it. To save his bill, Gardner made the point of order that Grosvenor's amendment was not germane. Perhaps an objective parliamentarian would have upheld Gardner. But the men who dominated the House were partisans. They were not objective; Watson, presiding in the chair, least of all. It was up to that courtier of the Speaker to rule on the acceptability of a point of order raised for the benefit of legislation which the Speaker considered harmful to his country. Watson astonished nobody when he announced that Grosvenor's amendment was germane. Thereupon the majority voted as Cannon wished, 128 to 116 for Grosvenor. "The Speaker is a great power," said Representative David A. DeArmond, Williams' silent Democratic partner on the Rules Committee, "and much of his power is due to the subserviency of those whose cringing abandonment of their legislative functions make the Speaker their untrammeled agent and omnipotent boss." So Cannon won his first objective. The House rebuffed the committee that had gone along with Gardner.

But Cannon's victory was by no means final. The Senate had approved the literacy test, and the Senate yet menaced Grosvenor's amendment, for the rules of the two branches of Congress provided Lodge and Dillingham with an opportunity for insisting that the House give in to them.

Like all bills passed in variant forms at the two sides of the Capitol, the immigration bill would go to conference, and in conference strong Senators could bend weak Representatives to their wills. Cannon therefore prepared to oppose strong Senators with stronger Representatives. His store of authority included the privilege of appointing the House members of the conference committees. For the immigration conference, he passed over Gardner in favor of the two lone dissenters on the Committee on Immigration and Naturalization, Bennet and Ruppert. With them he chose Benjamin F. Howell of New Jersey, chairman of the committee, who was bound by tradition to support the decision not of his own committee but of the House as a whole. Cannon did not instruct those three to persuade the Senate conferees, who included Lodge and Dillingham, to accept Grosvenor's amendment. He selected them for their defensive skill, to hold the line without flinching, against any suggestion by the Senators that the House should undo its work and restore the literacy test to the bill.

The conferees still disagreed when Congress adjourned in June. Uncle Joe blandly accepted the likelihood that holding the line would mean an endless deadlock and no bill at all. If there were no bill, there would be no literacy test, and it was the test that Cannon was bound to defeat. For the lack of a law Gompers and other union officials knew whom to blame.

On October 10 the Junior Order United American Mechanics sent Uncle Joe this letter:

This certifies that at the 34th annual session of the State Council of Ohio, Junior Order United American Mechanics, held at Canton, Ohio, September 11–13, 1906, a resolution was unanimously adopted protesting against your action in securing the defeat of the immigration bill through your personal solicitations, and we were directed to inform you that unless you assume a different attitude toward immigration legislation thirty thousand Ohio members of this organization would oppose your future political career with every effort in their power at any and all times.

Cannon paid no attention to the letter. In the Eighteenth District of Illinois he was safe from the Ohio Junior Mechanics, and from the Illinois Junior Mechanics as well.

The conferees resumed their meetings when the Lame Duck session came to order. How far would Cannon go—could he go —in forcing his will upon the Senate? Why, he would go to the very limit. The House conferees had the old instructions—no compromise with the Bostonians and Gompers. His patience gone, Gardner on February 2 introduced a resolution which, had the House approved it, would have authorized the conferees to accept the Senate bill. The resolution was sent off to the Rules Committee for burial. By that date the supreme authority of Cannon at the Capitol had gained such common recognition that even the Senators among the conferees abandoned hope. Lodge and Dillingham met with the House members perfunctorily, from a sense of duty.

Soon after Gardner's vain gesture, President Roosevelt sent his Secretary of State, Elihu Root, to call on Cannon with respect to the immigration bill. The purpose of the call was not to please Gardner or Lodge but to save the Mikado in Japan from a humiliation that might be costly to the United States. The San Francisco school board forbade the children of Japanese parents to attend classes with white children. The Japanese government took offense, and the legates of the Mikado informed the American government vaguely that he would demand satisfaction through diplomatic

channels unless the school board rescinded its policy. President
Roosevelt forthwith invited Mayor Eugene R. Schmitz of San
Francisco to visit him at the White House. There the two men decided that San Francisco would let Japanese boys and girls into
the schools and President Roosevelt would ask Congress to pass
at once the immigration bill mired in the conference committee,
with a new amendment prohibiting Japanese to enter continental
United States from Hawaii. The San Francisco school policy was
only one manifestation of a general California dislike for the Japanese, who were migrating to that state in large numbers. Customarily they did not come to the United States directly from
Japan but delayed their voyage across the Pacific by a stopover
in Honolulu. Roosevelt's Hawaiian formula could save the subjects of the Mikado from the stigma of direct exclusion, and at the
same time relieve, at least temporarily, the tensions between Japanese and white men along our Pacific Coast.

Roosevelt's agreement with Schmitz would mean nothing, however, until Cannon authorized his conferees to accept the immigration bill with the new amendment. That fact led to Root's visit
to the Speaker's rooms. The Secretary of State said that enactment
of the immigration bill had become necessary to the security of
the United States. Japan might go to war unless the school board
tolerated Japanese pupils, and the school board would become
tolerant only when Congress had approved the immigration bill
with the Schmitz provision. The arguments were powerful, but
rough Cannon, determined to gain the end he had sought when
he put Grosvenor up to introducing the amendment which killed
the literacy test, refused to approve Roosevelt's proposal unless
the Senate conferees would agree to rewrite their bill after the
House model, with the test removed. Cannon in 1907 was more
concerned by the thought of the damage he was sure a severe restriction of immigration would visit on the United States than he
was by Roosevelt's forebodings of war.

Having interceded with Cannon, Root visited Lodge. The Secretary of State approached the Senator as an emissary both of the
President and the Speaker. Indeed, his mission turned the President himself into the emissary of the Speaker. The President so
urgently wanted the restriction on Japanese immigration to become law that he was ready to sacrifice his old interest in the

literacy test in order to gain the paramount goal. If Cannon stood like iron, Lodge had to yield. Cannon's immovability was now so celebrated that nobody—President, Senator, or Representative— tried to move him. He could gain his way by a word. He had but to signify his wish, and it came true. The Senator gave up for his friend's sake what he had sought for ten years. Chairman Howell took his cue from Uncle Joe. In February 1907 the immigration bill became law in the only form the Speaker would accept.

CHAPTER ———•——— 7

Rather Be President

AT THE MOMENT the Lame Duck session adjourned on March 4, 1907, the oppressed members of Congress once more exposed the strange personal power of their oppressor by applauding him. The House members arose in their seats to cheer Cannon merrily and to praise him in nice speeches, and they gave a great demonstration for his white-whiskered lieutenant, General Grosvenor. Joy and sadness came over the latter, because the sound of Washington's noon bells, which mingled with the applause, tolled the knell of his public career. Grosvenor's return to private life bent Cannon's attention seriously to the problem of how he would keep on manipulating the House when his majority had shrunk and the opposition had infiltrated what he had left.

His goal was the routing of the agitators for change utterly, until they would mean no more in American life. Thus far he had been able to keep reform at bay—no more. The Speaker, even when he had expanded his authority within his office to a degree of which his predecessors never dreamed, had no means to stop the advocates of reform from storming his citadel. When Cannon rebuffed LaFollette on railway legislation or Gompers on immigration, LaFollette and Gompers at once reopened their assault on the Capitol with demands for railway legislation and immigration reform. He lived in perpetual siege. How could the Speaker clear the air outside the Capitol? He must be President.

Roosevelt fed this large ambition. For at the very time the Speaker had been repressing proposals to increase the power of the federal government, the President, with his office as a podium, had been reiterating the ideas which incubated those proposals. He so successfully spread the notion that the Republican Party was the nesting place for reform through political action that in Kansas the Populist Party, created to better man's economic lot by law, dissolved and its members by formal resolution joined the Republicans.

The more often Cannon balked Roosevelt's attempt to marry social consciousness to political science, the more the President insisted on the wisdom and rightness of his attempt. "Experience has conclusively shown the impossibility of securing by the actions of nearly half a hundred different state legislatures anything but ineffective chaos in the way of dealing with the great corporations which do not operate exclusively within the limits of any one state," Roosevelt told Congress in his Message on the State of the Union in December 1906. "In some method, whether by a national license law or in any other fashion, we must exercise, and that at an early date, a far more complete control than at present over these great corporations." He recommended the imposition of a federal inheritance tax, on grounds that "the man of great wealth owes a peculiar obligation to the state, because he derives special advantages from the mere existence of government. Not only should he recognize this obligation in the way he leads his daily life and in the way he earns and spends his money, but it should also be recognized in the way in which he pays for the protection the State gives him." He advocated also the restoration of the federal income tax which had been imposed by Civil War law in 1861 and resurrected by Congress in 1894, only to be pronounced unconstitutional by the Supreme Court. "The question is in its essence a question of the proper adjustment of burdens to benefits," the President said in presenting the case for the income tax.

In Cannon's Congress those proposals found their tomb. Bills for control of corporations, for the income tax, and for the inheritance tax were written and introduced into the House and seen no more. No committee considered them. No petition called for their consideration. Yet Roosevelt treated the proposals not as though they were dead but like sleeping beauties, subject to recall to life at some propitious moment. When Cannon's laboratory experiment in tyranny during the Lame Duck session was almost completed, the President on February 23, 1907, assured the Harvard Union that "those who invoke the doctrine of State rights to protect State corporate creations in predatory activities extended through other States are as short-sighted as those who once invoked the same doctrine to protect the special slaveholding interest. The States have shown that they have not the ability to curb the power of syndicated wealth, and therefore, in the interest of the people, it must be done by National action. Our present warfare is against special privilege. The men . . . who are prompt to speak against every practical means which can be devised for achieving the object we have in view—the proper and adequate supervision by the federal government of the great corporations doing an interstate business—are, nevertheless, themselves powerless to so much as outline any plan of constructive statesmanship which shall give relief."

In the quiet months after the Congressmen left Washington, the President never tired of stating his theses. When the Jamestown Exposition, celebrating the three hundredth anniversary of the landing in wild America of Captain John Smith and his little band of daring English settlers, opened in June 1907, there was Roosevelt pressing the equalitarian philosophy. "Most great civilized countries have an income tax and an inheritance tax," he said. "In my judgment both should be part of our system of Federal taxation. . . . As Lincoln pointed out, there are some respects in which men are obviously not equal; but there is no reason why there should not be . . . at least an approximate equality in the conditions under which each man obtains the chance to show the stuff that is in him when compared with his fellows." Sentiments in the same vein he aired at another national shrine marking another fundamental event in American history, the landing of the Pilgrims. At the laying of the cornerstone of the Pilgrim Memorial Monument in Provincetown, Massachusetts, on August 20, 1907, he observed, "Experience has shown that it is necessary to exercise a far more efficient control than at present over the business use of those vast fortunes, chiefly corporate, which are used (as under modern conditions they invariably are) in interstate business. . . . There is a growing determination . . . that a fortune, however amassed, shall not have a business use that is antisocial. Most large corporations do a business that is not confined to any one State. . . . I believe in a national incorporation law for corporations engaged in interstate business."

The use which Roosevelt was making of the presidency as a temple in which to expound a doctrine gave the Speaker an example and a goal. In such an office Cannon could come to grips with his adversaries outside the Capitol walls. The ideas which galled him he could combat in the open by unfolding his own conceptions of state and government in a program of affirmation. Those negative, defensive triumphs which he had gained by obstinacy hid from the public the fact—as he considered it—that he himself had a set of positive ideas. If his convictions were to prevail, he must spend more time in expounding his own thoughts and less in opposing the thoughts of others. The presidency was the great office for positive assertion. Only there could he make clear why he had dedicated himself in his old years to safeguard what he thought were the wellsprings of his country's great distinctions.

Early in 1907, however, nobody knew when Roosevelt intended to give up his office. Would he seek a third term at the quadrennial national convention of the Republican Party in 1908? Even in the midst of proving to the country that in the Capitol he had the power of a Khan, Cannon was humble enough to assume that it would be fruitless to race Roosevelt for the nomination. It was the President's for the asking. So until Roosevelt should renounce a third term, Cannon bound himself to silence. If there were no renunciation, Cannon could seek the office after such a third term. Until the leaves began to fall, he replied thus to all letters boosting him for President: "Frankly, the presidential 'bee' is not buzzing about my ears."

Yet as the price of his transformation into a symbol, Cannon was losing the privilege of making his own decisions. Tyrants do not belong to themselves. Their disciples try to possess them. The more he asserted his will in dealing with persons whose ideas he opposed, the less freedom he had to impose his will on his friends. Simple men who thought like him selected him to speak their piece for them. Most Americans alive in 1907 had lived in the era when it was accepted that a man owed his chief responsibility to himself, and some of them recalled the era nostalgically. They did not want to admit that men had failed to measure up to that responsibility, did not want to grant that men left to themselves become predators. As those longers for the misty past looked for someone to resurrect the era, or to prevent its further erosion, their eyes fell on Cannon. When he was approaching the conclusion that he would run for the presidency at the proper moment, they were insisting that he seek the presidency at once.

So "Little Mac" McKinley, without waiting to find out Roosevelt's intentions, disregarding the Speaker's wishes, seriously inaugurated Cannon's presidential movement in a conference in January 1907 with Charles P. Hitch, the editor of the *Beacon* of Paris, Illinois. Charley Hitch sat on Uncle Joe's Eighteenth District board of strategy with Son-in-Law LeSeure and with William R. Jewell, editor of the Danville *Commercial*. Jewell's reward for faithful service was the postmastership in Danville. His nephew, Payne Jewell, was deputy postmaster, and his grandson, Hosford Jewell, was a clerk in the Danville post office. Hitch was the U.S. Marshal for the federal District Court in eastern Illinois. He worked tirelessly for Cannon's interests. "You will have no trouble in carrying the state (Illinois) solid," Hitch reported to Cannon after the conversation with McKinley.

The number of Cannon supporters slowly grew. In April, when Uncle Joe, steadfastly resisting the temptation to promote his own cause, was convalescing on Vermilion Street from a spring cold and teaching his granddaughters to waltz, Representative Wesley Jones of Yakima, Washington, wrote that the Washington delegation in the House would support him as Roosevelt's successor. Senator Shelby Cullom of Illinois asked Uncle Joe to "let" the home state Republicans work for him. An Eighteenth District consumptive whom Cannon had thrust on the federal payroll in Arizona assured the Speaker that the Arizona territory delegation to the Republican convention would be his. "It is my conviction that with Roosevelt out of the way, you would make our strongest candidate, and I believe that New England can be brought into line for you," wrote Representative Dave Foster of Burlington, Vermont. North Carolina agreed. From Cannon's birthplace among the sweet hills in the Piedmont, Dr. L. L. Hobbs, president of the Friends' college at Guilford, North Carolina, offered Uncle Joe a helping hand to the presidency. Busy McKinley arranged a conference at the Union League Club in Chicago at the end of May, to which he invited Littauer and the great Republicans of Illinois. Subsequently McKinley hit the sawdust trail for Cannon in New Mexico, and made converts. Illinois Senator Albert J. Hopkins wrote that he had found friends for the Speaker even in Nebraska, where other visitors had tasted a strong LaFollette flavor. Cannon had support in Missouri, too, but his bland refusal to lift a finger in his own behalf got under the skin of his friends in that warm-tempered state.

"Let me say that the 'Barkis is willin' course will not win the next presidential nomination unless conditions in the party differ widely from what I now believe them to be," W. H. Wade wrote him testily from the Missouri House of Representatives toward the end of June. "At this stage the whole movement is premature," Cannon told Wade.

A letter from Tawney put a fleck in Cannon's sky. The handsome blacksmith wrote that in Minnesota the strongest candidate for the Republican nomination was William Howard Taft, the Secretary of War. Taft's name was heard elsewhere. A rumor was going around that if Roosevelt forbade his own renomination, he would designate Taft as his successor. Cannon could not take this report seriously. Not even Roosevelt "can put Taft across," he said. Presidents had ceased to choose Presidents after Andrew Jackson installed Martin Van Buren in his place. Uncle Joe had been looking at Presidents up close for forty-seven years since he had met Lincoln in Decatur, Illinois, in 1860. Lincoln had not designated Andrew Johnson to succeed him. Johnson had not picked Grant; nor Grant, Hayes; nor Hayes, Garfield; nor Garfield, Arthur. Benjamin Harrison had not called for McKinley, nor had McKinley taken any serious part in choosing the man who, by accident, followed him—Theodore Roosevelt. In Cannon's experience, the withdrawing President was by custom almost the last person consulted in choosing the next nominee for the office. As it had been with Lincoln, so it must be with Roosevelt. His appreciation of the present disturbed by his vision of the past, Cannon wrote his friend Representative Samuel W. McCall of Massachusetts: "If our great and good President is really out of the race, then it seems to me that it is anybody's race."

While the Speaker was waiting for Roosevelt to state his intentions, however, Taft might have the President's help in collecting a convention following large enough to overwhelm Cannon. This possibility burdened Uncle Joe as he traveled about during the summer. Two score years ago that was not a season for decisive action. Americans did not exactly take to the hills, like the English retiring to Simla, but they slowed down their rate of work. When they could, they sat still, waving fans in the shade of porches. They drank beer, and stayed out of upper berths. Cannon retreated to the cool woods on Isle Royal in Lake Superior, near Duluth, where he was Tawney's guest. He spent a week at Mackinac with daughter Helen. He headed for Lake Champlain, where, with his eyeteeth piercing his cigar from the vigor of his conviction, he struck briefly at the things Roosevelt had said in Jamestown and Plymouth. "It would be a crime if Congress should do anything at this time to upset business," he told a reporter from the New York *Herald* who had found him at Alexandria Bay aboard "Brother" Sibley's yacht, the *Valcour*. Roosevelt could decipher the cryptic statement as a forecast that Congress, under Cannon, would approve no income tax, no inheritance tax, no law for national incorporation.

Cannon's patient waiting for Roosevelt to announce his intentions ended on October 23. On that day the Knickerbocker Trust Company of New York suspended payments to its depositors, and a brief depression was born. The immediate cause was the failure of August Heinze and his two brothers to corner the market in the stock of United Copper. When Heinze ran out of cash and could not pay for shares he had bid on, depositors began to remove their funds from the bank of which Heinze was president, the Mercantile National. Heinze resigned from the bank, and the Clearing House Association of New York demanded that two directors of the bank, Charles W. Morse and E. R. Thomas, resign with him. The Clearing House accused the directors of using funds from the Mercantile and some twenty other banks in which they were interested to finance their personal speculations. Uneasy depositors visited the Knickerbocker Trust Company, the president of which, Charles T. Barney, was known to have had business dealings with Morse. The Knickerbocker, with deposits of $50,000,000, was the second largest trust company in New York. When Barney publicly appealed for financial help, the panic began in earnest. The Knickerbocker shut the windows at the tellers' cages. Bank runs spread over Manhattan and then over the United States.

The crash changed Cannon's attitude toward Roosevelt. The Speaker decided to seek the presidential nomination, even if his opponent in the contest should be Roosevelt, who still had not renounced a third term. The golden age of Cannon's prosperity was disappearing in the bank runs, and for that calamity Cannon blamed the President. At Plymouth and Jamestown, and in his earlier speeches and messages, Roosevelt had been destroying public confidence in American business. And now business was paying the price, to the detriment of America. No longer was it enough to oppose what Roosevelt advocated. The survival of American society in freedom from government supervision now demanded opposition to Roosevelt as a person.

Cannon therefore approved when, five days after the Knickerbocker suspended payments, the Republican members of the Illinois Congressional delegation met in the Auditorium in Chicago and publicly decided to enter him in the campaign for the presidential nomination. They chose McKinley chairman of the canvass for the Speaker, who no longer discouraged his faithful friend's efforts to line up the country for him. The following day the La-Follette Republicans in Wisconsin launched a presidential boom for their leader, but Cannon paid no heed. He hurried to Springfield, the capital of Illinois, where the legislature was in session, for his first contest with President Roosevelt.

Since October 14, before the panic, the legislature had been considering a bill sponsored by Representative John G. Oglesby which, in accordance with the sentiment recorded by the voters of Illinois on ballots cast on November 8, 1904, had been drafted to introduce into the state the direct primary system for selecting the party nominees for every state office. Cannon ignored the bill until the collapse of the Knickerbocker. Now he wanted the bill amended in order to strengthen his chances for winning the presidential nomination. Oglesby's draft listed the party delegates to national conventions among the officers to be chosen in primaries. Cannon was sure that delegates selected as they always had been selected, at district conventions, would support him at the national convention. But it was possible that the strange lot of delegates chosen in a primary election would back Roosevelt, or whomever Roosevelt favored, if Roosevelt actually should go so far as to designate his favorite.

In Springfield Cannon took rooms at the Leland Hotel, the successor to that Leland where he had sat uncomfortably almost nineteen years earlier, waiting vainly for the legislature to elect him Senator. To his parlors Charley Hitch brought one by one the Republican members of the Illinois Senate for interviews. Cannon's message to each was the same: amend the Oglesby Bill by excepting delegates to national conventions from the primary. The Speaker quickly demonstrated his faculty for having his way which he had made famous on the Potomac. This visit to the Leland succeeded. He had no authority in Springfield. No Illinois legislator, except those from his own district, was beholden to him. But his name, bolstered by dim suspicions that he had undefined power in Illinois and by his association with Illinoisans to whom some Senators owed consideration, carried the day. To impress the visitors, Cannon had at his side Daniel A. Campbell, the post master of Chicago, an Illinois politician who could make life miserable or sweet for many members of the legislature. The Illinois House of Representatives had approved Oglesby's bill, 102 to 27, before Cannon took an interest in it. Amid shouts that Cannon had devised a scheme "to cheat Roosevelt out of the Illinois delegation," the Senate on October 31 adopted Uncle Joe's amendment, and on November 1 it passed the amended bill.

Cannon crossed the state to Danville and left Hitch in Springfield to persuade the House to accept the Senate's bill. The assignment took patience. The legislature recessed. Governor Charles Deneen, his mind on 1908 and re-election, left the capital for a speaking tour of the whole state. Illinois House Speaker Edward D. Shurtleff opposed Cannon's amendment. In Washington the Roosevelt Administration obstructed the Speaker's maneuvers for the presidency. Attorney General Charles Bonaparte notified Hitch, who pro forma was an employee of Bonaparte's, that "it is settled policy of the Department of Justice to discourage any interference by federal officials in the proceedings of state legislatures." But Cannon kept Hitch in Springfield through the winter. The views of Roosevelt and his Cabinet officers no longer concerned the Speaker. It seemed almost beside the point when Roosevelt finally, on December 11, renounced a third term. The statement came three weeks after Cannon had written in a published letter: "If perchance the choice for the presidential nomination should fall upon me, there would be no alternative but to accept." The bee was buzzing around his head at last.

On January 30 the Illinois Senate and House ended their disagreement over the Oglesby Bill. Both accepted Cannon's amendment. Illinois apparently belonged to Uncle Joe.

The victory dazzled him enough to make the road to the nomination seem clear. After all, Senator "Pitchfork Ben" Tillman had told the papers that Cannon was going to be the Republican nominee. So did Representative Olcott of New York. Likewise Representatives Joseph W. Fordney and Edwin Denby of Michigan. An American judge in Egypt announced that Cannon was the modern Lincoln. Who was Taft? Exuberantly Cannon wrote to Representative Charles E. Townsend in Michigan that he doubted whether Roosevelt was "strong enough to arbitrarily pick out some one man, and say to the party in convention, 'Nominate this man.'" That opinion propelled Uncle Joe along new paths of experimentation with the force of his own personality.

CHAPTER ——•—— 8

The Scourge of Roosevelt

CANNON LOST the humor from his eye, and a grim tenseness hardened the look of his face. Preoccupation overlay the friendly manner which had made him everybody's Uncle Joe. As a mark of his single-minded determination, the long cleft that ran up his forehead from the bridge of his nose seemed to have deepened and turned permanently crimson by the end of November (a month after he began to run for the presidency), when he left Danville for Washington and the new Congress—the Congress that he was about to use to destroy public confidence in Roosevelt's ability to exercise political leadership, and to fix the thought that he, Cannon, was the new leader who counted.

History and experience told him that in times of panic Presidents made easy scapegoats. The financial crisis of 1857 helped unseat Buchanan. The crisis of 1873 helped Tilden win a majority of the popular votes cast for President in the contest with the Republicans' Hayes. The Republicans' Arthur had to take the blame for the crisis of 1884, and Cleveland became President. On Cleveland was heaped the blame for the crisis of 1893, and McKinley became President. But Cannon was playing a dangerous game, for national repudiation of Roosevelt could win the presidency not for Cannon but the Democrats. He set himself a delicate course.

He joined the issue when the Republicans of the House met in caucus in the chamber after supper on November 30. His party colleagues having unanimously nominated him for a third term as Speaker, he delivered a short speech in which, while he did not mention the President's name, he challenged the ideas Mr. Roosevelt had set forth at Harvard, Jamestown, and Provincetown and in his 1905 and 1906 messages to Congress.

"It is not wise to increase the revenues of the government, neither is it advisable to transfer burdens from the local and state treasuries to the federal treasury—to foster a centralizing power and responsibility, which of necessity develops quite fast enough," said Cannon. "We have been admonished by events that it is not a time for extravagance or excursions into the realm of experiment in legislation. It is my personal judgment that we should hold fast the principles laid down by the fathers, that the federal government is one of limited powers, but supreme where it has jurisdiction, and that we should leave to the people of the states the jurisdiction not granted to the federal government, and also leave upon them the responsibility and burden of taxation for the same."

With that platform for inaction, he aggressively introduced himself to the Sixtieth Congress and its enlarged complement of reformers. The Representatives quickly comprehended that, in sending them to the House, their constituents had given them, if not the power to legislate, at least the privilege of watching at close hand a drama of great meaning for the future of their country.

The President underscored the ideological issue when on December 3 he sent to the Capitol a Message on the State of the Union which called for many excursions into the realm of experiment in legislation. He quoted in it from previous addresses. Since the message followed the caucus speech by three days, the President in effect seemed to draw the lines of a jousting field, and isolated himself and the Speaker as the contending champions of the two great conflicting points of view. Whatever Roosevelt might have intended, the Speaker at least was out to crush his opponent. No longer was he interested, as he had been the preceding two years, in simply disappointing and frustrating the President. The battle of heroes had begun.

"No small part of the trouble that we have," the President told the country and the self-reliant, independent Speaker in his message, "comes from carrying to an extreme the national virtue of self-reliance, of independence and initiative in action. . . . Centralization in business has already come and cannot be avoided or undone, and . . . the public at large can only protect itself from certain evil effects of this business centralization by providing better methods for the exercise of control through the authority already centralized in the national government by the Constitution." The interstate commerce clause of the Constitution was the key to an "extension of federal activity."

The message was more than a re-singing of old songs. It was a medley of LaFollette and Gompers and Roosevelt. For the benefit of the labor leader, the President said that "instances of abuse in the granting of injunctions in labor disputes continue to occur." In the summer of 1906 Roosevelt had congratulated Cannon for campaigning in Rockland, Maine, on behalf of the pro-injunction Representative, Charles Littlefield, whom Gompers was urging the Maine voters to defeat. "A very manly stand," the President said of Cannon then. Gompers took heart from the President's new statement, because the Federation was defending itself from a suit for permanent injunction which the Buck's Stove and Range Company in St. Louis had brought against it. Striking on August 29, 1906, for a nine-hour day, the Metal Polishers, Buffers, Platers, Brass Molders and Brass and Silver Workers' International Union of North America, Local 13, St. Louis, had put Buck's on its "unfair list," and the name of the company appeared on the "We Don't Patronize" list which the American Federation of Labor distributed every three months from Washington. By those means the unions besought all its friends not to buy stoves made by Buck's. The company thereupon had requested the Supreme Court of the District of Columbia to enjoin the effort by the Metal Polishers in particular and the Federation in general to boycott its products. The company had powerful support from businessmen's societies of national influence—the National Association of Manufacturers, the Anti-Boycott Association, and the National Council of Industrial Defense. The economic customs which the members of those associations recognized were the customs which judges in the main had accepted before their elevation to the court, since most of them had been businessmen's lawyers in their pre-judicial days.

Roosevelt went further for LaFollette than for Gompers by asking Congress to authorize the Interstate Commerce Commission to make a physical valuation of the property of railroads. Other

Senators had departed for the cloakroom when LaFollette vainly recommended such powers during his speech on the railway rate bill in the spring of 1906. As long as the public had to accept the roads' own statement of their valuation, the public could not judge the merit of the railway rate schedules. Roosevelt was brought around to LaFollette's opinion by the discovery in the summer of 1907 that in the reorganization of the Chicago and Alton in 1899, E. H. Harriman and other members of the reorganizing syndicate had bought reorganization bonds at sixty-five and sold them thirty-three days later to the New York Life Insurance Company at ninety-six. The reorganizers privately declared a 30 per cent dividend, without reporting it to the Interstate Commerce Commission. They charged to "construction expenditures uncapitalized" the amount they distributed to themselves in the dividend. Such disclosures fed the discontent.

The President also tried to please business by a scheme abominable to the Speaker. He requested Congress to revise the tariff after the coming election. The National Association of Manufacturers had begun in 1907 to distribute pamphlets in favor of revision. Jim Sherman pointed out the fallacy of that position to James W. Van Cleave, the president of the association, but Van Cleave continued to press upon the President his opinion that the United States was able at last to compete with foreign goods. Van Cleave held that American industry had become so efficient that it no longer needed special high protection to balance the benefits which foreign manufacturers obtained from paying low wages. Lower tariffs appealed to businessmen who formerly had opposed them because the supposition was spreading that manufacturers could sell more abroad if the country would increase its imports. Moreover, manufacturers needed cheaper raw and semi-finished materials from foreign buyers. To please one segment of business interested in reducing the cost of its raw materials, the President recommended the immediate elimination of tariffs on wood pulp and newsprint—a suggestion that reached him from the American Newspaper Publishers Association. Reiterating what Postmasters General had been asking since 1871, Roosevelt recommended the institution of a postal savings system. He reminded Congress that a year earlier he had asked for currency reform, and, the panic having intervened to emphasize the need, he asked for it again. He recommended the enactment of a model employers' liability act for federal employees. Nothing in the list except the last request could Cannon approve.

Cannon heard the message with aplomb, because things were going his way. He was still pleased by a pleasant surprise he had received on the first day of the session, when he discovered that the opposition in the House, for all their increase in numbers, were not going to make trouble at once.

Henry Allen Cooper of LaFollette's Wisconsin did give him a bad moment. When prim Dalzell had finished his usual task of recommending approval of the rules of the preceding Congress, Cooper spoke up that the rules gave the Speaker "more power than ought to be given to any man in any government that pretends to be republican in form and democratic in spirit." Cooper was an emphatic man, but mannerly. Cannon had known him since 1893, when he arrived in Washington to represent a conservative district in Racine. He was the best musician in the House. He composed his own tunes. At that time he had been defying his constituents by bending in LaFollette's direction. But he was not ready in 1907 to defy the habits of the House. Having stated his disapproval of the rules, he announced that he would take no steps to change them then.

Cannon waited for more criticism. The Federation of Labor had issued a proclamation "to all organized labor," asking Cannon's defeat for the Speakership. Gompers had no influence in Congress, but would John Mandt Nelson of Wisconsin remain silent? He was a true-blue LaFollette man. He represented Madison in the House, and he had been born in Dane County. During the summer he had pictured Cannon to his constituents as "the vulgar old man who rules the national House of Representatives in the interest of the trusts." But the boldness Nelson showed in the West deserted him in Washington. He voted for the rules, and he voted with the majority for Cannon's re-election as Speaker.

When the vote of confidence was over, Cannon stepped jauntily down from the Speaker's table to the well. Addressing his colleagues as man to man, he assured them that they were members of a unique institution worthy of their pride. "Other departments of the government have lofty and important functions," he said, "but to this House alone belongs the peculiar, the delicate, and the all-surpassing function of interpreting and putting in definite form the will of the people." It was not really a strange remark for him to make. Like a chef who expects the diners to relish the minestrone which he himself finds delicious, the Speaker assumed that what he willed all people with clear heads willed also.

Cannon withdrew to his rooms, and, while trustworthy friends presided in his chair at the Speaker's table in the House Chamber, for days he was scarcely seen except by the members of the court. He had an apartment of offices on the main floor of the Capitol in the southwest corner. The reception room was large, lined with chairs for the endless stream of visitors, and anchored at the corners and in the center with five great desks. Doors led from the reception room into the Speaker's private office and into small offices for Lincoln White Busbey, the Speaker's secretary, and for Asher Hinds, the parliamentary clerk, who strengthened the Speaker by providing him with precedents for his rulings from the chair. The two counsellors spent many hours in the Speaker's own office, where he had more space than he needed. At one wall was a red leather couch, but he seldom lay down on it. He wanted his visitors to think of him as vigorous and youthful. The sprightly septuagenarian ran down the gridiron and kicked a football from placement as part of the pre-game pageantry of a game played by Danville High in the autumn of 1907. To arm himself with answers for voters who held his age against him, he had the Library of Congress search for essays and studies tending to show that one's years need have no precise relationship to one's true age. Instead of reclining, he worked away at his desk in a corner. Like the desk at Danville, it was chipped at the edges from the heels of his boots. When he was in his office, most of Washington lay at his feet. The tall windows gave on the hill which the Capitol crowns. Through them Cannon could glance downward in the direction of the White House, its flag waving a mile away, and toward every other executive agency, for they were all on the flat beyond the hill, all below him.

There Cannon stayed in retreat more than two weeks. It took him that long to decide how, since the voters had affected the make-up of the House by their discontented desire for change, he could hold under his thumb the chosen representatives of the 80,-000,000 Americans. Could he somehow distribute the diminishing number of his friends through the committee structure in such a way that they would dominate every battlement of the Speaker's wing of the Capitol? If so, they could make certain that as long as the country sent more Republicans than Democrats to Congress (and thereby kept the Republicans, represented by Cannon, in command of the organization of the House), nothing would happen in those representative halls except what pleased Uncle Joe.

But his scrutiny of Representatives' names aroused no hope of recapturing the kind of control over all the standing committees which he had enjoyed before the Sixtieth Congress. Instead, he took the risk of leaving in chairmanships a number of Representatives who sympathized with one or another of the President's theses. He kept Hal Cooper as chairman of Insular Affairs. He let another opponent, Halvor Steenerson of Minnesota, continue to be chairman of Militia. Rebel Charles Newell Fowler of Elizabeth, New Jersey, stayed on as chairman of Banking and Currency. President of the Equitable Mortgage Company, Fowler was a solitary, unpopular know-it-all who often said that the United States would be damned unless its currency system were reformed. Cannon satisfied himself with naming a reliable standpatter, Theodore E. Burton of Ohio, to the banking committee, with expectations that Burton would keep him up-to-date on Fowler.

The members of the two great committees, Ways and Means and Appropriations, interested him more than the chairmen of all other committees. He took pains to name to those two committees a full complement of Republicans who would support him unanimously. To Littauer's old place on Appropriations he appointed a country banker from Salamanca, New York, Edward B. Vreeland, whom Jim Sherman recommended. To Ways and Means he assigned Longworth, the President's son-in-law, and Joseph Fordney, a lumberman from Michigan, who in October had persuaded his Congressional district, in the Saginaw neighborhood, to advocate Cannon for President in gratitude for Cannon's high tariff attitude toward sugar, which Michigan grew in the form of beets.

The upshot of those decisions was that the Speaker henceforward relied less on the standing committees than on the Rules Committee and on himself alone to continue his domination of his fellows. The most important of the appointments which the Speaker announced on December 20, when he reappeared from the Gethsemane of his office, was that Sherman would succeed Grosvenor on Rules. At the same time he commenced the practice of giving strained and arbitrary interpretations to the rules governing debate in the House. He became mean and unfair. In the past he had been domineering but usually he had observed the amenities of parliamentary procedure. Now he was in the mood to treat all as he once had treated Representative William T. Zenor of Indiana. When Zenor from the floor asked the Speaker if a certain bill could not be passed, Cannon replied: "This House could pass an elephant if the gentleman in charge of it could catch the Speaker's eye." He then shut his eyes and called for the next order of business. The Speaker followed this capricious course so successfully in the Sixtieth Congress that when a citizen asked Representative Nathan Hale for a copy of the House rules, Hale sent in return a photograph of Cannon.

The recognition of Cannon's position as the contestant of Roosevelt's leadership in the Republican Party spread quickly as the Speaker held the House at a standstill. One desperate member of Roosevelt's cabinet, Postmaster General George Von L. Meyer, visited the Speaker at the Capitol with a request for enactment of a postal savings scheme, but Cannon refused to budge. Postal savings meant government intrusion into the banking business. The bills inspired by Roosevelt's message were sealed in their vaults. When the Committee on Agriculture gave signs of readiness to report one measure which Roosevelt had been seeking more than a year—authorizing the federal government to buy lands in the Appalachian and White mountains and control them permanently as forest reserves—Cannon sent the bill to the more dependably standpat Judiciary Committee with a request for a report on its constitutionality. Thus he won a delay.

Inactivity dropped a pall over the whole Capitol. The Senate, which the Speaker had so often put in its place, was as inert as the House. The Senate leaders, Nelson Aldrich of Rhode Island and William B. Allison of Iowa, were Cannon's brothers under the skin. Federal judges continued to see the country through Cannon's and Aldrich's eyes. A week after Roosevelt recommended softness in issuing injunctions, the District of Columbia Supreme Court enjoined the American Federation of Labor from carrying on its boycott against the Buck's Stove and Range Company, and justified its decision by an opinion which William Howard Taft had written in 1893. Everywhere men in public life were reincarnating the old, while the public called for something new.

Snow still covered Washington when Cannon began to achieve the distinction of replacing reform itself as the major political issue in the United States. His patience gone after being shut out for almost two months, the President on January 31, 1908, sent a special message to Congress reiterating, in stronger language than before, all his admonitions and requests of December 3. Never had he been so emphatic about the abuses heaped on labor. "It is all wrong," he said, "to use the injunction to prevent the entirely proper and legitimate actions of labor organizations in their struggle for industrial betterment, or under the guise of protecting property rights, unwarrantedly to invade the fundamental rights of the individual. . . . This matter is daily becoming of graver importance and I cannot too urgently recommend that the Congress give careful consideration to the subject."

It was a wax dart thrown against Gibraltar, but it brought John Nelson of Wisconsin, that Nelson who had been silent in December, to his feet in the House, where he said:

In no other country of the world, be its government in form republican, monarchical, or imperial, has there been such a complete surrender of powers and prerogatives by one of the representatives of the people in the one chamber to its presiding officer. . . . The policies advocated by the President are indeed of vast importance to the American people, but the most important, the most pressing, the most agonizing need of the country today is not one of these policies, but reform in the House.

De Armond went to New Haven and told the students in the Yale law school:

One man, the Speaker, exercises a veto power greater than that of the President. The Speaker enslaves the majority and minority indefinitely. When the opportunity comes to you, young gentlemen, to deal with czarism, don't trouble yourselves about Russia but direct your efforts against the czarism which flourishes in the House of Representatives of our own country.

The effort to obstruct reform grew boisterous. In the Committee on Election of the President, Vice President, and Representatives in Congress, two Democrats tackled at the ankles two Republicans who were running from the committee room in order to spoil a quorum. The sprinters intended to prevent the committee from favorably reporting a reform bill requiring political party organizations to name the corporations from which they obtained money. The committee could not vote in the absence of a quorum. Those fleet-footed conservatives, Gerrit Diekema of Michigan and Francis Burke of Pennsylvania, did not realize, however, that their standard-bearer, having won recognition as the hero who defied the President, was slightly changing his tactics.

Hoping to attract support for his presidential aspirations from the least enthusiastic backers of reform, Cannon began carefully to create the illusion that he favored some reform measures. Ambition, slightly rusting that fine frankness of his, was tempting him to prove an observation of William Graham Sumner's: "It is thought to be the triumph of practical statesmanship to give the clamorers something which will quiet them, and a new and special kind of legislative finesse has been developed, viz., to devise projects which shall seem to the clamorous petitioners to meet their demands, yet shall not really do it." He did this either by stating that he was for action in the future or by following Representative Mann's practice of offering half a loaf. He even spoke up for tariff revision, to be carried out "at the earliest possible day" —after the presidential election. Such statements forestalled the movement, agitated in the Senate by Beveridge, to set up at once a permanent commission of experts to study the tariff schedules and recommend changes in the duties.

Cannon magnanimously encouraged the House to pass a bill requiring political parties to make public reports of the donations they received and the names of the donors, after he arranged for inclusion in it of an extraneous section which one could know would mean its sure death in the Senate. His friend, Representative Samuel W. McCall of Massachusetts, sponsored this bill, which not only called for publicity but required every person elected to Congress to report whether citizens in his district were freely permitted to vote, and, if that right were denied them, to set forth the extent to which the franchise was suppressed and the methods which made suppression possible. It was a blow to the restrictions on Negro voting in the southern states, and southern

Senators persuaded their northern colleagues to let the bill languish. When Representative George Alexander Pearre introduced an anti-injunction bill pleasing to Gompers, Cannon had Payne introduce one which did not satisfy Gompers but which might dupe the casual voter into thinking that Cannon was harkening to public demand.

Driving forward under the goad of his ambition, Cannon became a stranger to many of his old friends. He cultivated only those who could help him on. He sacrificed even his long-standing, warm-hearted friendship with his ebullient little colleague from Mississippi, John Sharp Williams.

By spring the time was ripe for Democrats to take partisan advantage of the President's inability to make his promises come true. Archie Butt, Roosevelt's military aide, wrote a friend that he thought the Democrats could win the next presidential election if they picked the right candidate. In that propitious atmosphere Williams undertook to attract voters to the Democratic Party by disgusting them further with the party in power. On April 2 he made a motion that the House instruct the Speaker to distribute to the interested committees the President's message of January 31, to which Cannon had paid no attention. With that move Williams and his party colleagues in the House launched a filibuster, for the avowed purpose of preventing the passage of appropriation bills (without which the federal government would cease to function) until the Republicans had legislated the reforms which Roosevelt besought of them. Instead of helping Roosevelt, of course, the maneuver only emphasized Roosevelt's helplessness and nourished doubts about the competence of Republicans to govern.

"Every time anybody wants to pass any of this reform legislation," Williams said to the Republicans, "you cry, 'After the election.' You remind me a little bit of a piece of poetry my boy picked up the other day somewhere at the public school and brought home and recited to me:

When I asked my girl to marry me, she said:
"Go to father."
She knew that I knew her father was dead.
She knew that I knew what a life he had led,

She knew that I knew what she meant when she said:
"Go to father."

Williams managed his filibuster cleverly. He wasted the time of the House by demanding roll-call votes at every opportunity, and each roll call took nearly half an hour. He demanded roll calls on the approval of the journal, which briefed the activities of the preceding day. He demanded roll calls on motions to adjourn, and he demanded roll calls on demands for roll calls. One day he forced the House to go through twelve roll calls, taking up almost six hours in the monotonous calling of names by the clerk. It resembled the filibuster which had aroused Speaker Reed eighteen years earlier, and Cannon met the problem like Reed. He called for new rules. Hinds and Dalzell wrote the new rules, Dalzell explained them, and the House approved them. But they failed. The dilatory tactics continued.

A sickening tension spread through the House Chamber as the filibuster went on, because the antagonists were Williams and Cannon, two faithful comrades. Which ought to be the stronger in them—the sense of responsibility of the public servant, or the sense of responsibility of the friend? Neither man hesitated to choose the former. Could they collide in pursuit of their public duty without damaging their personal relationship? The answer came on April 20. It was Saturday afternoon. The Republicans were restless, longing to leave the Capitol. Williams forced them to suffer for the sins of their leader by keeping them in session. Sunset was coming when the Speaker heard a motion to adjourn. As he accepted it, Williams called, "Division"—meaning a show of hands on the motion. Another device for delay. Cannon ignored it. He declared the House adjourned. As the members filed out, the Speaker stepped down to the well and approached Williams, who was standing in the aisle.

"Sharp," he said, putting out his hand.

Williams, biting his mustache, turned his back on his old companion.

Williams spent a miserable week end, condemning himself over and over because he had refused to speak to Uncle Joe. Early Monday he wrote a note of apology.

"I think you did a public wrong," he told Cannon, "but I know

I followed it with a private wrong, a sense of which has not added to my happiness. Enduring personal friendships in this world are too infrequent, too difficult to form and too precious when formed to be lightly shaken off."

But the precious thing was gone. When the House met Monday afternoon, Williams asked for a vote of censure of the Speaker, on the ground that he had arbitrarily adjourned the House without ruling on Williams' request for a division. "Mr. Speaker," said Williams, "you are one of the best men in the world, but a long and undisturbed power, whose lesser abuses have been good-naturedly passed over, has made you despotic and somewhat intolerant of opposition." The motion of censure failed. One hundred and forty-six Representatives voted against it, and one hundred and nineteen for it. Cooper and Nelson voted for it.

The bitter truth revealed in Williams' sad analysis of power's destructive effect escaped the Speaker. He continued to force his likes on his friends and on the nation, and he continued to do what he could to humiliate Theodore Roosevelt. Late in April the President sent to Congress a new message, urging the Senators and Representatives to provide an adequate appropriation for the Interstate Commerce Commission's administration of the Hepburn Act, which had standardized the railway rates, and repeating the oft-repeated request for a postal savings system and the redistribution of wealth through taxation. The new message, in stronger words than Roosevelt had used before, asked Congress once more to release labor from the leash of the injunction. Gompers had new reason to resent the punishment of the courts. The Supreme Court had just announced that, for boycotting their employers, the Hatters' Union must pay triple damages. The cause of unionization was in danger, because unless organized workers could strike and boycott without fear of having their treasuries depleted by judicial orders, the unions would be helpless to improve pay scales and working conditions for their members.

It was late in the day when the messenger from the White House arrived at the Capitol with the communication, and Cannon refused to interrupt the proceedings of the House by having the message read then. When the House met the following day, Cannon let the message lie on his desk in his office, and not until midafternoon did he deign to present to the members the words

of the President. The message having been read, Cannon referred
it to the Judiciary Committee, which many Representatives now
called "The Morgue" because the Speaker used it as a catch-all
repository for legislation he did not want to bring to life. The
Judiciary chairman, John Jenkins, was a Wisconsin man of the
Spooner and Sawyer School, a thorn to Cooper and a rose to Cannon. The Interstate Commerce Commission obtained its appropriation, through the intercession of the Senate, but the offensive dis-
dain which the Speaker showed for Roosevelt's message, and the
failure of the House to murmur even the mildest rebuke, caused
the New York *Herald* to comment, "Congress no longer stands in
awe of the President."

When the rules on which Cannon founded his despotism worked
against him, he suspended the rules. Thus he got around the barrier in his progress to the mountaintop of despotism which the unsympathetic chairmen and the unreliable committees put in his
way. The Speaker demonstrated his superiority over those committees by his manner of dealing with Chairman Fowler of Banking and Currency. Fowler and most of his committee colleagues
crossed Cannon on the question of currency reform. Fowler in
the fall of 1906 had appointed a committee of fifteen bankers to
study the country's financial problem for him, and they had recommended that the federal government set up a central bank to
oversee all banks. When Fowler introduced a bill based on the
recommendations, Cannon refused to have it brought before the
House. "What the hell does this howling in Wall Street amount
to?" Cannon asked Fowler. "The country don't care what happens
to those damned speculators. Everything is all right out west and
around Danville. The country don't need any legislation."

In the year Booth killed Lincoln the Treasury had tried to subordinate banks to the will of Washington, but the influence which
the federal government exerted in 1908 through the National Bank
Law of 1865 was micrometric. Many bankers managed their affairs to suit their own caprice. They did not often regard themselves as agents of the public filling a role useful to society. They
kept their banks local in outlook and local in control as business
grew national in scope. In this situation, the country lacked enough
currency to take care of nation-wide business needs. American
economic activity had outpaced the increase in currency needed

to carry on that activity during the golden age which stirred Cannon's boasts. As a result, when millions asked the tellers to turn their bank deposits into cash after the Knickerbocker incident, the banks could not produce the currency, and the debtors suffered when banks suddenly demanded payment of their loans.

Moneyless in the midst of wealth, Americans could sing an economic version of that ironic line, "Water, water everywhere, and not a drop to drink." The clamor for legislation that would make the currency more elastic and subject the banks to some common superior authority increased even as the country recovered, about the time of Williams' filibuster, from the panic.

The brief brush with hard times was driving back to their original homes abroad many of the immigrants for whom Cannon had held open the door into the United States, and expectation of some new collapse disturbed the Americans who stayed here. If the money and the banks had failed the country once, they could fail it again. City bankers were beginning to think that they had an excess of freedom in the conduct of their banks. At the height of the panic, John L. Hamilton, chairman of the currency committee of the American Bankers Association, told the Illinois Manufacturers Association that "our present distress is due to the lack of proper banking laws. . . . Our system is practically the same as it was in 1865, . . . and it is not in keeping with the business necessities of the time."

Soon after he fell out with Williams, Cannon attempted to quiet the cry for banking reform with a spoonful of sugar water. He continued to blame Roosevelt for the panic, and he connected even the most conservative arguments for currency reform with economic quackeries that had been hawked to the voters in the last years of the nineteenth century by political wondermen who seldom found their nostrums a key to public office. They were the Greenbackers of the 1870's and Dick Bland and William Jennings Bryan and the other silverites of the 1890's. They all attributed almost magical qualities to currency expansion. They were mystics who absorbed their knowledge by inspiration. They conceived of a monetary system as the single panacea, at very least a kind of economic penicillin, for soothing all the troubles of a national society. Cannon had campaigned successfully against Greenbackers, although he himself had once advocated the restoration of bimetallism, which the United States abandoned in the year he took his seat in Congress. But as soon as William Jennings Bryan incorporated bimetallism in the articles of Democratic faith, the single gold standard had become an integral part of Cannon's Republicanism.

The Speaker nevertheless thrust those prejudices from his mind and guided through Congress legislation that seemed to reform the currency, in order to prevent Congress from passing legislation that would have wrought serious changes in the currency and the management of banks. Comment like Banker Hamilton's, agitating the nation, had induced Aldrich to sponsor and the Senate to pass, before Cannon fell out with Williams, a bill that crossed the limits of Cannon's tolerance. To stave off the Senate bill, Cannon was willing to provide his own bill.

In the form Aldrich had written it, the bill simply authorized national banks to issue currency based on their securities, authorized the Treasury to keep such currency out of circulation except in times of emergency by a high tax, and established a National Monetary Commission, to be selected only from members of the House and Senate. That bill would father little new currency, and it promised to silence the clamor for federalizing the banks until some vague future time when the Commission, reflecting Congressional views, chose to write a report. But LaFollette had ruined the bill for Cannon. He had tacked on a prohibition against banks' lending money to firms of which an officer of the bank was an officer or director. The bill also required banks to keep 30 per cent of their deposits in cash. "If it becomes law, it will surely put about forty per cent of the country banks out of business," J. W. Gates, the owner of the First National Bank, Port Arthur, Texas, wrote to Cannon.

The Speaker, the honorary president of the Danville National, knew a thing or two about country banks, and he was in complete agreement with Gates. For something better than the Aldrich Bill, however, the Speaker could not turn to his own Banking and Currency Committee. There squatted the bossy Fowler, dinning out his demand for a central banking system like Germany's. Fowler did not trust Congress to analyze the shortcomings of the banking and currency problem. He, too, proposed the establishment of a National Monetary Commission, but his would consist of twenty-one experts drawn from outside the Capitol as well as twenty-two members of the House and Senate. Cannon drew back from resort to experts as an affront to the American system of government, a compromise with the privilege of Congress to study as well as to legislate on the banking and currency.

Cannon needed a law custom-made for his country-banker, small-government, optimist's conceptions. He encouraged Representative Vreeland, who was president of the leading bank in the Indian reservation country in southwestern New York—the Salamanca Trust Company—to introduce a currency bill that fitted the Speaker's requirements. It hardly differed from the bill Aldrich had written. LaFollette's amendments were expunged. The unbearable provisions pushed by Fowler were left out. It set up the Monetary Commission as a Congress monopoly, and it authorized banks to form National Currency Associations (ten banks to an association, one association to a city), to which the federal Controller of the Currency could issue new paper money. The securities held by the banks in each association would back this Vreeland-Aldrich currency. Bankers and businessmen in the cities cried out in anguish. The *Journal of Commerce* said that the bill would bring inflation, since securities on which the currency was to be based could fluctuate in price. The Merchants Association of New York sent a letter of protest to Cannon and every other member of the House: "If Congress passes the Aldrich Bill or any portion of it, we feel sure that it will have to reckon with the vigorous and practically unanimous disapproval of the entire body of commercial and financial thought." What the merchants said about the Aldrich Bill applied equally to the Vreeland Bill. Even some small-town financiers objected to the measure. "The Vreeland Bill is a panic breeder because it puts no check whatever on the amount that may be issued of bond-secured currency," J. G. Vivion, an investment broker in Galesburg, Illinois, wrote to the Speaker. Cannon put away the protests, and referred the bill to Fowler's committee.

The committee promptly tabled the bill, the members voting twelve to three against recommending that the House pass it. Burton, faithful to Cannon, voted for Vreeland and persuaded John W. Weeks of Massachusetts to go along with him. Otherwise Cannon's maneuver would have had no Republican support on the committee. Fowler called the bill a "makeshift," "another stumbling block to real reform of our currency and financial practices." He mentioned that Vreeland, who was not a member of the committee, had never before sponsored a banking bill, although he had been in the House eighteen years. Fowler's comments did not anger Cannon. They meant that in the bill he had the harmless palliative that he sought.

The rules prevented the House from considering legislation which the standing committee, possessing proper jurisdiction, refused to approve. One afternoon at half-past twelve in the middle of May, however, a week after Cannon's seventy-second birthday, Vreeland sent to the Speaker's desk a resolution calling on the House to ignore the rules, to discharge Fowler's committee from responsibility for either his bill or a similar one sponsored by Williams, and to pass the bill by 5:00 P.M. The resolution bore the stigmata of Dalzell in the phrases that called for action now. A speech by Burton showed the House that not all Banking and Currency members agreed with Fowler. The House performed as requested. It voted to suspend the rules, and by sunset it approved Vreeland's bill. Fowler and Cooper and Nelson voted against both propositions, which looked like the handiwork of Cannon himself as well as Vreeland. But then they were voices in the wilderness. Within a week the Senate accepted the House bill, and it was law. In sponsoring legislation as well as by smothering it, Cannon portrayed himself as the scourge of Theodore Roosevelt.

CHAPTER —•— 9

Poker and Prayers

CANNON's success in championing his own cause had its disappointing feature, however, in that it did not enable him effectively to champion himself. The President tantalized the Speaker by serenely declining to complain openly about Cannon's responsibility for the shabby treatment his program was receiving. The proddings of his Cabinet officers did not stir Roosevelt from this policy. The exasperated Postmaster General Meyer enlivened a Cabinet meeting, in May 1908, by stating that the Congressmen were taking their do-nothing cue from the Speaker and urging that the Speaker be called to account. Roosevelt listened and then forgot. By silence Roosevelt facilitated the Speaker's repression of the proposals contained in the stream of messages which passed from White House to Capitol. But he confounded the Speaker's effort to run for the presidency.

Cannon so expertly frustrated the President's program and the President so politely accepted the frustration that Cannon was unable to come directly to grips with Roosevelt the person. The country could plainly see that Cannon was engaged in battle against what Roosevelt represented, but the conflict was shadowy as long as Roosevelt stayed away from the tournament. Having in December laid out the jousting field for the struggle with Uncle Joe, Roosevelt was content to let the field be used only as a battleground for ideas, and he refused to put on his armor and

106

ride out to the rescue of the ideas. Since Cannon could not go after Roosevelt the man, he could not openly go after Roosevelt's protégé, Taft, either, although by the end of January the politicking out in the states on the part of the federal officeholders not beholden to Cannon made it plain that Roosevelt really was going to try to put Taft across. "The Speaker" was not a precise label for Cannon's office. During and before Cannon's day the Speaker was customarily one of the most silent officials in government. He aired his opinions in the actions and inaction of the House rather than in his own assertions. In remaining aloof from personal controversy Roosevelt disclosed his astuteness. A joust by lances with Cannon would certainly have unloosed the Speaker's tongue, divided the Republican Party, and jeopardized Taft's chances of victory. As it was, Taft had opportunities to expound, without being too specific, the things he stood for, and to relate them to the aspirations and recommendations of Roosevelt, while Cannon became increasingly famous for the things he stood against.

Cannon nevertheless began the year 1908 in a cheerful frame of mind about the presidency. "Frankly, the more I see of the situation the better I am satisfied, from the party standpoint as well as the standpoint of the best interest of the country, that the field should be larger than Brother Taft in the national convention," he wrote on January 16 to Captain Henry King, editor of the St. Louis *Globe-Democrat*. To B. M. Chiperfield, a constituent in Canton, Illinois, he wrote: "It seems to me that if Illinois shall present in good faith my name to the convention, it will have more than an even chance of being successful."

Dick Yates, the turn-coat Republican who had campaigned against Cannon for Congress in 1906, came out for Cannon for President in January 1908. Representative William S. Greene of Massachusetts told the New York *Sun* that "only two things stand in the way of Joseph Cannon's triumphant nomination and election—his age and his profanity. The former cannot be helped, while the latter should not really be held against him, because it is not real irreverence, but merely a habit of speech." In February the *Inter-Ocean* reported that Cannon and Taft were the "two leading candidates." The other aspirants were Charles Fairbanks of Indiana, the Vice President; Governor Charles

Evans Hughes of New York, and Senator Philander Knox of Pennsylvania. A mock Republican convention conducted by the students of the high school in Hazleton, Pennsylvania, nominated Cannon on the second ballot. He received a good word even from Wisconsin: "You have acted like a statesman should throughout. Republicans of Wisconsin have good reason to blush for persons like Cooper, who are simply Democrats masquerading as Republicans." A few words from John C. Spooner, LaFollette's old foe, implied that in the nation as well as in Congress, Cannon was becoming the leader of conservatives. "I have been immensely pleased with your attitude during the present session," wrote Spooner.

The loyal Republicans of Illinois in convention in the Arsenal in Springfield on March 26 unanimously endorsed Cannon for the presidential nomination, as the Speaker had expected they would when he opposed the Oglesby Primary Bill. Jewell presided over the resolutions committee, which was fretting with a tariff plank when a knock came at the door of the conference room. It was a messenger who whispered to Jewell the news that the Leland Hotel, where most of the delegates to the convention had rooms, was afire. Jewell smiled at his colleagues, closed the door after the messenger departed, and kept the information to himself. He did not want the committee members to leave before they had completed their work. But an hour later they were still fumbling for the precise words. They had worked out a statement that satisfied Jewell, but the debate went on about the need for changing a word here and there. Impatiently Jewell interrupted their discussion.

"Perhaps some of you will be interested to know that your grips and other property are in the Leland Hotel, and I have been told it is burning," he said. "You had better adopt the resolution and adjourn." Throwing back their chairs, they tossed the resolution to Jewell with a shout that they now approved it as it was, and hurried away to the hotel. The tariff plank thus precipitately accepted was a series of suitably ambiguous sentences which mirrored both the sentiment of the times and the celebrated convictions of Cannon. It said:

The very success of the present tariff demonstrates the wisdom of revising it to conform to the improved conditions which it has produced. We believe that the people of the United States will profit by a new tariff, but it must be a Republican tariff, a protective tariff, a tariff which recognizes in all its parts the difference between American and foreign wages, the difference between the high scale of living of American wage earners and the scale of living imposed by insufficient wages upon foreign workmen.

Nobody was playing jokes on Uncle Joe, but the graph of his race for the presidential nomination showed a curve on the rise at the beginning of the year and then a sharp decline. As they say for horses, he had "early foot." When winter edged toward spring, the optimism for Cannon's chances began to dull. Even during the most cheerful period he seemed to be making little serious headway outside Illinois. Those friendly letters he was receiving from all over were not the equivalent of votes in the convention.

The most ardent members of his cheering section complained that his canvass was not being pushed vigorously enough. Did McKinley really have what it takes to line up votes for a presidential candidate? He was such a mild little man, with his two gentle mottoes: "If you can't speak a kind word, keep still," and "We must be polite even to our friends." Little Mac was a hard and competent worker, with a record of reaching his goals by ingenious and persistent assault on the obstacles in his way. When he failed to obtain a right-of-way for his interurban line into St. Louis over existing bridges, he ran for Congress in order to sponsor a bill authorizing the construction of a new bridge across the Mississippi River. His constituents elected him, Congress approved the bridge, and his trains rolled into St. Louis. But Cannon's partisans were dissatisfied. Captain King wrote to Cannon that he better get busy lining up Arkansas, and the *Inter-Ocean* gave this advice in an editorial: "The observed facts should suggest to the men in charge of the Cannon campaign not so much a dress parade in Illinois—where it is all over for Mr. Cannon but the shouting —as active and constructive organization in other great Republican states which have no 'favorite sons.'" An anxious note crept into the communications from his friends. "My only fear is that you are remaining too reticent as to your southern campaign," wrote an admirer in the capital. Cannon's agents were tardy about making up lost time. On March 19 John H. McGraw, a Cannon campaigner, reported to Busbey from Seattle:

I arrived here the evening of Saturday the 14th inst. and immediately took up the work of preventing an endorsement of any candidate for the presidency by our State Central Committee. I was too late, however, and soon discovered that the friends of Mr. Taft had been actively engaged in gathering up the proxies of the members who would be unable to attend the meeting, and that an instruction [for Taft] was probably a foregone conclusion.

Cannon, in drawing attention to himself as the champion of conservatism, was making enemies outside the Capitol at a faster rate than he was attracting supporters. Perhaps this untoward development, rather than any inadequacy of McKinley's, accounted for the slow progress of the canvass for the Speaker. As early as December 1907 Jewell had written to Busbey that "Mr. McKinley finds that there is considerable opposition developing against Mr. Cannon on account of his supposed unfriendliness to organized labor, and especially to organized railroad labor." The Speaker doubted that the rail men were turning against him. Evidence in support of his confidence in them came from William Bosley, a Big Four hogger living in Mattoon, Illinois, who on March 4 sent Cannon a resolution of criticism adopted by his lodge of the Brotherhood of Locomotive Engineers. He followed that communication with a letter to McKinley: "Personally, I have the highest regard for Mr. Cannon and believe that he is sincere and honest in every way and that he endeavors to handle the business of his office in such a manner as will bring about the greatest good to the greatest number."

But the rising tide was the tide of complaint. In their hearts as well as in public thousands of Americans were growing hostile to Uncle Joe. Their temper was tersely analyzed by a stranger, J. E. Forbes, a traveling salesman, who wrote to the Speaker late in April, after the Williams filibuster, from the heart of the old Populist country, Ottawa, Kansas. "The public mind is not now in a condition to tolerate the arbitrary control of Congress," said Forbes. "Any Republican Congressman standing for re-election in a close or moderately close district has got to pledge himself against Cannonism or go out of office. Ought to pass the Theodore Roosevelt program. Need bill on publicity for corporation contributions to campaigns, postal savings, federal licensing for state corporations, open all banks to government inspectors, let the Attorney General name receivers for insolvent railroads. Turn over a new leaf."

Cannon's new enemies included the temperance fanatics, who were daily growing in number and influence, and the publishers of several hundred newspapers. The dries advocated government enforcement of total abstinence from alcoholic beverages, including ales, beer, wine, and patent remedies (topers unable to buy whiskey could ease their nerves with a "purely vegetable" tonic which contained 41.6 per cent alcohol or various stomach bitters which averaged 45 per cent). The cause of enforced abstinence had been taken seriously since the organization of the American Anti-Saloon League (soon changed to the Anti-Saloon League of America) in Washington in December 1895. Four years later the League opened a legislative office near the Capitol the better to influence Congress, and in 1901 it persuaded Congress to eliminate canteens (liquor stores) from military reservations. The League's "Wet and Dry Map" of the United States for January 1, 1908, showed four states which prohibited the sale and consumption of liquor—Maine, Kansas, Georgia, and Oklahoma. All other states but nine (New Jersey, Pennsylvania, New Mexico, Utah, Nevada, Idaho, Wyoming, Montana, and Washington) had passed local option laws which permitted the residents of municipalities and counties to hold elections on the question of imposing abstinence in their particular political subdivisions. Twenty-five counties in Illinois, among them Edgar County in Cannon's district, voted dry in the spring of 1908.

That progress, however, left the temperance campaigners dissatisfied, and for their continued dissatisfaction they blamed Cannon. The inhabitants of dry states, dry cities, and dry counties were free to buy and drink all the intoxicants they could stomach, without fear of punishment, despite the strict prohibition in the local laws, as a result of the interstate commerce clause of the Constitution. The courts had decided that liquor shipped in its original package to an addressee in a dry area was subject not to the police power of the states but to the interstate commerce clause, which was enforceable only by the federal government. Since the federal government did not prohibit the shipment of liquor anywhere except to Indian reservations, the federal government in effect forbade the dry areas to enforce their local laws by seizing liquor in transit. Flouters of the local law not only could drink the interstate commerce gin with impunity, but they could sell it without fear of arrest or fine, provided the sale was made in the original package. The express companies regularly increased the size of their agencies in counties which had voted dry, in order to put themselves at the interstate commerce service of the minority which remained wet.

Cannon irked the Anti-Saloon League because he prevented the House from voting on a bill which would have permitted prohibition and local option states to forbid the delivery to the addressee of alcoholic liquors which entered the state or local option areas in interstate commerce. In the first session of the Fifty-ninth Congress the Judiciary Committee refused to report the reform bill. In the second session the committee reported the bill to the House, but the Rules Committee did not authorize consideration of it. In the Sixtieth Congress the bill again languished in the Judiciary Committee because the Speaker wished it to. The author of the bill was a teetotaler, that same Charles E. Littlefield of Maine whom Cannon had helped to save from Gompers. "Today the temperance people all over the world are looking to Maine as the leading state in outlawing the liquor traffic," Littlefield remarked to the editor of the 1908 *Anti-Saloon League Yearbook*.

The first suggestion that Cannon's opposition to the Littlefield bill was politically indiscreet came in a letter from a Cannon supporter, H. L. Sheldon, of Rock Falls, Illinois, on February 20. Sheldon had heard a rumor about Cannon and the temperance bill. "I have been all over the state," wrote the correspondent, "and I have been surprised to see the deep feeling existing among the Republicans upon this question, and I am writing you this simply to remind you that these men cannot be safely ignored." Cannon already, moreover, had dismayed the foes of "ardent spirits" by advocating, in an address in November 1907 in Chicago at the banquet of the Naval Academy Alumni Association, the return of the canteen to military reservations "for the good of the service." Cannon argued that it was better to have the canteen, with proper restrictions on its use, than to tempt soldiers and sailors to leave the reservation in search of a drink. The Reverend A. S. Buchanan, pastor of the First Presbyterian Church in Cairo, Illinois, read news reports about the speech and warned the Speaker that he could "depend on the most intense opposition from the whole Presbyterian ministry in your campaign for the presidency. We are not Democrats but would a hundred times rather see a Democrat elected to that place than a man who holds such a low idea of morals." And the *Northwestern Christian Advocate,* the Chicago organ of the Methodist Episcopal Church, asked editorially whether Cannon "meant deliberately to insult the ministers and members of the Christian Churches of America who entered their protest against the canteen." The furore about Cannon's honest attitude toward military drinking intensified the ill will which he aroused in temperance circles by his smothering of the Littlefield bill. The sincere drys in local option areas became his opponents. And Methodists everywhere officially bridled at his name after May 1908, when the General Conference of the Methodist Episcopal Church, meeting in Baltimore, resolved:

We stand for the speediest possible suppression of the beverage liquor traffic.

The Methodist church had more members than any other Protestant sect.

Cannon also angered newspaper publishers by his refusal to support President Roosevelt's recommendation that the tariff be abolished on newsprint and on the wood pulp of which newsprint is made. For this stubbornness the publishers, from the spring of 1908 onward, portrayed Cannon to every newspaper reader in the United States as a mulish, narrow, mean, self-seeking Czar. The editorial picture of the funny, friendly pioneer gradually disappeared. Gompers and the total-abstainers and the midwestern reformers could agitate only in restricted circles of Americans with special separate interests. The papers affected the opinions of all. In his defiance of the publishers, Cannon made possible the beginnings of that slow coalescence of his opponents who, when they had combined, overwhelmed him and what he stood for.

The publishers won the President to their cause by identifying it with conservation. Free trade in print and pulp, they said, would save the American forests, since the raw materials would come from Canada. That was a new twist in an old campaign. Since 1894 the American Newspaper Publishers Association had been asking for special tariff consideration in order to cut the costs of doing business, not to promote conservation. They lobbied at the Capitol during consideration of the Dingley Tariff, but the Congressmen, disregarding the publishers, set duties of $6 and $8 a ton on newsprint. The publishers' interest in free trade for newsprint grew when the International Paper Company and the General Paper Company were organized in 1898 as near-monopolies; they manufactured most of the newsprint used in the United States. As far as paper was concerned, even the most conservative publishers adopted the argument of LaFollette that the tariff was the mother of trusts. They blamed the newsprint duties for the power of International Paper.

In the summer of 1907 the price of newsprint which Publisher Herman Ridder bought for his paper, the New York *Staats-Zeitung,* rose from $35 to $49 a ton. Ridder, who was the president of the American Newspaper Publishers Association, on September 18 called a special meeting of the organization, which resolved to seek again the repeal of the print and pulp tariffs and to ask the Department of Justice to make another investigation of the "paper trust." An investigation in 1905 of General Paper had resulted in a court order in 1906 dissolving the company. The dissolution briefly but not permanently depressed newsprint prices. After the meeting a committee of the association saw Roosevelt and converted him to the movement for tree trade in pulp and print, and when Congress convened, Representative Frederick Clement Stevens of Minnesota introduced a bill to carry out the summer resolution of the publishers' association.

Ridder was a bland-looking German-American, large, fair-haired, and moon-faced. His vigorous determination to have his own way won him a label, "That German Devil." He was president of the publishers' association because, contrary to the tradition of the society, he had forced a fight for the office on the floor of the annual convention in the spring of 1907 and had won. Although many publishers had habitually called for lockouts and strike-breaking to force their economic will upon printers, pressmen, stereotypers, or photo-engravers, Ridder persuaded his newspaper colleagues to arbitrate their labor disputes and keep peace on the papers.

He opened his campaign for passage of the Stevens bill on March 9, when he wrote Cannon asking for his co-operation in protecting newspapers from the "combination" of companies that made up the American Paper and Pulp Association which, Ridder said, were responsible for "extortionate increases in the price of newsprint paper." The Stevens bill had been referred for consideration to Sereno Payne's Ways and Means Committee and had never reappeared. On March 21 Payne notified Ridder that his committee would not consider the newsprint tariff during that session of Congress. Cannon said nothing, but he quietly opposed the Stevens bill and Ridder's request for many reasons. Above all, Ridder was putting the protective tariff in jeopardy. To consider a free trade bill for the benefit of newspaper publishers would incite a horde of other special interests to demand free trade on goods they bought. Then, Cannon was not a conservationist. Besides, the Stevens bill would not change the publishers' situation because the Dominion government and many of the individual Canadian provincial governments imposed export duties on pulp, in order to encourage Canadians to manufacture newsprint at home. Those duties, beyond the reach of the United States publishers, had as much effect as the American tariff on the price of paper, and Canada indicated that it would retain, even increase, export duties whatever action the United States took. Furthermore, Cannon suspected, because Ridder was an active leader in the Democratic Party, that he had partisan political motives for his free trade campaign. Cannon received letters from some newspaper publishers opposing tariff abolition. Cannon did not know whether the paper trust really was extortionate. A New York lawyer interested in the pulp business told him that International Paper was only the largest of sixty-eight competing paper manufacturing companies in the United States. The arguments on both sides were inconsistent. Ridder argued that behind their tariff protection the newsprint manufacturers were ruthlessly destroying the forests and that they were at the same time severely restricting production. The paper manufacturers asserted that the lifting of the tariff would not affect the prices paid by Ridder et al., except that it might cause a ruinous reduction of prices.

In that confusion Ridder saw Cannon early in April. The Speaker had introduced a resolution calling on the Attorney General and the Secretary of Commerce and Labor to send the House all papers bearing on the affairs of print paper manufacturers and to report what steps their departments had taken to investigate the charges of "trust" which the publishers leveled. That was not enough for Ridder. "We now appeal to you," he wrote Cannon on April 9, "to aid us by favoring a resolution instructing the Committee on Ways and Means to immediately report the Stevens bill to the House for its consideration." The letter failing to move Cannon, Ridder called in person at the Speaker's office.

Ridder has left no record of that meeting, but according to the "Personal Memoirs of Uncle Joe Cannon, as told to Dorsey Richardson, Esq.," a typescript in the Illinois State Historical Library in the Centennial Building in Springfield, Ridder told Cannon that if he would support the Stevens bill, the publishers would launch his campaign for the presidency at a dinner in Washington and put him in the White House.

"Ridder," said Cannon, according to the Memoirs, "I remember reading in a book when I was a boy—induced to read in it by my mother; I have not read as much in that book perhaps as I ought to have read—about a certain individual taking another individual up into a high mountain and waving his arm and saying to him, 'I will give you all this if you fall down and worship me'—when he knew that he did not own a God-damned foot of it."

"Then we shall destroy you," Cannon remembered Ridder rejoining. "You will never be Speaker again. You will never be elected to the House of Representatives again. And we will destroy the Republican Party unless this is done."

Cannon sent for his colored messenger to escort Ridder from the office. "Get out of here and don't you ever enter my room again," the Speaker said to the departing publisher.

Cannon stood pat. Instead of frightening him into taking action for print and pulp, Ridder had only weakened the whole case for general tariff revision. "I am satisfied that most of the tariff revision 'hurrah' comes from newspapers that want cheaper printing paper," Cannon said in a note to Busbey. One hundred and sixty-four Representatives, among them John Sharp Williams, signed a petition for the disinterment of the Stevens bill from the Ways and Means Committee graveyard and for its consideration on the floor, but the Speaker was granite. While the American Newspaper Publishers Association was holding its annual convention in New York City late in April, Cannon sponsored and the

House approved a resolution establishing a special committee to investigate the charges of monopoly and price-fixing by the paper industry. The passage of the resolution was the requiem for the Stevens bill as far as the Sixtieth Congress, First Session, was concerned. Cannon named his favorite, Representative Mann, to the chairmanship of the special committee. The publishers treated the resolution as the final effrontery visited on them by the Speaker. They called it a "subterfuge," and, in the midst of the campaign for the presidential nomination, the newspaper attacks on Cannon began.

Until then the newspapers had taken calmly Cannon's high-handed behavior. Most of them tolerated the repression of others' interests. With a few rare exceptions, publishers of Republican papers had supported him or ignored him and publishers of Democratic papers had criticized him as a matter of course. The new critical attitude of the publishers, irrespective of party, influenced the readers of the newspapers. When the Chicago *Post* condemned Cannon's refusal to heed the petition for the Stevens bill, a member of the the Union League Club, the inner circle of Republicanism, wrote the Speaker:

You are making tens of thousands of Republicans dissatisfied with the party, and I truly believe as I have heard many men say you were making more anarchists at the present time than could be manufactured in all the cities of the world.

Charley Hitch reported that the Chicago *Record-Herald* and the *Tribune* "are about as mean as they can be and doing all they can against you." Medill McCormick, editor of the *Tribune*, was a member of Ridder's special publishers association committee for the Stevens bill. Frank B. Noyes, part owner of the *Record-Herald*, was an owner as well of the Washington, D. C., *Star*, the managing editor of which, Samuel H. Kauffmann, was also a member of Ridder's committee. The newspaper criticisms extended far beyond Chicago. Lawyer Frank Lindley, an old friend of Uncle Joe's in Danville, who had helped William P. Cannon organize his public utility companies many years earlier, confessed that he suffered "extreme regret" at finding, in his reading of daily papers "from the Atlantic to the Pacific and from the Gulf to the Lakes," that they were full of "bricks" for Cannon.

Newspapers which remained friendly to Cannon could not always save the name of the Speaker in their circulation areas, because national magazines which criticized him offset the influence of those papers. Frank P. MacLennan's Topeka, Kansas, *State Journal* was friendly, but MacLennan informed Cannon that an editorial in the *Outlook* of May 2 was making an impression in Topeka. Now defunct, the *Outlook* was a weekly journal, edited by Lyman Abbott, with a large following.

Abbott, a lawyer, a Congregational minister, and an author (he wrote a book a year for thirty years), reviewed Cannon's behavior temperately but sardonically. The Speaker irked him by suppressing not the Stevens bill but the bill to establish the Appalachian and White Mountain forest reserves (which today we know as national forests). The effect on the reader was the same: Cannon in any case was presented as an absolutist exercising powers he should never have possessed. About Cannon and the forest bill, the *Outlook* said:

> It is not necessary to consider the motives which actuate Mr. Cannon in his obstructive tactics except to say that no one suspects him of corrupt motives. His motive is immaterial. It may even be that he is right in thinking the legislation inexpedient, extravagant or unconstitutional. That also is immaterial. The fundamental question is not, Is this bill wise? but, Have the American people, through their properly constituted representatives, a right to pass on its wisdom? The *Outlook* protests against substituting government by oligarchy, however wise it may be, for government by the people, however unwise they may be.

The problem of the forests also provoked *Collier's* magazine to print two articles condemning Cannon late in May. William Hard, the *Collier's* author, could not escape the old man's crusty charm. He found the Speaker a "lovable Philistine, . . . racy, . . . virile, . . . magnetic." His eyes were "tender," and he had a good voice for camp-meeting hymns. But his faults outnumbered his attractions. Americans in the midst of an aesthetic revival read in *Collier's* that Cannon was a crude hater of beauty, who damned architects for considering the appearance as well as the efficiency of the buildings they planned. He advocated a prohibitive tariff on foreign paintings. The use of public grounds for parks instead of productive facilities outraged his sense of thrift, and he proposed covering LaFayette Park, a lovely open green spot opposite the White House, with a stony pile of government offices. "No amount of massage can rub a new idea, like the Appalachian National Forest, in through his pores," said *Collier's*. Hard reported that Congress had received petitions for the establishment of forest reserves from the National Association of Manufacturers, the American Cotton Manufacturers Association, the National Lumber Dealers Association, the National Lumber Manufacturers Association, the Carriage Builders National Association, the National Slack Cooperage Association, and the National Association of Box Manufacturers. But since Cannon was "the most unimaginative man that ever rose to so high a public position in this country," the petitions did not move him or affect Congress.

The controversy over forest reserves was old, and for most Americans, dull until Cannon transformed it into a question of vital interest by including it among the proposals under his personal ban. Here we begin to see how his exciting personality could give a quivering animation to public issues which otherwise left the average citizen cold or which puzzled him because they concerned matters outside his direct experience. For city dwellers it took an effort of mind to grasp the meaning of forests to their daily lives. For farmers ignorant of good soil practices those trees in the forest not needed for stove wood often represented simply an impediment to cultivation. Cannon himself as a child had watched his father and their neighbors in the primeval woods of Indiana ring trees by the hundreds to make way for fields of corn and wheat. Gifford Pinchot, the United States Forester and the initiating genius of the conservation movement in America, might say, as he did with perfect truth, that Americans would bequeath a poverty-stricken country to their posterity if they exhausted their forests and other natural resources, but such a statement brought little more than a shrug before the problem became identified in reverse with Cannon. As he impressed more and more people by his despotic conduct, the problems which he despotically thrust aside attracted ever-increasing notice. After the spring of 1908 those who saw bad in Cannon saw good in whatever he opposed, and those who discerned the good in him opposed whatever and whoever opposed him. "Not one cent for scenery," said Cannon in squelching a request for funds for some modest federal undertaking in conservation. He admired natural beauty. When he visited the state of Washington, he arranged to have himself awakened on his train soon after dawn so that he could get a good long look at Mt. Rainier, which he had seen before only for a few moments. Nothing pleased his eye more than the tall corn waving in the fields in August. But scenery was not to be bought and improved at public expense.

Lyman Abbott in 1908 could write his editorial that aroused Topeka, because in 1901 the legislature of North Carolina had authorized the United States to acquire title to state land in the Appalachian Mountains, along the western rim of the state, for use as a forest reserve. Soon Georgia, Alabama, and Tennessee passed similar measures. A year later the Society for Protection of New Hampshire Forests advocated the establishment of a White Mountain Forest Reserve and an Appalachian Forest Reserve. Thus commenced the movement for the protection of 18,000,000 acres of eastern forestland from commercial exploitation. In the West the federal government had already set aside 39,000,000 acres of forest reserves, administered first by the Interior Department and subsequently (over Cannon's objections) by the Agriculture Department. In those reserves no Sawyers, no railroads harvested the trees for private gain. The government managed them for the public advantage, to improve waterways, provide facilities for recreation, and safeguard the precious top soil, the great source of wealth to which America owed its status as a civilized nation. No sooner had the Society for the Protection of New Hampshire Forests published its suggestion when the conservationists began recommending to Congress that it pass the proper legislation for the federal acquisition of the properties. In subsequent years the Senate and the House both passed the bill but they never passed it in identical form in the same session of Congress. As a result of that aimless lack of co-operation, the bill had not become law by 1908. Many times it had died in Congress without any special exertion on Cannon's part, and the public was not aroused.

Cannon did not favor the bill. He held to his old dictum of "not one cent for scenery." To administer the reserves would be a waste of public money. Furthermore, if Congress should authorize the White and Appalachian Mountain acquisitions, the citizens of how many dozens of other regions would soon be beseeching Congress to set up reserves for them? Texans who had heard about the eastern proposals were already asking the Speaker for a public forest of their own. Even if the eastern reserves cost little to develop and oversee, billions of dollars would perhaps be spent on all the reserves that in time the federal government might conceivably organize. On behalf of the Speaker, Parliamentary Clerk Asher Hinds tried to explain the headaches in regional discrimination to E. F. Baldwin, a member of the *Outlook* editorial staff: "You may say that Congress need not go beyond this bill. Well, you may buy one of your five daughters—providing Heaven has so blessed you—a Paris gown and make the other four wear their last season's raiment. Of course, you can do it; and he would be a very illogical person who should deny your power. And yet what do you think of it?" As Cannon was refusing to permit the change by law of 18,000,000 Appalachian and White Mountain acres in the east into forest reserves, President Roosevelt, by Executive fiat, was turning 148,000,000 acres of western lands into forest reserves. He could do that because the acres were part of the public lands, which the President controlled. Yet Cannon did not abandon the struggle. If it created the eastern reserves by law, Congress would be surrendering to those who believed that the purpose of government was to protect the people who maintained the government. The forest planners were among the earliest advocates of the welfare state. "The idea that the Executive is the steward of the public welfare was first formulated and given practical effect in the Forest Service by its law officer, George Woodruff," Roosevelt said in his *Autobiography*. That alone was enough to turn Cannon from conservation.

The Appalachian-White Mountain question fell directly under Cannon's influence in 1907, when he was proving, during the Second Session of the Fifty-ninth Congress, that he could control the fate of legislation at will. The Senate passed the reserves bill unanimously and sent it to the House. There Cannon assigned it to the Agriculture Committee, although its chairman, Gilbert Haugen of Iowa, leaned toward the ideas of Pinchot and his little band of professional conservationists as a result of interest on the plains in the preservation of the top soil, the farmers' gold. Haugen did not immediately report the bill to the House for consideration because Congress in 1907 authorized the Secretary of Agriculture to determine the area that the two forest areas should embrace and appropriated $25,000 to finance the inquiry. Tolerance of that inquiry was a diversional tactic on Cannon's part. When Haugen's committee early in the Sixtieth Congress indicated its readiness to present the bill to the House, Cannon assigned the question to the Judiciary Committee with a request for an opinion on the constitutionality of the proposal.

In that instant Cannon arrogated to himself the authority not only of the House, the Senate, and the President, but also of the Supreme Court, which for more than one hundred years had been the agency for determining the constitutionality of laws. Not even Jenkins, the Speaker's legislative funeral director, nor the other members of the Judiciary Committee disapproved the bill. They reported that it was constitutional, because in administering the reserves, the federal government would be controlling the watersheds of navigable streams, and such streams lay in the jurisdiction of the federal government. Undaunted, Cannon now buried the proposal himself in his own Rules Committee. The President recommended the establishment of the eastern reserves. The Senate approved their establishment. Two House committees were willing to support their establishment. But Cannon opposed it, and that ended the matter.

In opposing it, however, he made it famous. After years of obscurity from all but specialists, the technical issue of watersheds suddenly became part of the human issue of Cannon, and publishers of the serious magazines like Abbott's and of the hostile newspapers saw to it that everybody appreciated that issue. Since Cannon opposed the forest reserves, the unfriendly publishers took forest reserves to their hearts. After Cannon had dashed their hope for tariff relief, the publishers continued to portray free trade in pulp and newsprint as a matter of national concern because the future of the forests was at stake, and the papers explained the meaning of the reserves to every man. In that way Cannon the tyrant stimulated the education of the public in the issues which they had been willing to ignore.

As Cannon was making enemies, Taft was winning support. Probably Taft would have forged ahead even if Cannon had not so independently rebuffed citizens whose yearning for change he did not share. Roosevelt was the most popular of all Americans, and because Roosevelt was for Taft, the Rooseveltians were for Taft. That left few Republican supporters for any other candidate. The professional politicians did not find him attractive, but they bowed to the President. Almost every federal employee was at Taft's disposal for the canvass. Gradually Cannon's great expectations dwindled. In spite of the good wishes of Guilford College, the Republican convention in Guilford County, North Carolina, Cannon's birthplace, instructed its delegates to the national convention to vote for Taft until nominated. Even Illinois proved disloyal. Two Chicago delegates to the national convention announced in April that they belonged to Taft. The encouragement which Cannon had received from his friends in Massachusetts soured. There Augustus Peabody Gardner was leading Taft's campaign, and he found the going easy. In the first week of April the New York *Herald* estimated that already four hundred and four delegates were certain for Taft, who needed only four hundred and ninety-one to win. Cannon led the "allies," as he, Hughes, Fairbanks, and Knox were called, but he could count on only sixty delegates.

Cannon complained that Roosevelt and Taft were playing both ends against the middle. Roosevelt was not among those "advanced" representatives of humankind described by George Santayana who "will rather die than surrender a tittle of their character." When the stake was great—such as saving his office from occupancy by a professed opponent of reform—he could equivocate on issues and make his peace with the kind of men he had denounced at Plymouth as the malefactors of great wealth. To Taft he attracted Wall Street and the eastern businessmen, whom Roosevelt, for all his speeches and messages, had not really harmed. Outside Manhattan, Cannon could pass as a city man, but he still had too much hay in his hair for the very New Yorkers whom he protected from Roosevelt and the opposition. Cannon wrote A. E. Clarke in Boston that the President, a tariff revisionist in Washington, had inspired the resolution adopted by the New York Republican convention praising the existing tariff schedules, which satisfied the up-state voters beyond the New York City area. The "so-called plutocrats in New York" and others labeled "the criminal rich are, under the direction of the President, supporting Mr. Taft. In the meantime, the so-called Civic Federation Bill (anti-injunction), the product of Mr. Gompers, Seth Low, and attorneys Morawitz and Stetson, representatives of the criminal rich, is pending before the House Judiciary Committee for consideration," said Cannon with more asperity than clearness.

"In other words, poker and prayers are being played from the same hand."

The combination was formidable. When the Republican National Committee early in June decided in favor of Taft four contests between rival delegates from Arkansas and Alabama for seats at the national convention, Jim Sherman passed the word that Taft was in. Cannon, however, headed for the convention a week later with hope still faintly gleaming. He always ran out his hits.

CHAPTER ———•— 10

A Hero in Chicago

CHICAGO was the Republican Convention city. There in June 1908 Cannon found vindication for his experiment with power.

The city was always exhilarating for Cannon. It signified victory. There he watched the Republicans nominate Abraham Lincoln in 1860. He was able to be a spectator of that portentous action because the generous Illinois Central stationmaster in Tolono, Illinois, wrote out a pass for him. He was too poor to pay his own way. He returned to Chicago in style for the nomination of three other successful Republican candidates for the presidency—James A. Garfield in 1880, Benjamin Harrison in 1888, and Theodore Roosevelt in 1904.

Chicago meant the metropolis of culture and money to him. For years the great summer event for Cannon's constituents had been the railroad excursion to Chicago for a sight of its elevated train lines, its museums, its massive buildings of brick and stone, and the waves dashing its shore. It was the economic center of the Wabash world. It set the price for the corn which grew in the Eighteenth District. Chicago bought Vermilion County coal. The banks in Danville followed the lead of banks in Chicago so closely that when Speaker Cannon satisfied President Cannon of the Danville National, he could be sure that he was at the same time satisfying the great bankers in the metropolis. A letter which G. M. Reynolds, president of the Continental National Bank, Chicago, wrote to Cannon in June 1908 shows one source of the Speaker's inspiration:

Now that Congress has adjourned and the onerous duties devolving upon you, as Speaker of the House, have been for the time being laid aside, I wish to congratulate you upon the great amount of work accomplished by the House in its closing days, and especially do I want to congratulate you upon the passage of the currency bill.

On behalf of thousands of western bankers I desire to thank you for the assistance given to that bill, for we all well know that without your support it would have been impossible to have secured any legislation at the last session of Congress.

Thank you personally for your courtesies to myself and associates when we called on you to discuss this matter with you.

The sight of the city always brought back the supreme moments of Cannon's life. He and Molly Reed Cannon had gone there on their wedding trip, and they bought the furniture for their first house from Marshall Field, then clerking in a Chicago store. In Chicago Cannon boarded the train for Washington to take the oath of office for the first time. He was thirty-seven then, and the charred city was recovering from the fire. But the city that flames destroyed was the city which afterwards astounded the world by the beauty and magnitude of its Exposition celebrating the four hundredth anniversary of Christopher Columbus' landing on the soil of the new world. Chicagoans were the rugged urban cousins of the rural pioneers who in company with the Cannons civilized the wilderness of Indiana. They built their city in defiance of the blustery lake winds that knifed one in the winter, and they over-rode disappointment and rebounded from setback. Chicago had the optimism which vitalized Cannon.

It was considered unseemly in those days for a candidate for a presidential nomination to attend the convention which he hoped would choose him. Honoring the coy custom, Taft, Hughes, Fairbanks, and Knox (and also Roosevelt) all kept their distance from Chicago. But Cannon, who had no shame for his ambition, arrived there on the morning of June 9, one week before the convention was to open.

The city already was crowded for this fiesta dedicated to the saints of self-government, and most of the delegates and many of the spectators arriving early treated Cannon like a hero. Mark

Twain, on the scene, compared him favorably with Lincoln. The delegates in the main shared Cannon's conservative opinions and admired his skill in defending them. The enemies he collected only swelled their affection for him. The dirges of discontent audible in the nation left them cold. They did not take the criticisms in the newspapers seriously. Some of them had won campaigns of their own in the face of newspaper protest, and they despised the papers. Some of them had lost campaigns because newspapers opposed them, and they hated the papers. Most of them were pledged to nominate Taft, but that did not mean they had to go out of their way to further the Roosevelt crusade through Taft. These delegates were the party, and they preferred Cannon's leadership to Roosevelt's. Most of them were men of the old order, professional politicians and prosperous businessmen who had cultural and economic stakes in the preservation of private enterprise from government interference. Their presence turned Chicago into congenial ground for Cannon, for they agreed with the sentiments, expressed in a note which he received after he reached Chicago, from an investment specialist, Carsten Boe, in New York:

I have for the past months tried to make the people see that you and only you are the man to save the country from the revolution now threatened.

Cannon flouted tradition and went to Chicago for three reasons. The first was to satisfy his own ambition. The second was to arrange the nomination of James Schoolcraft Sherman as vice president. The third was to make sure that the convention did not adopt a resolution favoring the exemption of labor from writs of injunction issued under the aegis of the Sherman Anti-Trust Act. McKinley announced that Cannon was in the fight for the presidential nomination to the finish. But the presidency no longer gleamed with the importance which it possessed when McKinley opened his canvass. Even if the convention selected Roosevelt's man Taft as the presidential nominee, the choice of Sherman for vice president would save the Republican ticket from falling entirely into the hands of men who favored a protective government. And Roosevelt's eagerness for change would lead nowhere if the Republicans adopted a set of platform resolutions that pleased the standpatters. Cannon might not become President, but if he dictated the platform, the chances were that any Republican President would be his representative.

Roosevelt was at odds with Cannon on every item of business that took him to Chicago. The President had his own allies in the city, which was thronged with opposition as well as with Cannon's admirers. The reformers all had designs on the platform committee that conflicted with the Speaker's. Hal Cooper of Racine had with him a special set of resolutions which the LaFollette Republicans in Wisconsin commissioned him to present to the convention. Wisconsin was asking the national Republican Party to take a stand for evaluation of the railroads' physical property, and for restriction of the authority of judges to grant injunctions in labor disputes. Gompers was carrying about the city an injunction resolution which he and the other members of the executive council of the American Federation of Labor drew up at a special meeting in Chicago early in June. He had reason to think that it was time responsible representatives of political parties listened when he spoke. The Federation had two million members in one hundred and twenty national and international unions which were made up of twenty-seven thousand locals.

Seth Low, who represented the National Civic Federation at Chicago, took seriously both the size of Gompers' following and the merit of Gompers' case against the injunction. Low's was a familiar name to Cannon, for at the Capitol this private citizen was Roosevelt's unofficial representative. He had drafted, or supervised the drafting, of bills to carry out most of the reforms about which the President had exhorted Congress, but he never encouraged Roosevelt's tendency to denounce elements in society whose conduct struck Roosevelt as beyond the pale. Low saw evil all around him, but he also saw possibilities of good in every evil thing. He was willing to work with the "malefactors of great wealth."

As far as issues were concerned, he was the chief dealer in Roosevelt's game of poker and prayers. He employed his organization as an instrument for attracting others to his belief that men could attain prosperity and contentment through co-operation instead of conflict. He was confident that a point of harmony existed for reconciling the differences between the groups in society that usually rub one another the wrong way—the wage-earner and the wage-payer, the farmer and the city-dweller, the debtor and the creditor, tenant and landlord. The purpose of the Civic Federation was "to organize the best brains of the nation in an educational movement toward the solution of some of the great problems related to social and industrial progress." Low tried to extend its influence to every quarter. When the Civic Federation held a conference on trusts and corporations in the autumn of 1907, delegates came from ninety agricultural, labor, commercial, and economic associations.

He was the most interesting reformer of them all. He symbolized the national conscience, tortured by dark thoughts of the mistreatment which Americans meted out to Americans in the race for wealth and power which characterized Cannon's golden age. The social abuses of the time did not touch his own tangible interests. He grew up in comfortable circumstances as the son of a tea merchant, and was the president of the tea company after his father died. But in ethical revulsion against the corruption and human exploitation which he sensitively perceived around him, he took upon his soul the guilt that belonged to others. Public corruption and squalor which he discovered in his home city of Brooklyn awakened his interest in betterment. Abandoning commerce, he was elected mayor of Brooklyn, New York, when Brooklyn was a city apart. An educator, he was president of Columbia University until 1900. He had been mayor of New York City. He was at this time president of the Civic Federation.

The Federation gratified his hunger for reform by enabling him to propound remedies for national wrongs as well as municipal shortcomings. He was supporting many projects at Chicago. One was the case for the Appalachian-White Mountain forest reserves, to which Roosevelt gave increasingly vigorous verbal backing. A few days after the publication of the *Outlook* editorial criticizing Cannon for preventing the House from voting on forest reserves, the President called to order an Inland Waterways Congress at the White House. Vice President Fairbanks, the members of the Cabinet, many Congressmen, the nine justices of the Supreme Court, and the governors of forty-one states took part. The purpose of the congress was to emphasize the interlocking character of our natural resources, to make clear to the unconcerned public the intimate relationship between good forestry, the preservation of the soil, the banishment of destructive floods, and the utility of streams and rivers for navigation and as a source of power, and thereby to invigorate public interest in the necessity for the expansion of the national conservation program under government management. Soon after the congress, Roosevelt established the National Conservation Commission, with Pinchot as its chairman, and charged it to carry on a continuing study, financed by public funds, to determine what new conservation programs the Republic should undertake in order to make sure that Americans then and in future decades would use prudently the resources which lay at the foundations of their country's power. The enthusiasm which the Inland Waterways Congress generated bolstered Low's confidence that the convention would speak up for the forest reserves.

The strongest coupling that linked the rich and poor, conservatives and changers, in Low's poker-and-prayers program was the tariff. The case for revision of Dingley's eleven-year-old schedules was accepted by the National Association of Manufacturers, the American Federation of Labor, and the New Idea Republicans in Wisconsin. Even Cannon seemed to accept it, but his views were misted by a semantically intricate discussion of the form revision should take.

You had your choice between the "maximum and the minimum" and the "minimum and the maximum" tariff. Cannon chose the maximum and the minimum. So did Roosevelt's friend Senator Lodge. So did the American Protective Tariff League, which was backing Cannon for President. The propositions differed like candy and spankings, reward and punishment. The maximum and minimum formula stood for punishment. Congress would fix minimum tariffs by law and authorize the Executive to raise them, in spanking retaliation for foreign discrimination against imports from America, to a maximum level stated in the law. The minimum and maximum represented reward. The tariff schedules approved by Congress would be the uppermost levels, and the Executive would be empowered to lower them to a minimum defined in the law, as he saw fit. The controversy about minimum and maximum and maximum and minimum blew fog over the tariff problem at Chicago. The real question was, Is there to be revision? And, Is revision to go up or down? Low wanted revision downward.

Cannon's maximum and minimum implied revision upward.

The tariff issue at Chicago had another refinement. Van Cleave, the president of the National Association of Manufacturers, took to the convention a sheaf of resolutions which a formidable number of businessmen's societies had passed recommending the establishment of a tariff commission. Cannon had not given an inch in his disapproval of the commission idea. In Chicago as well as in Washington he no more trusted businessmen to determine what was good for themselves than he trusted his colleagues in Congress to determine what was good for the people they represented. Besides his own association, the organizations backing Van Cleave included the American Meat Packers Association, the National Association of Agricultural Implement and Vehicle Manufacturers, the Indiana Republican Editorial Association, the Massachusetts State Board of Trade, the Merchants Association of New York, the Chicago Association of Commerce, the American Hardware Manufacturers Association, the Millers National Federation, the National Piano Manufacturers Association of America, the Western Association of Shoe Wholesalers, the National Boot and Shoe Manufacturers Association, the Board of Trade of Chicago, and the Carriage Builders National Association. By opposing the commission during the Congress session, Cannon drew a thunderous salvo of denunciation from Van Cleave, who wrote to Jim Watson:

Speaker Cannon is approaching eighty years of age. His mind became standpat back in the sixties, in the days of fraudulent army contracts and much corruption. His extreme and picturesque profanity is not a matter of mouth only but of intellectual attitude toward things up to date and clean. Physically and mentally he is a veritable Don Quixote, and a spectacle to the nation as he fights against the windmill of progress, moved by the helpful, onward breath of heaven.

He is a political horse trader, loose in promise and action, saying to one man he is in favor of a tariff commission, to another, he will not oppose it, and goodness knows what to a third.

Back of Cannon we see the great interests described by Payne: sugar, steel, petroleum and others. . . . Those interests are the fat men who hit the chestnuts, letting fall upon the political standpatters enough crumbs in the way of political contributions and preferments to keep them active and subservient.

No radical ever matched that outburst, but Cannon could not take the tirade seriously. A lot of the insinuations and assertions were untrue. Van Cleave was more his ally than his enemy. The president of the National Association of Manufacturers was also president of that Buck's Stove and Range Company which had won an injunction against the American Federation for boycott. In Chicago Van Cleave fought Gompers' ideas about the injunction much more fervidly than he fought the Speaker's ideas about the tariff. He had to rely on Cannon to suppress Gompers.

At Chicago it appeared possible in the first hours of the convention that Low would have victory as well as right on his side and that he would guide the country then and there, through its dominating party, toward reform. But it turned out that he was in advance of his time. He was not the light of reform himself, but he was the voice by which the news of the light, of the change to come after him, was transmitted. He helped prepare the country for acceptance of change, but other men brought the change about.

The personal authority of Cannon, increased by the discords among the reformers, overwhelmed Low and all the men and things he stood for. The Civic Federation members and officers did not form solid ranks. The businessmen in the Federation could not stomach Low's support of Gompers. Roosevelt was glad to work through Low, but he pushed off other changers and specifically dissociated himself from the Wisconsin movement, his wintertime support of LaFollette's railroad program sacrificed to his exigent need to win conservative backing for Taft. Roosevelt always made it easy for Cannon at the crucial moment. As Senator Henry Cabot Lodge departed for Chicago, he received a note from the President expressing hope that the convention would not admit to the Republican platform the "LaFollette type of fool radicalism." Reform still lacked central leadership, and Cannon knew what he wanted and how to get it.

The convention opened in the Colosseum on June 16. Nine hundred and eighty delegates and several thousand alternates, friends, spectators, and flunkies filled the auditorium. When Senator Lodge, who was the permanent chairman as well as a delegate from Massachusetts, mentioned Roosevelt, the delegates applauded and cheered for forty-seven minutes. They admired Roosevelt for his dramatic ability to hold the party together, but only a few of them blessed him for his views. When aged Julius Caesar Burrows, the temporary chairman, tried to utter Roosevelt's name, he stammered and choked as though he were gagging on the syllables. The standpatters let Roosevelt know who was in charge of things in his party the moment Burrows began to speak. The injunction was the rope in the tug of war between President and Speaker, and Burrows took the Speaker's side. He presented the issue as choice not between hurting and helping labor but between upholding or damaging the integrity of the courts. While the agents of the President were running themselves ragged at the Auditorium Annex Hotel to push an anti-injunction plank into the platform, Burrows was saying:

The courts are the safeguard of the individual and the republic. If constitutional government and civil liberty should ever be imperiled in this country and driven to bay, they will find their true refuge and defense within the impenetrable fortress of the supreme judiciary of the United States.

The Chief Justice presiding over the supreme judiciary in 1908 was Melville Fuller, who had pronounced the income tax unconstitutional, discovered that the Sherman Anti-Trust Act did not apply to many business undertakings, and regularly upheld judges of subordinate courts who chastised the unions through the Sherman Act. Whoever defended Fuller's integrity questioned Roosevelt's.

The Speaker had many helpers besides Burrows. To a man his Congressional intimates showed up in Chicago. They conferred with him every day at the Union League Club, and through their personal friends on the platform committee and on the Republican National Committee they diligently undercut Taft, Roosevelt, Gompers, and Low. Cannon controlled the highest level of the platform committee. Before the convention was organized, it became known that Senator Albert J. Hopkins of Illinois wanted to be chairman of the platform, but he could have the post only if the Illinois delegation selected him to represent his state on the platform committee. The chairman of the delegation was Senator Shelby Cullom, an elderly, pinch-bearded contemporary of the Speaker's and one of the earliest serious backers of his presidential boom. With Cullom's acquiescence, Cannon told Hopkins that the

delegation would support him provided he agreed to oppose a resolution for modification of the injunction. The newspapers of the
time reported that Hopkins accepted the bargain. Illinois nominated him to the committee, and the committee named him chairman.

But Hopkins was only one of fifty-two members of the committee, and the platform was still in the making when the convention
opened. A minority kept the committee in protracted debate by
insisting that the views of Roosevelt and not of Cannon should
prevail. Roosevelt had sent Wade Ellis, the attorney general in
Taft's home state of Ohio, to Chicago with instructions to draft
reform resolutions dealing with labor matters. He was loyal to the
President. He sympathized with Gompers' aim to have labor excluded from the injunction process, and he fended off Cannon as
best he could. Cannon took his case to the public through one of
the few newspapers which still admired him, Captain King's St.
Louis *Globe-Democrat*. "If the legislation he [Gompers] demands
were enacted, destruction of property by irresponsible persons in
such controversies would increase," he told Captain King's convention reporter. "Again, if such legislation were enacted, under its
cover vicious and irresponsible people belonging to the criminal
classes not engaged in labor, nor seeking to labor, would avail
themselves of this opportunity, in the name of contesting labor, of
destroying property, and the owner thereof would be without
remedy."

Cannon's refusal to lie down fascinated the anonymous *Globe-
Democrat* reporter, who wrote in the paper of June 16:

Never in the history of a great party gathering has there been a
situation with relation to the party expression which begins to ap-
proach that offered tonight. There is evidence that the fight is the fight
of President Roosevelt and not of Mr. Taft, and that it means simply
the transferring to this city of a fight which has been going on at the
national capital for the past two years.

The row in Hopkins' committee over the injunction was still
raging when the convention, in its third day, began to vote on the
presidential nomination. But Ellis was losing control. Hopkins
fobbed Gompers off on a subcommittee instead of giving him a
hearing before the full committee. The subcommittee members

followed instructions from Washington, but they listened to the labor leader coldly. Their unfriendly manner resembled the attitude which Cannon had shown when Gompers presented him with "Labor's Bill of Grievances" in the spring of 1906. "You are not the whole shooting match," Cannon said then. "You are not the only pebble on the beach." Lodge at Chicago agreed with the Speaker. The effort of Roosevelt's supporters on the platform committee to muster a majority failed. If Hopkins did not put the platform before the convention soon, the country might jump to the conclusion that the party was irreparably divided. Such a reputation could cost the Republicans the election in November. The committee accepted Cannon's injunction formula. The American Federation of Labor, Low, Roosevelt, Wisconsin—all had fallen once more before Cannon the Czar.

The resolution which Gompers and Low recommended until the committee's final vote would, in practical effect, have committed the party to the reforms described in the Pearre bill. That bill, lying deep under the sod of the Judiciary Committee in Washington, asserted that the Sherman Anti-Trust Act should not in the future be "enforced so as to interfere with or restrain the right of employes to strike or to combine or to contract with each other or with employers for the purpose of peaceably obtaining from employers satisfactory terms for their labor."

The resolution which the platform committee recommended to the convention at the behest of Cannon read:

The Republican Party will uphold at all times the authority and integrity of the courts, state and federal, and will ever insist that their power to enforce their decisions and to protect life, liberty and property shall be preserved inviolate. We believe, however, that the rules of procedure in the federal courts with respect to the issuance of the writ of injunction should be more accurately defined by statutes, and that no injunction or temporary restraining order should be issued without notice except where irreparable injury would result from delay, in which case a speedy hearing should be granted hereafter.

This life preserver for the labor injunction did not displease all members of Low's National Civic Federation. Nicholas Murray Butler, the president of Columbia University (having succeeded Low), and chairman of the Industrial Economics Department of the Civic Federation, wrote to Cannon:

I want to send you a line of personal thanks and congratulations for your most effective leadership in the struggle to prevent our party from being committed to a declaration in favor of extreme radicalism, particularly as concerns the federal courts. You have once more rendered to the Republican party and the nation a most conspicuous service, and not only I, but many others who feel as I do, thank you from the bottom of our hearts.

The platform bore other evidence of Cannon's influence. The Speaker failed to prevent the adoption of a resolution favoring the establishment of postal savings banks, and Postmaster General Meyer was happy for a change. But while the Republicans were willing to say that they endorsed the conservation movement, Cannon persuaded them not to recommend establishment of the eastern forest reserves. The tariff resolution plugged Cannon's maximum and minimum and omitted mention of the tariff commission. It asserted that the party was "unequivocally for a revision of the tariff by a special session of the Congress immediately following the inauguration of the next President." But—as few tariff reformers, blinded by exultation, noticed then—it did not say revision *downward*. It pledged change, but it did not promise change for what Van Cleave and his colleagues considered the better. The convention rebuffed Cooper when he presented the Wisconsin resolutions in a report dissenting from the decisions of Hopkins' committee. Hopkins said Cooper's planks were "socialistic" and "democratic" (meaning the spawn of the Democratic Party). But those resolutions were a portent of Cannon's and America's future.

The full convention accepted Cannon's injunction plank and the other resolutions on June 18. But the men who honored Cannon's opinions did not honor his ambition. The delegates nominated for the presidency the man they knew Roosevelt favored, Secretary of War William Howard Taft. Taft won the honor on the first ballot, with seven hundred and two votes. Cannon received fifty-eight, of which fifty-one came from Illinois, three from New York, three from New Jersey, and one from Michigan. The defeat of hopes nurtured more than half a year, however, did not depress the resilient Speaker. If he could not be President, perhaps he could control the President. Having put an obstacle to one side of Taft by giving him the kind of platform he did not want, Cannon now proceeded to thrust on him a running mate he did not choose.

When the convention opened, Taft's agents were beating the bushes for a vice president who, if he did not stand for reform, at least had no ties with Cannon. They specifically excluded Sherman from their list of acceptables. Roosevelt in Washington and Lodge in Chicago both campaigned against his nomination. The President preferred Senator Jonathan Dolliver of Iowa, who was an ally of the New Idea Republicans. When Dolliver turned down the opportunity, the Taft men sought Hughes, but he declined their offer of the vice presidential nomination as emphatically, if not so pungently, as Cannon had declined a similar proposal in 1904. After Taft had been nominated for the presidency on June 18, he still was looking for a partner. In desperation he asked Fairbanks if he would take a second term. No. He tried Senator Chester I. Long of Kansas. The answer was the same.

Taft's trouble in recruiting a partner meant advantage for Cannon. The Speaker and his colleagues at the Union League Club slowly organized a large following for Sherman among the delegates. The New York *Tribune* had opened Sherman's vice presidential boom on May 28, and conservative businessmen at once rallied to him. His tariff views were identical with Cannon's, but the National Association of Manufacturers wired him: "All our people in Chicago will wave the Sherman banner for the high office of vice president for our New York friend." J. D. Crary, secretary of the New York Lumber Trade Association (an opponent of free trade for pulp), wrote Sherman: "This Association, being one of the many which opposed the special legislation which was offered on behalf of organized labor and other special interests at the last session of Congress, desires to express to you its appreciation of the part you took in consideration thereof." The testimonials of approval which Sherman attracted only underscored Cannon's wisdom in pursuing his tyrannical course in Congress. The accolades for Sherman really belonged to Cannon, for Sherman's acts carried out Cannon's thoughts. On the Rules Committee Sunny Jim had stood with the Speaker like a rock against Roosevelt, the opposition, and reform. After Cannon appointed the committee to investigate the pulp and print business, Sherman diligently looked for witnesses who could confound Ridder. He suggested that Chairman Mann consult with Carvello, William Randolph Hearst's business manager. "He represents a string of papers which have been fighting the proposed movement (for tariff relief)," Sherman told Mann. Sherman presiding over the Senate, as vice presidents do, would give Cannon at last an ally at the north end of the Capitol and ease his task in controlling Congress.

Littauer took a vacation from his glove works to push the cause in Chicago. Some westerners complained that Sherman, fat, baldish, with his side whiskers, round red face, and pince-nez, looked so much like an English country squire that he would cost the Republicans votes in he-man country like Colorado, Wyoming, and Utah, but a meeting between Sherman (dressed in one of the white cashmere suits which he had bought in Bermuda for $11 each) and the protestants erased those prejudices.

The delegates met on June 19 for their final session in the great roasting oven that the Colosseum had become. The fans barely agitated the hot air. The sweaty crowd wanted to nominate a vice president and go home. Lodge stepped down from the stage and placed before the convention the name of Governor Curtis Guild, a leading agitator for tariff revision. Timothy Woodruff of New York presented Sherman's name. Then a kind of tension seized the throng. The delegates, who had been leaning back in limp discomfort, sat up straight in their chairs. A familiar bearded figure was walking down the aisle, from the section of chairs set apart for the Illinois delegation, toward the stage, with that hitching gait that was his trade mark. It was Cannon, full of fight, a hated man for many who called him "czar," but the symbol of the good days gone past by which most of the delegates in the hall measured their contemporary world. A nominating convention fills a party member with a sense of fraternal brotherhood and a tingling sensation of something like tribal loyalty on a great feast day. Cannon was the champion of the tribe, the party. He had always been true to the Republican brotherhood. He was the fraternity incarnate, and the delegates cheered enthusiastically.

Uncle Joe stepped upon the stage to second Sherman's nomination. His left trouser leg was inside his shoe and his right trouser leg hung over his shoe. The sleeve of his coat was caught inside his double cuff. "I would rather be a doorkeeper in the House of the Lord than to dwell in the tents of the wicked," he began. He glorified Sherman:

He is big enough, industrious enough, patriotic enough to fill the great office of the vice presidency. And if in the chapter of happenings, which God forbid, the President should be called across the river, measuring my words, there is no man of my acquaintance that I would sooner trust, from all the tests of good citizenship and ability, to worthily fill the first place instead of the second place in the Republic.

It was a treat to see him speak. He pranced across the stage with his left arm pumping up and down as of yore to accent each word. As he neared the front of the stage, he stood in one spot, rocking back and forth on his toes, as though preparing to spring into the audience. With his right hand he brushed again and again at his wispy hair as if he were trying to loose it from his scalp. He was with friends and he had made himself their hero. The delegates forgot Taft and Roosevelt and Guild. On the first ballot they chose Sherman. The Presidency was to be Taft's, but the Republican Party was Cannon's. Uncle Joe took the train for Danville.

A Villain in the West

THE STING of Cannon's easy conquest of Theodore Roosevelt at the convention was too painful to bear in the Upper Mississippi and Missouri Valleys. The farmers in Wisconsin, Minnesota, Iowa, Kansas, Nebraska, and the Dakotas felt more keenly than any other Americans the oppressive one-sidedness of the struggle between the powerful enterprisers who set prices and wages and the millions who had to fit their scale of living to these prices and wages. Things had scarcely improved in 1908 beyond the conditions in 1900, when LaFollette won the governorship. From the vantage point of Madison the United States appeared still to be divided in gross inequality between a few wealthy exploiters of land, forest, and mines who fixed the life pattern (to the extent that economic conditions could fix it) of all their compatriots. The lumbermen, the owners of elevators, the millers, the manufacturers of farm implements, the processors of fertilizers, and the railroads—always the railroads above all—hovered beyond the reach of state governments. Ten years had passed since Hazen S. Pingree, the governor of Michigan, disclosed that the railroads which owned more than a third of the property in Michigan paid less than one-twentieth of the taxes collected by Michigan, but in a large part of America the railroads were still contributing little and taking much from the population that relied on them as the indispensable sinews of the nation. Pingree had pushed through the Michigan

140

legislature a law authorizing a board to value the property of all corporations (including railroads) and to tax them equably, and years had gone by since LaFollette got his Railway Commission in Wisconsin. Yet the flavor of the new century continued to resemble the flavor of 1890 as described by Justice John F. Harlan of the Supreme Court of the United States: "The conviction was universal that the country was in real danger from another kind of slavery, namely, the slavery that would result from the aggregations of capital in the hands of a few individuals and corporations controlling, for their own profit and advantage exclusively, the entire business of the country, including the production and sale of the necessaries of life." The mid-continent Americans were lonely in their struggle against that kind of slavery as long as they could use only state laws for weapons. They were cornered without the help of the federal government.

Clearly it was Cannon who prevented the federal government from equalizing the distorted relationship between the rich and the aspiring. His despotic control over the House had given him control over the political affairs of the United States. His repeated snubs of the President's messages requesting authority to evaluate the physical property of the railroads kept the users of the rails at the mercy of the operators of the rails. The roads had fallen into the custom of issuing stocks and bonds against property which did not exist. The Interstate Commerce Commission reported in 1907 that the roads were capitalized at $68,000 a mile, but their actual indebtedness amounted to $73,000 a mile. The overcapitalized roads had to charge high fares and high freight tariffs in order to pay their capitalization charges. "The greater the capitalization, the more of its earnings will be absorbed in fixed charges and less can be paid for maintaining the service," said one opponent from the Mississippi-Missouri Valley, Representative Andrew J. Volstead of Minnesota. The valley men looked for some relief in the development of the inland waterways system. With the Mississippi open to commerce in all its length, "every man who can summon enough capital to build a boat may become one of the common carriers of the country," Governor Albert Baird Cummins of Iowa forecast to the Upper Mississippi River Improvement Association. But Cannon refused to have the House consider a bill for financing the waterway development.

Cannon attempted to cut the few life lines that Washington had thrown to the states. In the session of Congress just ended he excluded from the House version of the Sundry Civil Service Appropriation Bill the funds which the Interstate Commerce Commission needed in order to enforce the Hepburn Rate Act. The Senate barely saved the situation by belatedly amending the bill after the President intervened with Congress for the Commission. The disgruntled in the Mississippi and Missouri Valleys took seriously Cannon's opposition to federal control of the forests. They had seen the forests felled so fast that lumber tracts rose from eight dollars to sixty dollars an acre in Minnesota in twenty years. Having watched the railroad operators damage agriculture by despoiling the woods, the discontented inhabitants of the midcontinent came close to sharing the opinion which the Free Soil Democrats set down in their platform of 1852: "The public lands of the United States belong to the people, and should not be sold to individuals nor granted to corporations." And the discontented among the valley men did not trust Cannon to expedite the revision of the tariff schedules down to levels that would satisfy the principles of protection without encouraging greed. The tariff was the keystone in the structure of abuse and privilege. The tariffs bolstered monopoly, and the monopolists ran the railways. "There has been in later years that intimacy between railway management and the industrial combinations of the country which renders them [the railways] powerless to escape," said Cummins in 1905. It was much the same in 1908.

The Chicago convention destroyed the hopes of the men in the valley states that they could reach their goals by fighting out the issues. The questions of the railways and the forest reserves and the trusts had to wait on resolution of the question of Cannon. An engagement between men had to take the place of the engagement between ideas.

To wage the struggle in terms of personalities was a dangerous venture, for the valley region was predominantly Republican, and the promoters of change would risk the ruin of their party by launching an open fight against a party leader. But what was the paramount consideration? The salvation of party? Or the salvation of country? Like other sectionalists before them, the valley men interpreted the national needs in terms of their own needs, and in June 1908 it was clear to them that their party would never release them from the oppression imposed by those who controlled the nation's wealth as long as the party continued to follow principles which satisfied the needs of Vermilion County. The reformers would remain as helpless as Roosevelt, devoted to grand new conceptions but unable to institute them, until they captured the party. The risk of party rupture was indispensable to reform, and in the summer of 1908 they took the risk. Tawney felt the impact of the new spirit and wrote to Cannon:

I have never known a time . . . when there was such an unsettled condition in the public mind in this part of the country as there is today. Nor have I known a time when there was so little sentiment for the principles and policies of the political parties. We seem unconsciously to have drifted into a condition of purely personal politics.

The commanding personality in the new condition was LaFollette's. Cooper's submission of the reform resolutions at Chicago gave "Fighting Bob" the status of general leader of all the discontented in the valley states, whose inhabitants had come to know him as a result of the long series of Chautauqua lectures he had been giving in that region for three years. He helped himself to make his mark by pleasing the Scandinavian-Americans, especially the descendants of the equalitarian Norwegian immigrants. These new Americans were insatiably discontented, ever ready for change, experimentalists in agriculture and politics. For years the Koshkonong Prairie settlement in LaFollette's Dane County was the Norway headquarters in the United States, and from Koshkonong the Scandinavians had pushed out to the other valley states. It was possible to travel hundreds of miles in Wisconsin, northern Iowa, Minnesota, and North and South Dakota without leaving land owned by Scandinavians. They had numbers and determination, and everywhere they demanded reform. Their chronic rebelliousness stirred a cyclone that whirled LaFollette forward. In June 1908 he launched the fight against Cannon and the traditions of party and Nation in the hilly corn country around his wife's home city, Baraboo, Wisconsin. Irvine Luther Lenroot, a fair-haired, handsome young man of Norwegian ancestry, who had been Speaker in the Wisconsin House when the legislature accepted LaFollette's state reforms, announced his candidacy for the Republican nomination for the seat in Congress which Representative John Jenkins, Cannon's reliable chairman of the Judiciary Committee, occupied. Lenroot asked the Republicans of Baraboo to abandon Jenkins and to choose him because he would vote against the re-election of Cannon to the Speakership in Washington. He stood for tariff reform, restriction of the injunction, and more effective regulation of trusts and monopolies. But the heart of his campaign was opposition to Cannon and to Jenkins as Cannon's creature. LaFollette himself spoke in Baraboo on behalf of Lenroot. That was fitting, because the whole pre-primary campaign was a contest between LaFollette and Cannon through the symbols of Lenroot and Jenkins. LaFollette's symbol won. At the primary election on August 31, the Republicans in Baraboo and vicinity chose Lenroot.

LaFollette was shrewd in choosing the Baraboo district as the site for beginning his attack on Cannon because the prohibitionists, aroused by the suppression of the Littlefield Interstate Commerce Liquor Bill in Jenkins' committee, ranged their awful might behind Lenroot. The directors of the Wisconsin Anti-Saloon League did not unanimously support LaFollette's movement for the New Idea Republicanism. But the magic of the Cannon name was making allies of Americans who disagreed about political theory. The drys were intensive campaigners, who went from door to door and farm to farm placidly stating the case for the retirement of Jenkins. The victory excited temperance leaders far from Wisconsin. David Thompson, editor of the *Northwestern Christian Advocate* in Chicago, told the delegates at the West Wisconsin Methodist Conference, which met in Ashland a few days after the primary, that the defeat of Jenkins was the strongest blow the United States had struck for temperance. The success in Baraboo encouraged the drys to range further and to try to destroy the authority of Cannon by removing all his supporters from the House. It made no difference whether the supporters were intimately identified with the liquor issue. It was enough that they stood by Cannon. Tawney had no hand in the burial of Littlefield's bill, but "the ministers of all Protestant denominations who quietly and effectively, without noise, accomplished the defeat of Jenkins, are moving in on Tawney's district now," Henry Casson, the sergeant-at-arms in the House, who was a "stalwart" (anti-

LaFollette) Republican from Madison, Wisconsin, wrote Cannon early in September.

West of Wisconsin the LaFollette revolutionaries had the help of the conservative Republican newspaper publishers who snarled at the name of Cannon because of his opposition to Ridder's free pulp and paper program. Cannon received from Sherman at the end of July a memorandum submitted by an anonymous friend, who reported that Victor Rosewater, publisher of the Omaha *Bee*, was contemplating the calling of a conference of editors of Republican papers in the western states to talk about starting a campaign for the nomination of Republican candidates for Congress who would agree to vote against Cannon's re-election as Speaker and to vote for a change in the rules of the House. The memorandum said that Republican editors in Iowa and Minnesota favored the idea.

Rosewater, whose father founded the *Bee*, ran one of the most clearly written newspapers in the United States. In 1908 he was only thirty-seven years old, but he had controlled the paper for thirteen years. He had a doctor of philosophy degree from Columbia University. He was a member of the Republican National Committee from Nebraska, and he attended the Chicago convention as a Nebraska delegate. He had nothing in common with the discontented except their distaste for Cannon. He approved the platform resolutions of the convention, and he found even the nomination of Sherman palatable; he described it in his paper as "happy and satisfactory." Roosevelt suited him completely without enrichment by LaFollette "radicalism," and he was confident that Taft would follow Roosevelt's lead like an arrow.

His state was not seething with Republican discontent like Wisconsin. "The people do rule," Nebraska Governor George L. Sheldon declared complacently in his address to the McKinley Club in Omaha in mid-summer. "Never has there been a time when the affairs of the nation have been more equally distributed and never before has a man occupied the White House who has stood closer to the people than now." Sheldon two years earlier was a reformer, but his reform had run its course. He had the railroads where he wanted them. During his administration the legislature in Lincoln had enacted laws forbidding railways to give away passes and establishing a railway commission. He reduced by 15 per cent the freight rates in Nebraska on grain, livestock, fruit, lumber, and coal. He reduced express rates by 25 per cent, and brought passenger rates down to two cents a mile. He sponsored a state-wide primary law. New statutes forbade lobbying in the state Capitol and forbade corporations to damage their competitors by reducing prices in one area of competition and raising them in another. Nebraska was prosperous. Crop yields were off, but corn and hog prices were higher than usual. Instead of closing down and throwing Nebraskans out of work, the Union Pacific and Burlington railroad shops had worked at reduced time during the panic. Nebraska had more automobiles per person than any other state in the union.

In that atmosphere it was easy for Rosewater to praise Republican doctrines as disclosed in the decisions of the Chicago convention while he criticized the man responsible for the conservative quality of the Chicago platform and for the Chicago vice-presidential nomination. Nebraskans who were discontented looked to the Democratic Party for relief. Representative George Norris of McCook was one of the few Nebraska Republicans who had a serious affinity for LaFollette's ideas, and his fellow party members sneered that he was no better than a Democrat. William Jennings Bryan, the Democratic opponent of Taft in the contest for the presidential election, lived in Nebraska.

Rosewater the conservative ironically sped the disintegration of the Republican Party because he could not stomach Cannon, the conservative scourge of Roosevelt. When the Democratic National Convention in Denver adopted a resolution denouncing Cannon, the *Bee* remarked that "the domination of the House by the Speaker and a select Committee on Rules is as obnoxious to Republicans as it is to Democrats." Frank Hitchcock, the chairman of the Republican National Committee, appointed Rosewater to his Taft campaign executive committee and named him director of the Republicans' western literary bureau. That gave him control of Republican publicity in the valley states, where the Republican reform movement was already fattening on antipathy to Cannon. The presence of an active enemy in Republican headquarters irked Cannon, but Tawney tried to cheer him up. "Confidentially," the Winona blacksmith wrote to the Speaker, Rosewater "is what we would call a half-baked ass."

But others took him more seriously. "I have written Mr. Sherman today asking him if there was any way conceivable to head off Rosewater of Nebraska from exacting pledges of candidates under threat of defeat to vote against you for Speaker. The importance of having this done cannot be overestimated. . . . I think in some way notice should be served on this gang that they have got to haul down their black flag and do it quick," Cannon read in a letter from Casson. The Speaker took it up with Taft, to whom he wrote that "the matter is only unfortunate as it tends to promote discord where, at least from now until the election in November, there should be unity of action and warfare only against the common enemy."

Taft himself shuddered at the thought of Cannon. "Confidentially, the great weight I carry in this campaign is Cannonism," Taft wrote privately. "Of course, it would not do for me to express such a desire publicly, or to anybody but a very few friends, I should not be at all disappointed if a new Speaker were elected in the next Republican House, if it is to be Republican." Rosewater endeavored to satisfy Taft's desire. He persuaded many small town papers in Nebraska to exact from Congressional candidates the pledges of anti-Cannonism which the *Bee* proposed. The campaign succeeded. Representative George Norris of McCook announced that he was "opposed to the re-election of Mr. Cannon as Speaker, not because I doubt his patriotism or question his ability but because he uses the power of his high position to prevent the consideration of legislation asked for by the people and desired by a large body of the membership of the House of Representatives. The most serious objection in my judgment to his re-election as Speaker is that he is opposed to any change in the present rules which would take away or modify the unreasonable and arbitrary power now possessed by the Speaker." All but one of the five Nebraska Republican candidates for Congress followed the lead of Norris, and papers in Iowa, Missouri, and Kansas exacted Rosewater pledges from candidates in those states.

Iowa was seething like Wisconsin in dispute about the nature of government until controversy over Cannon brought the conflict to a decisive end. In the sudden death in mid-summer 1908 of William Boyd Allison, who had been Senator since 1873 (he and Cannon took the oath of office at the Capitol on the same day), Iowa lost the leader of its traditionalists, and the state Republicans divided in two for a struggle between his disciples and the followers of Governor Cummins. Cummins' public and private career had been spent in fighting privilege. A Pennsylvanian by birth, he joined the westward movement when he was twenty-two years old (in 1872), studied law in Chicago and there gained admission to the bar, and pushed on to the newer city of Des Moines on Iowa's rich prairie. There he became the legal champion of the farmers. On their behalf he conducted a famous suit against the barbed-wire monopoly, which the Supreme Court in Washington ordered dissolved on the strength of Cummins' presentation. The railroads and the regular Republican organization defeated him when he sought election to the Senate in 1894, but the grateful farmers elected him governor in 1901, in 1903, and again in 1906.

Cummins was a reformer in the image of LaFollette. He was not satisfied, like Governor Sheldon of Nebraska, to stop with remedying obvious abuses. His state laws needed the bolstering of federal laws if they were to be truly and lastingly effective. In pressing through the Des Moines legislature laws which weakened the grip of monopolists and railroads on the economy of the farmers and the machinery of state government, Governor Cummins had constructed a rough-hewn system of thought about political science. He stood for a way of life, emphasizing the responsibility of every American to play fair with all Americans, and the central government was the instrument for carrying out the responsibility. Iowa did not permit him to go quite so far as LaFollette in espousing a comprehensive realignment of economic relationships in America. The farmers of the state wanted no part of the proposal for a law restraining the courts from issuing anti-labor injunctions. Unions recently had irked the farmers by trying to organize farm hands. Cummins was working a revolution for small capitalists.

The conservative Iowans were numerous enough in the Republican Party to select Allison and reject Cummins in the senatorial primaries in the spring of 1908. Allison's death revived Cummins' ambition to enter the Senate, but the traditionalists appeared still to be so strong that the governor, having stated that he wanted Allison's seat when reporters gave him news of the vacancy, then coyly retracted the assertion. By the summer's end, however, he found it expedient to bring his ambition boldly into the open. A change was coming over his state. The excitement about Cannon, generated by the disgruntled publishers, added numbers to the Republicans who opposed Cannon's political philosophy. As the candidates for national office stressed not local Iowa issues but the question of Cannonism, the traditionalists fell into the minority. The problem before Iowa was not only whether Cannon could be forced to permit the country to veer in a new political direction but whether he was demoralizing the representative institutions that had existed from of old. "There are scores of Congressmen who very gladly take shelter under the alleged tyranny of the Speaker from personal responsibility for measures coming before Congress," Representative E. H. Hubbard said through the newspapers in Sac City, Iowa, as he announced to his constituents that he would oppose Cannon's re-election to the Speakership. Swayed by the hostility to Cannon, the Republican Iowans who had rejected Cummins in the spring primary voted for him, by a majority of 42,000, in an autumn primary. The legislature elected him to Allison's seat in the Senate, where he buttressed LaFollette and the new Republicanism.

The temperance politicians had a hand in undercutting Cannon in Iowa, and they were busy elsewhere. In Minnesota, Tawney told Cannon, "they even went so far as to circulate among the ministers of the Methodist Church that I was going to have my wife and daughter withdraw from that church and that we would all join the Episcopal Church for political reasons." The Epworth League of the two Kansas Citys (Missouri and Kansas) called on Representative Edgar C. Ellis with a demand that he state his position on Speaker Cannon. The Kansas City *Star* published his wriggling reply: "I must needs prefer to support some other than Mr. Cannon."

The *Star*, published in the city on the Missouri side of the Kaw by the enormous William Rockwell Nelson, had more influence on political attitudes in Kansas than any journal published in Kansas itself. During the summer of 1908 Nelson ran many editorials picturing Cannon as a czar who "carries the United States in his pocket." By tradition the state was dry (the home of Carrie Nation) and for reform (the western stronghold of populism), and in the hullabaloo about Cannon the Republicans in the Kansas Legislature retired the conservative Chester I. Long from the

Senate and chose in his place a reformer in the Sheldon mould, Joseph Bristow. LaFollette had visited Kansas before the primary to speak against Long.

The states east of Montana and west and north of Illinois which touched on the Missouri and the Mississippi Rivers formed the center of the New Idea Republicanism which was feeding on the villainy of Cannon. But the Speaker in 1908 became a national issue also in states far from the mid-continent heartland. Few easterners then were ready to accept the political theory of the New Idea Republicanism as expounded by LaFollette, and the east in the main took calmly the failure of Roosevelt to turn his novel proposals into law. But the despotic manner in which Cannon rebuffed Roosevelt aroused some easterners and prepared them for later acceptance of the Twentieth Century political conceptions repugnant to the Speaker. Cannon offered to campaign in Ohio, Taft's state, on behalf of Republican congressmen running for re-election, but John F. White, of the Ohio State Republican Central Committee, asked Cannon to keep out lest he turn away the labor vote. The Methodist Conference in Lancaster, Ohio, passed resolutions denouncing Cannon, and the Anti-Saloon League caused the defeat of a Cannon supporter and member of Jenkins' Judiciary Committee, Representative Reuben O. Moon, in the Republican primary election in Portsmouth, Ohio. Cannonism stirred New Jersey. When Representative Wayne Parker of Newark refused to take a Rosewater pledge, his Democratic opponent told the voters that in voting for Parker's re-election, they would be "voting for the retention of Uncle Joe as the ruler of the House. . . . That is practically the only issue before the voters of this district."

The campaign taught this lesson—that at last the country had an issue around which the majority of Americans might conceivably rally in support of the reformers and thus change the course of American history by revising the political philosophy underlying American government. For years the discontented had been lonely and divided. Greenbackers, the Farmers Alliance, the Anti-Monopoly Party, and the Populists had risen and fallen, intense in feeling, weak in numbers. No wonder that LaFollette hearkened joyfully to the rumbles coming from the plains of Kansas and Nebraska and the factory cities of the east and said in exultation:

It is my hope and my prayer that Joe Cannon will be defeated. If there is a man who is a traitor to the government and who deserves to be defeated, it is Joe Cannon. The voice of the people is strangled and stifled by this man. There is a tyranny there that makes men cringe and crawl, that makes cowards of the Republicans of the House.

C H A P T E R —·— 12

The Contest at Home

<hr/>

THE OUTLOOK for Uncle Joe appeared now good, now drab. He unwaveringly held to his course. The comments of his enemies failed to change him. He almost pitied the critics as men in the grip of error when they exploited his name as a new word for villainy. He continued to regard himself as a hero, boldly bucking the tide of opinion for the sake of righteousness. "Did it ever occur to you that Lincoln was the the most hated man in the country during the [Civil] War?" He addressed that plaintive question to an unidentified correspondent in 1908. He further revealed the state of his mind in a letter he wrote during the summer to the Congressional Republican Campaign Committee:

When somebody says the Speaker is an autocratic leader, and somebody says the Speaker of the House has organized the House that he may be an autocrat, no man deserves to be Speaker who is moved by accusations of that kind. No man deserves to be Speaker who does not organize the House, when that duty is given to him, . . . as safely and sanely as it can be organized . . . and thereby bring forth the best results for the party. And the Speaker who, in the organization of the House, finds some man upon some committee in former congresses who has turned Democrat while he calls himself a Republican, who has not the courage to put him off and put some true Republican on, is not fit to be Speaker.

Cannon took comfort also in the belief that might as well as right was with him. The success of the opponents did not appear so great, seen from the perspective of Danville, as it did when scrutinized in Madison or Des Moines or Kansas City or Omaha. LaFollette might crow over the defeat of Jenkins, but the stalwart Republicans remained strong in Wisconsin. The primary law enacted at LaFollette's behest was not helping the cause of progress. LaFollette asked the Republicans to vote against Isaac Stephenson, a stalwart and a lumberman (who in a flirtation with novelty had financed LaFollette's first gubernatorial campaign), when they designated in the primaries the man they preferred as the party candidate for the United States Senate, but Stephenson won. The primary dealt LaFollette a harsher blow by ending the political career of his young Norwegian protégé, Herman Ekern. Stephenson's victory meant that LaFollette would continue to have a stalwart as his colleague in Washington, and Ekern's defeat put in danger LaFollette's own Senate seat. Ekern was a Representative of Trompealeau County in the Wisconsin General Assembly, where he strongly supported the New Idea Republicanism and opposed the stalwart program of LaFollette's unsympathetic successor as governor, James O. Davidson. Ekern lost in the primary by a handful of votes to a protégé of Davidson's, A. J. Twesme. LaFollette endowed that obscure contest with major importance by asking the Trompealeau Republicans to repudiate the decision which they had recorded in the primary. He said that the admission of Twesme to the General Assembly would encourage Davidson (one of the few conservative Wisconsin Norwegians) to ask the legislature in Madison in 1909 for election to LaFollette's seat in Washington. He attributed the majority for Twesme to the conniving of insurance companies, twenty-six of which had abandoned their offices in Wisconsin rather than accommodate their ways of doing business to the requirements of LaFollette's state insurance law. He persuaded Ekern to run as an independent, and he asked the Republicans who had voted for Twesme in the primary to vote for Ekern on election day. On Vermilion Street the meaning of the desperate maneuvering in far-off Trompealeau County seemed plain. If LaFollette could not control the Republican Party in his own state in 1908, why should one think that he and the various forces accidentally allied with him would be able to control the Republican Party in the United States?

Cannon found further reason for cheer in the behavior of the acknowledged leaders of the party. While they declined to interfere with Rosewater, they were expounding the point of view which Cannon had forced on them in the resolutions adopted at Chicago. President Roosevelt, Nominee Taft, and officials of the Administration defended the injunction in labor disputes as though they had agreed with Uncle Joe all along.

Taft began to buoy Cannon when he formally accepted the presidential nomination in Cincinnati on July 28. Labor may strike, Taft said in effect, but it may not take the steps necessary to win the strike. For labor must not injure an employer's business "by use of threats or methods of physical duress against those who would work for him, or deal with him, or by carrying on what is sometimes known as a secondary boycott against his customers or those with whom he deals in business. . . . Threatened unlawful injuries to business can only be adequately remedied by an injunction to prevent them." Thus, more than eight months before his inauguration as President, Taft began to disclose that opposition to change which later caused Mr. Dooley to comment, "Taft throws the brakes well, but he ain't very familiar with the power."

Roosevelt himself was transformed from the President of the reform messages and from the President who prodded Wade Ellis to put across a reform platform at Chicago, into a President sympathetic to Cannon. In October the newspapers published a letter from Roosevelt to Senator Philander Knox of Pennsylvania in which the President defended the Chicago resolution on the injunction. Was the Roosevelt crusade coming to an end? Or was William Jennings Bryan, running against Taft for the presidency, forcing the Administration to pose as the standpatters' friend?

The Democratic Party had assumed the role of the party of reform. The convention in Denver which nominated Bryan accepted the resolutions of discontent which LaFollette and Gompers had vainly urged upon the Republican delegates at Chicago, and only by decrying reform did the Republicans defend their past failure to give the discontented the laws they demanded. Bryan refrained from campaigning in Wisconsin because he said that his principles matched LaFollette's (except that in tariff matters Bryan was a free trader and LaFollette was a protectionist, although he favored the revision of Dingley's duties). Gompers gave up the traditional American Federation of Labor non-partisanship. He campaigned vigorously for Bryan and asked all union members to vote the Democratic ticket in gratitude because the Democrats had resolved thus in Denver: "Experience has proved the necessity of a modification of the present law relating to injunctions. . . . Labor organizations and their members should not be regarded as illegal combinations of restraint of trade." The resolution called for little more than Roosevelt had requested of Congress in his April message. But what Bryan favored, the regular Republicans turned against. Roosevelt told Knox that Gompers and Bryan were "fooling" labor when they implied that they could produce the kind of law recommended in the Denver platform and win the courts' approval for it.

When the Roosevelt crusade was young, Elihu Root, the Secretary of State, had, in a roundabout way, warned the courts to uphold the constitutionality of the Roosevelt laws or suffer—in some manner not defined—for not doing so. "Constructions of the Constitution will be found that vest the power where it will be exercised—in the national government," he said in December 1906. The standpatters considered the speech an invitation by Roosevelt to the Supreme Court to assist him in overthrowing "the balance of the Constitution and to regulate each and all of us from Washington." The note of, "Judges, you had better decide that our laws and the powers the Executive assumes are constitutional," rang clear. But in the campaign of 1908 Root declared that the courts must be free from the influence of Presidents. "If Mr. Bryan has the opportunity to reconstitute the Supreme Court, he will make it the instrument of his own destruction and an accomplice in the surrender of that great judicial safeguard against the momentary influences of popular excitement, which has been the chief element in the security, the stability, and the progress of the American Republic," he said in a campaign speech in Durland's Riding Academy in New York.

The Democrats themselves had strengthened Cannon with Roosevelt by attacking the Republican Party through him. John Sharp Williams attended the Denver convention of the Democrats as a delegate from Mississippi. He was through with the House. The legislature in Jackson had elected him to the Senate. But the stings of his old friend's tyranny in the Speaker's chair still burned. The Denver platform showed it.

"The House of Representatives, as controlled in recent years by the Republican Party, has ceased to be a deliberative and legislative body, responsive to the will of a majority of its members, but has come under the absolute domination of the Speaker, who has entire control of its deliberations and powers of legislation," said the platform. "We have observed with amazement the popular branch of our federal government helpless to obtain either the consideration or enactment of measures desired by a majority of its members. Legislative government becomes a failure when one member, in the person of the Speaker, is more powerful than the entire body. We demand that the House of Representatives shall again become a deliberative body controlled by a majority of the people's representatives and not by the Speaker."

The Democrats rang the changes on that theme until the last day of the campaign. "The overwhelming issue is, 'Shall the people rule?'" Bryan said in accepting the Democratic nomination. "They cannot do so unless they can control the House of Representatives and through their representatives in the House give expression to their purposes and desires." "Cannon is a strangler," John Worth Kern of Indiana, the Democratic candidate for the vice presidency, said in his acceptance speech.

As the first step toward the revision of the powers of the Speaker, Bryan recommended the removal of Speaker Cannon from Congress. Accordingly he visited Cannon's district to urge the defeat of Uncle Joe in his nineteenth campaign for re-election. The bombardment exchanged between the presidential candidate and the Speaker did not raise the tone of American electioneering. Cannon sneered that Bryan, the candidate of the poor man, had made $1,000,000 in "selling wind and ink," through his Chautauqua lectures and his writings. Bryan, replying that the value of his possessions came only to $150,000, accused Cannon himself of being the millionaire. And how did the Speaker win this fortune? Bryan, ignoring the history of pink-eyed brother Will, hinted at corruption which he could not prove. "During the last forty-seven years he has held office more than forty years, and about thirty-five years of that time he has been a member of Congress, and has been drawing a salary that the members of Congress thought so inadequate that the salary has recently been increased," Bryan said of Uncle Joe. "Will he tell us what he has been selling, to whom he has sold it and how much he got for it? . . . He has been greatly hampered in the accumulation of money by the strict attention to public duties, and yet he is reputed to be wealthy."

The childish exchange distressed Taft. When he learned that Cannon was going to campaign for Republican congressional candidates in Kansas, he beseeched the Speaker by letter to avoid all mention of Bryan. While Taft was swallowing Cannon's opinions, he found the man hard to take. Prodded by his wife, he grumbled about him throughout the campaign. The Speaker's manners were revolting. He was so cheerfully honest that he seemed cynical to men more accustomed to cant. Filled with "blackguardism," Taft muttered. But neither Taft nor Roosevelt publicly blamed the Speaker for ruining the President's efforts to make his party the party of reform. To denounce Uncle Joe would have relieved the spleen but it might have been a costly exercise in heroics.

Cannon in the summer and early autumn of 1908 was not a deserted figure to be attacked with impunity. On the contrary, he continued to be the magnet of the hopes of the large number of Americans who, like him, had a nostalgic confidence in the old ways. Good standpatters who approved of Cannon managed the canvass for the election of the Republican Congressmen. McKinley had succeeded Sherman as chairman of the Republican Congressional Campaign Committee, and Loudenslager was the committee secretary. If Taft disclosed openly his sentiments about Cannon, he could unsettle McKinley's and Loudy's work, and find himself Republican President with a Democratic Congress.

Neither Bryan's insinuations nor Cannon's petulant accusations affected the outcome of the election in the Eighteenth Illinois District. The foes of whom Cannon had to beware were amateurs, representing special interests without clear-cut permanent party affiliations. Trades unionists, the prohibitionists, and the conservationists, all of whom had suffered in Washington from Cannon the Czar, assumed leadership in the task of opposing Uncle Joe from Kankakee to Paris. They were not constituents of Cannon's. Hundreds of Americans who had never seen or heard of Vermilion Street before wended their way into Danville and away again during the campaign to shoot oratorical poisoned arrows at John Joseph Gurney Cannon. Some of the arguments they left behind sounded strange to Cannon's constituents, who were used to opposing him or supporting him on grounds of what he did or failed to do for the Eighteenth District, not because of his attitude toward the questions that excited their countrymen in other districts, other cities, and other states.

At the outset of the campaign in September, Cannon's new status as a national issue threatened to harm him in the Eighteenth District. "Prospects were not as good as heretofore," the Speaker's manager in the town of Watseka wrote him. The troubles of LaFollette and the conservative expressions of Taft and Administration leaders could bring Uncle Joe no lasting joy or benefit if the Eighteenth turned against him.

The outsiders' invasion of Cannonland began on Labor Day with the arrival of Samuel Gompers. Cannon was dozing on his porch, his hat tilted over his forehead, his feet on the railing, when the parade in honor of Gompers began to pass his house along North Vermilion on the way to Lincoln Park. In the parade was the man selected to benefit from the invasions, Henry C. Bell, the Democratic candidate for Cannon's seat, who was distributing all through the district plain white cards bearing three words:

CANNON THE STRANGLER

Bell clung to Gompers for support in hopes that the leader of the American Federation of Labor could persuade the Republicans among the trades unionists to vote for him and not for Cannon. "I believe in the absolute right of labor to organize for its own protection and well-being," said Bell. "I do not believe that injunctions should issue in labor troubles, except in rare cases." It was an academic assertion for Bell, because he had no direct interest either in the effectiveness of strikes and boycotts or in the sanctity of courts. But Gompers had personal cause to be roiled. His magazine, the *American Federationist*, had criticized the issuing of the injunction in the Buck's Stove and Range Company case, and now he had been judged guilty of contempt. If Congress had passed the Pearre bill, he would be beyond the reach of the courts. For the smothering of the bill he blamed Cannon, and he told the throng standing in the grass and dust in Lincoln Park:

You know Uncle Joe very well, or think you do. He comes to you once in a while and stays with you for a while, and you see that mask, you see that genial smile. You do not know what is hidden behind that smile. We who are in Washington and constantly keeping our gaze upon him know his various changes of feature. If we were offered the privilege of eliminating Aldrich [Nelson Aldrich, the conservative leader of the Senate], Rockefeller [John D. Rockefeller, president of Standard Oil, the stock symbol of privileged abuse of wealth and corporate power], or Cannon from influence in America, without hesitation we should choose Cannon as the most dangerous of the three . . . It is quite evident that Cannon controls the banks, the business, and the booze of Danville . . . If you love him so much, you will do the American people a great political service if you will keep him at home with you.

Throughout the history of the United States, trade union leaders have failed again and again to deliver the votes of their members to the candidates whom the leaders bless. Dues-paying wage-earners vote as individuals moved by many considerations besides their class-conscious interests. In 1908 unionists had not long been free from onerous subjugations to the political opinions of their employers, who during the Nineteenth Century often required their workers to vote for the bosses' candidates. Men who remembered that political dictation were reluctant to accept the new political dictation of the officers of their unions. Moreover, the fear existed that unions which become political organizations endangered their existence as labor organizations. The declining Knights of Labor had expired into nothingness when they allied themselves with Populism in 1892. So few trades unionists followed Gompers into Bryan's party. The Democrats at Denver asked John Mitchell of the United Mine Workers to be their vice presidential candidate, but he spurned the opportunity and later in the summer formally declared his independence of all party affiliations. H. R. Fuller, president of the Brotherhood of Locomotive Engineers, joined Bryan with Gompers, but members of his union established the Railway Men's Independent Taft Club. A few weeks after the Gompers speech in Lincoln Park, the

Chicago branch of the Railway Men's Taft Club notified Cannon that it was going to send some engineers into the Eighteenth District "to build up steam" for the Speaker.

Cannon counted on such dissidence to nullify Gomper's call for his defeat. He (and Taft and Roosevelt) felt sure that Gompers could not deliver labor to Bryan or Bell. He had labor friends of his own. The locomotive firemen were grateful to him because, reversing his congressional practice of repressing legislation, he had supervised the enactment of a bill which made the trade of fireman safer by requiring railroads operating in interstate commerce to equip locomotives with self-dumping ashpans. No longer did the fireman have to crawl beneath the firebox to dump the ash hopper, exposing himself to danger of injury, or even death, by burning. At Cannon's request, Representative Stevens of Minnesota—the author of that free pulp and paper bill beloved by Ridder—sent a representative of the conductors' union to Danville as an advocate of Cannon's re-election.

Would the driving of such wedges into the membership of labor enable the Speaker to command more unionists than the president of the American Federation of Labor? Cannon struggled forward on the assumption that it could. "We may fight and fail, but men have fought and failed before and yet made great contributions to civilization," he wrote in one of those inspirational memoranda which he set down for himself frequently during the tremblingly uncertain months of the campaign. He reshaped the injunction issue to suit himself. Let Gompers talk of judges' mistreatment of laborers. The question was whether the fundamental American principle of equal treatment for all was going to survive. With his good left hand hammering the air, he replied to Gompers: "The offense that brings me under his condemnation is that as a Representative in Congress and Speaker of the House, I have refused to take orders from him and to agree to a scheme of legislation which would make one law for one set of Americans and another law for all other citizens."

Collier's magazine joined the invasion of Cannonland by mail. Provoked by Cannon's hostility to public measures for the conservation of natural resources, *Collier's* throughout the campaign posted anti-Cannon broadsides to newspapers in the Eighteenth District with the suggestion to editors that the welfare of the nation required them to use the material for the purpose of retiring Uncle Joe to Vermilion Street. "The Roosevelt republican who can enthuse over the candidacy of Judge Taft cannot, with any conscience, vote for Mr. Joseph G. Cannon," Richard Lloyd Jones of *Collier's* editorial staff wrote to the editor of the Hoopeston *Daily Chronicle*. The magazine had influence in Washington. But neither it nor conservation aroused the voters in the Vermilion Valley.

What did stir them, and excite Cannon with the fear of defeat, was prohibition. The Littlefield bill became the campaign's main issue. The wrath of the godly all over the United States fell on Uncle Joe and poured strength into Democratic Bell.

The general conference of the Methodist Episcopal Church, meeting in Baltimore on August 12, passed a resolution demanding Uncle Joe's defeat in his campaign for Congress, as the preface to the election of a new Speaker who would permit the enactment of the Littlefield bill. Other Protestant bodies seconded the demand. The Presbyterian Synod of Nebraska condemned Cannon. President Hurley of the Illinois State Baptist Association opened the organization's sixty-fourth annual convention with the statement that Uncle Joe must be "kicked into oblivion." The Women's Christian Temperance Union chapters in the Eighteenth District dedicated themselves to winning Cannon's seat for Bell. The drys were not divided like the trades unionists. The Anti-Saloon League backed Methodists, Baptists, Presbyterians, and the W.C.T.U. in a coalition against Cannon, and the Prohibition Party candidate for Congress withdrew from the race in support of Bell. The alignment of dry women and dry clergymen was frightening. While the women lacked the franchise, they crystallized the opinions of timid and undecided husbands. The great majority of Cannon's constituents were Methodists, Baptists, and Presbyterians, and many of them quickly responded to the suggestion of bishops and synods. "The Methodist clergy are making quite a stir in this county (Iroquois) and, of course, are having some effect against your candidacy," B. F. Shankland, one of Cannon's campaign managers, wrote the Speaker.

To quiet the ecclesiastical outcry, Cannon said that it was no fault of his that the Judiciary Committee had not reported the Littlefield bill. "I have neither the power nor the disposition to control the action of the various committees of the House of Representatives, including the Judiciary Committee, touching bills of the character of the Littlefield bill or any other of the twenty thousand bills introduced in the House and, under the rules, referred to the appropriate committees," he wrote to Methodist Bishop John Hamilton of Boston, an old friend. In the middle of September Littlefield himself went to the Speaker's defense. "To one who has an elementary knowledge of the rules, it is hardly necessary to say that there are no rules, there is no Committee on Rules, and there is no Speaker that can prevent a majority of the House from taking up any measure and acting upon it at any time," Littlefield wrote Uncle Joe. Cannon sent a copy of the letter to David Thompson, editor of the dry, Methodist *Northwestern Christian Advocate,* which had appealed in an editorial in its issue of September 9 to all Methodist and temperance voters all over the country to ask their candidates for Congress to vote against Cannon for Speaker if Cannon remained in the House. Loudy had one hundred thousand copies of the letter distributed in every Congressional district where the *Advocate* was read.

Bishop Hamilton believed Cannon, and he refrained from joining sixteen other Methodist bishops in signing an anti-Cannon editorial which appeared in the *Illinois Issue,* the official organ of the Illinois Anti-Saloon League, on September 11. But few other clergymen believed either Cannon or Littlefield. It was known too well that the Speaker did have the authority, and the disposition, to control the actions of the various committees. The drys carried on their fight.

At Cannon's request, the Reverend E. C. Dinwiddie, former legislative representative in Washington of the Anti-Saloon League, wrote to the Reverend J. S. Dancey, pastor of the First Methodist Church in Danville, which Cannon attended, that the Speaker had always been a friend of temperance and had helped Dinwiddie draft legislation for the control of the liquor trade in the District of Columbia and in Indian Territory. Dinwiddie's successor as the legislative representative, S. E. Nicholson, wrote Dancey that what Dinwiddie said was false. Dinwiddie said that he had resigned from his job in Washington, and the Anti-Saloon League said that he had been fired.

Cannon methodically paid personal calls on most of the ministers in his district in order to counter the temperance crusade for his sacrifice. He pointed out that Tuscola was dry when he lived there forty years earlier, and that he had sat two years on the Tuscola Common Council without trying to have the temperance ordinance rescinded. He said that his only objection to the Littlefield bill was that it was unconstitutional, and that the courts, once it was enacted, would not permit its enforcement. He drew attention to the fact that no law forbade the shipment of liquor within Illinois from a wet zone to a dry zone.

His assertions were futile, but the drys could not down him. Sentiment, not argument, aided him. The appeal of the drys began to weaken when they attacked Cannon as a drunkard.

"Whereas it is a well-known fact that Mr. Joseph G. Cannon is a man of intemperate habits, is financially interested in the liquor business and therefore opposed to all anti-liquor legislation, and whereas it was mainly through his influence that the Littlefield-Hepburn Bill, so much desired enacted by temperance people, was defeated, therefore be it resolved, that the women here consider him unfit for the position of trust he has held and earnestly pray the voters of the district to defeat him at the polls in November." So resolved delegates to the Iroquois County convention of the Women's Christian Temperance Union on September 24.

It was a gross exaggeration, an untruth. Cannon's constituents began to feel sorry for him as a maligned and abused man. He was a moderate drinker. He drank openly and heartily, but seldom too much. He needed a clear head by day to manage his affairs, and a clearer head by night to make the best of his poker hands. Nobody had ever seen him drunk. The Reverend S. S. Jones of the Church of Christ in Danville, who twice had run as the Prohibition Party candidate for Cannon's seat, wrote to friends in Watseka that Uncle Joe was not intemperate. While bishops and clergymen outside the Eighteenth District went on with their lambasting of Cannon, the clergymen within the District came to his support. If his detractors would lie about his personal drinking habits, perhaps they were lying about his behavior as Speaker. W. L. Biggs, the postmaster at Westfield, wrote the Speaker,

I have had a personal talk with the leading members of the M. E. Church and they assured me that they was for you to a man. This report that Bell is going to carry this Westfield is a dam lye, and you can tell any man or preacher so.

Bell, like Cannon, was old. He had fought in the Civil War, and in 1908 he had been receiving a pension of $12 a month for forty-three years as compensation for losing a few teeth and suffering a heart ailment after his enlistment in the Union Army. He had worked in Washington for twelve years, in jobs of steadily decreasing responsibility in the Bureau of Pensions. He was anti-injunction, anti-liquor, and pro-conservation, a friend of the income tax and a general believer in centralism, but as a candidate he had a flaw, or at least it was said openly that he did. People believed that he drank too much. The fact that even temperate men in the Eighteenth District thought that Cannon was not a lush when he was accused of being one, and thought that Bell drank although he was speaking up for temperance, brightened Uncle Joe's prospects as election day neared. The Anti-Saloon League grew worried whether the combined influence of bishops and ministers of many sects would be sufficient after all to shake the respect of the Eighteenth District for their Congressman.

"We are aware of the fact that much criticism has been offered of Mr. Bell, the opponent of Mr. Cannon, . . . but after all is said and done it is the great principle back of the men that we are fighting for. Mr. Bell stands for that principle and has pledged himself to that end," the Anti-Saloon League wrote to the clergymen on its mailing list.

In those days Americans read newspaper editorials with more serious attention than they do today, and the editorials as a result had a greater influence in political controversy than they do now. Cannon had a strong battery of papers on his side in his district. Publishers in Danville, Watseka, Kankakee, Hoopeston, Paris, and Toledo did not join Ridder and Rosewater in scoring Cannon because he refused to help them gain tariff concessions. Let the price of paper touch the sky, and Postmaster Jewell and Marshal Hitch would still be at his side. But one paper which was carefully read in the district did oppose him. It was the Chicago *Tribune*.

It was published one hundred and twenty-five miles north of Danville, but the early morning Chicago and Eastern Illinois Railroad train for Evansville put it in Cannonland every day in time for breakfast. During the thirty-five years since Cannon first arrived in Washington, he and the *Tribune* had been usually friendly but sometimes at odds. The paper and the Congressman had had their most serious quarrel in 1890, when Cannon lost his campaign for re-election. The *Tribune* blamed Cannon's failure to take its advice for his defeat. He had, in the *Tribune's* estimation, fallen for eastern blandishments in voting for high duties in the McKinley Tariff on commodities which the paper considered too dear already—woolens, linens, glass, and tinplate. Cannon blamed the *Tribune* for his defeat. "What the party needs," he said then, "is a cheap Republican paper that could reach the masses of the people. The *Tribune* does us more harm in four years than good."

The *Tribune* that contributed to Cannon's defeat in 1890 seemed likely to defeat him again in 1908, because it drew together the case for the discontent with Cannon and reminded the Eighteenth District daily that their Representative had many enemies. It also circulated widely in the pastures of discontent in Wisconsin and Iowa, where it strengthened anti-Cannonism. It was not like today's *Tribune*. It printed political news without much bias. Its editorial columns were plastic and foreward-looking instead of petrified as they are now. Its editor was Joseph Medill McCormick, thirty-one years old, who later became vice chairman of the Progressive Party National Committee. The *Tribune* had treated Speaker Cannon well when Robert Wilson Patterson edited the paper, but shortly before the 1908 campaign began he gave way to young McCormick, with his enthusiasm for novelty, and the *Tribune* grew hostile.

Apparently Cannon asked for help from William G. Beale, the paper's attorney, and on October 8 Beale interceded for Cannon with Medill McCormick. "I would like to have the *Tribune* commence giving support to Speaker Cannon," wrote Beale. "A vicious fight is being made on him, and while I do not think his defeat probable, one can never be sure about such a thing, and the *Tribune* ought to help him. . . . (He) is a strong, courageous force on the conservative side of things, and in these days of radical tendencies he is greatly needed at Washington to help keep the balance right. . . . He ought to be re-elected to Congress and the Speakership."

McCormick was reluctant to praise Cannon. "In other congressional districts than his own Speaker Cannon is an issue," the *Tribune* editorial page said on October 14, six days after Beale sent his letter. "It may be said of him that in his own district his opponents have sought to make him an issue, but that in all probability they have failed and he will be re-elected. . . . The charge against the Speaker is that he is a reactionary. We are inclined to the view that he may be called a 'stationary.' . . . It is easy to damn a man. Mr. Cannon himself is reported to have damned many, but the people of the Eighteenth District will not fail to re-elect a man who has served the district for seventeen years and who today is the Speaker of the House."

That feeble attempt at praise angered both Beale and Cannon. "The *Tribune* was my most efficient supporter when I was first elected Speaker, but for the last year it seems to me that its tone and attitude have been substantially unfriendly," the Speaker wrote to Beale. "This has been unfortunate, in my judgment, for the party, not on account of my personality—which is but of little consequence to any one except myself—but from the fact of my being Speaker of the national House of Representatives." Beale requested McCormick to make the future editorials stronger. But McCormick was stubborn. "It has been charged against the Speaker that he was the friend of special interests," the *Tribune* said on October 20, "It is time for somebody to say that he has been attacked by special interests. . . . None except a few has suggested that the Speaker, whatever his position may have been from time to time, was actuated by any but honest motives. . . . His constituents should return him to Congress because of his long record as a public servant and because of his courageous adherence to his convictions."

Beale's rage at that insipidity boiled over into a steamy telegram to McCormick:

I am not at all satisfied with political attitude of *Tribune* and want it changed at once from feeble lukewarm attitude to emphatic and vigorous support of Republican party, including strong support for Speaker Cannon for Congress and Speaker. Editorial this morning weak and ineffective. Please notify editorial writers accordingly, and if they will not obey orders discharge them, and, if necessary, I will get your uncle [Robert Patterson] to take up his pen again.

McCormick resisted no more. The editorial he wrote for the Sunday *Tribune* of October 25 satisfied Beale and Cannon. It contains a fair summary of the reasons why, in the face of the demonstrably true statements by LaFollette, Bryan, Gompers, the Methodist Bishops, Rosewater, the conservationists, and all the other outsiders who devoted themselves in 1908 to proving to Vermilion County and environs that Cannon in office menaced his country, the inhabitants of Vermilion County nevertheless reasserted their confidence in Uncle Joe. They liked him for himself. The editorial said:

The *Tribune* is for the re-election of Joseph G. Cannon as a member of Congress and as Speaker of the House of Representatives:
1. Because he is honest
2. Because he is courageous
3. Because he is capable and efficient.
The district cannot decently desert him. The state cannot afford to let him go. The nation cannot completely fill his place.
The *Tribune* earnestly desires his re-election by a big majority in his district and by a unanimous vote for Speaker by the Republicans in the next House of Representatives.
'Jo' Cannon has been standing like a stone wall against every kind of jobbery and corruption in the House of Representatives for a generation. . . . Speaker Cannon can cast up his political accounts when his long and useful career is ended with confidence of finding an immense balance in his favor. . . . If he is to be blamed for not passing unconstitutional measures regulating interstate liquor traffic, then he must be praised for passing the pure food bill, under which the percentage of alcohol over a certain amount contained in every kind of patent medicines is plainly printed on the label—an act that has no parallel in any other country that we know of.
. . . 'Jo' Cannon has got character. That is why we like him and respect him even when we differ with him, and that is why we want him to be re-elected to Congress by the biggest majority he ever had and re-elected Speaker by the vote of every Republican member.

He had won the election more easily in 1906. But when the votes were counted on November 3, 1908, Uncle Joe had a safe plurality of ten thousand above Bell. For two months his constituents had heard constantly about the despotic way in which he repressed the will of America, and they made it clear that they did not care. He had licked the opposition because the constituents' fondness for his character and his person outbalanced their disapproval of his methods of conducting his office. Who could say now that his opponents really represented the will of America? The opponents had made him the national issue, and on that issue he, not they, had won. In saving his own career, he proved again to his own satisfaction that America stood by the tradition of limited government which he upheld by his tyranny. The Ben Hur band played old settlers' tunes in the street in front of his house, and two thousand of his friends in Danville serenaded him on the night of victory.

CHAPTER ———•——— 13

Contest in Washington

SURVEYING 1908 from the watchtower of today, we can see that
the victory in Danville was the indispensable prelude to the later
enthronement in the United States of new conceptions of political
science which were not dreamed of by the founders of the Republic in the eighteenth century and which were rejected over and
over by those responsible for the government of the Republic in
the nineteenth century. The victory strengthened the alliance
between the true reformers of the LaFollette tribe and the incidental anti-Cannonites, the drys, the dissatisfied easterners, the
Rosewater-like followers of Theodore Roosevelt, and the host of
others whose confederation would certainly have fallen apart if
they had been able to remove Cannon from the scene in 1908. Hostility to Cannon was their only bond. The LaFollette reformers
neither in 1908 nor ever afterward had following enough in their
own society to control the Republican Party or authority enough
to persuade Americans to accept the new idea, that the central
government was their defender against inequality and privilege
and the protector of the public interest against individual private
enterprise. But as long as Cannon ruled, the number of anti-
Cannonites increased, and as long as those true reformers had the
wickedness of Cannon to exploit, they could continue to enlarge
their coalition of anti-Cannonism into one awful movement. LaFollette regarded anti-Cannonism as the doorway to the new political

science. He said a few months after the election, the "battle of
the people's forces against one-man rule" must come before the
settlement of the "great fight to determine the future of this American Republic—whether the machinery of government shall be in
the hands of men who represent the public interest or men who
represent private interests."

The elections of 1908 encouraged the agrarian and Scandinavian reformers on the plains and in the forests of the mid-continent
valley states to hope that their alliance would soon be overwhelming in its might. The anti-Cannonites took the victory in Danville
calmly because they won so many congressional contests outside
Danville. Tawney survived in Minnesota, but in the same state
Representative J. Adam Bede, an admirer of Cannon's personality
if not his opinions, had lost the Republican nomination to Clarence Miller in a campaign featured by Miller's exaggerated claim
that Bede was a "hide-bound Cannon man." The Indiana voters
defeated all but two of the Republican incumbents running for the
House after campaigns in which the drys attacked every one of
them as agents of Cannon. Harassed by the same accusation,
Jim Watson failed to win the governorship of Indiana. Nebraska
showed the depth of its interest in fundamental reform by electing
three Democratic Congressmen who satisfied the voters that they
had a more intense and sincere interest in change than their Republican opponents did. What an ironic result for Rosewater's
campaign! The Omaha editor not only injured Cannon but also
endangered his own conservatism, because he whipped up enmity
for Cannon's opinions. The strong vote against Cannonism raised
doubt as to which party had been victorious. Formally it was a
Republican year. The nation chose Taft for President, and it maintained the Republican majority in the House, where the division
in the Sixty-first Congress would be two hundred and eighteen Republicans and one hundred and seventy-three Democrats. The
Democrats clearly had gained ten seats, and perhaps they had
gained many more. For the anti-Cannonites among the Republicans numbered at least two dozen. If they supported the Democrats, and if the Democrats supported the new idea, Congress
could institute at last the reforms which the Speaker had repressed
so long.

The goal which the leaders among the allies set themselves immediately after the elections was the removal of Representative Cannon from his great office in Washington. "The real issue as regards Mr. Cannon is not his re-election to Congress but his re-election to the Speakership," the *Central Christian Advocate,* one of the Methodists' temperance-minded journals, coolly told its readers the day after the trouncing of Mr. Bell. Within a week Norman Hapgood, the editor of *Collier's,* which was rapidly becoming the eastern spearhead of the drive LaFollette and Cummins led in the West, was asking every Representative by mail: "Are you willing to let us know your opinion of the advisability of electing as the next Speaker some other than Mr. Cannon?" From his home in Elizabeth, New Jersey, Fowler, the frustrated chairman of the Banking and Currency Committee, assisted the Methodists and Hapgood and LaFollette by inaugurating a campaign for his own election to Cannon's position.

Believing as I do that there must be some change in the method of bringing forward legislation in the House of Representatives, to reflect better the opinion of the whole country, to conserve better the welfare of all the people, and also to insure the election of a Republican House in 1910, in order that President Taft may be supported throughout his entire term by a Congress working in harmony with him, I am writing you to ask your support of my candidacy for the Speakership for the Sixty First Congress upon the following platform:

The House of Representatives shall elect a Board of Managers, consisting of seven members, which shall be charged with that direction of legislation which is now assumed by the Speaker of the House.

Sincerely hoping that you will agree with me that it is essential that this reform shall be effected now, I remain very respectfully yours, Charles N. Fowler.

Fowler sent that recommendation in a circular letter to all members of the Sixty-first Congress, which was expected to convene in the following March. President-elect Taft had said that immediately after his inauguration (March 4) he would call Congress into extraordinary session to revise the tariff.

Cannon sensed the intimations of revolt. The success of the Democrats and the discontented at the polls had destroyed the complacence which had prompted him to write Sherman during the summer: "If you except ten men at the outside, followers of

LaFollette, some of them 'D.F.s', the House is o.k." At the request of Littauer, he left Danville the day after the elections for New York City, where he consulted with Litt, McKinley, Loudenslager, Bennet (Uncle Joe's supporter on the immigration bill), and Sherman. Sherman had almost died of a gall-bladder attack two days after his nomination for the vice presidency in June; but his health was blooming in November, and he was hopeful that Taft could be used to save Cannon and the paramountcy of the conservative tradition. The meeting over, Cannon wrote to Captain King of the *Globe-Democrat* and to his Chicago *Tribune* friend, Robert Patterson, that he would probably receive the votes of all the eastern Republican Representatives except Fowler's and Augustus Gardner's. Payne reported to Cannon that he had written to the twenty-six New York Republican Congressmen, that three-fourths of their number had replied, and those who replied were all for Cannon. The Speaker understood that many Representatives who once disliked him were driven by their own ambitions to support him. Representative J. Sloat Fassett of New York, a lieutenant of Theodore Roosevelt's, wrote him early in November recommending Representative James Breck Perkins of New York as chairman of the Committee on Foreign Affairs, a post which would be vacant in the Sixty-first Congress as a result of the swamping of Charles Landis in the Indiana deluge. A few days later Perkins wrote to Cannon that he had heard from Fowler but he would vote for the Speaker's re-election.

Soon after the meeting in New York, Vice President-elect Sherman departed for Hot Springs, Virginia, where President-elect Taft was perfecting plans for his execution of the presidential office. Ridder's New York *Staats-Zeitung* and the New York *Tribune* published rumors that Taft favored the ditching of Cannon from the Speakership. But Taft was an amiable man who longed always for harmony. Sherman predicted to him drably that his term in the White House would be wasted, empty of accomplishment, if he thrust his party into internecine war by forsaking the leader of one of its strongest factions, Cannon. Now that the election was over, should the new President invite discord? It was hard for him to make up his mind. Roosevelt himself advised Taft not to support the anti-Cannon faction among the Republicans. What strange instructions, pregnant for the future! Who will unravel the mystery of Theodore Roosevelt? How could he write those messages of 1907 and 1908 and defend the man who murdered the messages? Did he have an ounce of sincerity? No matter. He was at least by accident the friend of Joseph Gurney Cannon, and that is what counts here. In October and November he gave his counsel that Taft accommodate himself to Uncle Joe. And when Tawney told Roosevelt that Cannon wished to talk with Taft, Roosevelt asked Taft to submit to the interview. That advice from the retiring President fixed the course of Taft's presidential career. The gradual subjugation of Taft to Cannon disclosed Cannon's wisdom in having readily accepted the inevitable at the Chicago convention: his own inability to win the presidential nomination. While he had been able only to frustrate Roosevelt, he could capture and guide Taft. There was not much practical difference between being President and telling the President what to do. If the Speaker could induce the President to stop bleating for reform, then the buffeting of the Capitol by other howlers after reform might cease, and Cannon would no longer have to hold at bay the friends of change. Bryan, on a visit to Danville, went so far as to predict that Cannon, already the leader of the party, would be the presidential candidate of the party in 1912.

Unaware of Roosevelt's counsel, the friends of change in the House counted on Taft to back any undertaking aimed at turning Cannon out of the Speaker's office. Confident, almost exultant, they gathered in Washington and laid their plans for rebellion a few days before Congress was to convene in the Lame Duck session. They had until March to perfect the plans, for no opportunity to harass Cannon would arise in the Lame Duck meeting. They vowed either to oust the Speaker or to deprive him of his power, and in the autumn most of them hoped to do both. They counted thirty absolutely reliable anti-Cannonmen in their cabal. That was more than enough to destroy Cannon's party majority, provided they could make a temporary alliance with the Democrats.

Expecting some defections from the camp of the enemy, Burleson, the Texan who had greeted Uncle Joe so cordially at the Arlington on his seventieth birthday, spent the autumn at ease in Washington in order to be on hand for whatever extraordinary developments might occur. Toward the end of November he fell in with Norris, the Nebraskan, who cautiously suggested the possibility of an understanding with Representative Champ Clark of Bowling Green, Missouri, the Democrat who, it was taken for granted, would succeed John Sharp Williams as floor leader. The Republican rebels did not care at that moment who might become Speaker, as long as it wasn't Cannon. Many of them were indifferent to the future of their own party. They recalled the first days of the Republic, when men banded together temporarily in support of an opinion and not of a party. "The regular Republican in Congress, as distinguished from his brother progressive, is one who is a party man before he is a citizen," said Representative Charles Augustus Lindbergh of Little Falls, Minnesota, father of the aviator. "One of the fundamental principles" of the rebellion, said Representative Asle J. Gronna of Lakota, North Dakota, "is that each Representative is responsible to his constituents for his actions in Congress and not to any party organization." No matter how the Speakership fight might come out, the rebels wanted Democratic support for their plan to change the rules, so that whoever should become Speaker would not possess the all-pervading authority that Uncle Joe had at his command. Burleson arranged a meeting. Assured by Norris that the rebels were serious, Clark agreed to help them amend the rules. A change would be useful to him. It would increase the opportunity for the Democrats to influence the decisions of the House as long as their party was in the minority.

The rebels were a varied lot. At their core was the group of valley men under the spell of LaFollette. They were beginning to call themselves "progressives." Their leader was Victor Murdock, the wavy-haired red-head from Wichita, Kansas, where the farmers and millers grumbled that the big railways discriminated in Kansas City's favor on freight rates for wheat and flour, and where independent oil producers cursed the might of the Standard Oil. Less explosive but equally determined on changing the course of the Republican Party was Norris. With them stood five Republicans from Wisconsin, headed by Cooper, who looked vaguely like a bearded Toscanini, and John Mandt Nelson. There were others from Minnesota, Iowa, and North Dakota. The pledge-signer from Missouri, Edgar C. Ellis, bolstered the group. Miles Poindexter of Washington was a true progressive, and so was Everis A. Hayes of California. The distinction that set the progressives apart from the other rebels was that they opposed Cannon and the rules not merely because they wished to reform the procedure of the House but because they considered it vital to the nation's survival to enlarge and revise the powers of government in dealing with social and economic inequalities. To a man they were tariff revisionists. Their immediate purpose was to render Cannon helpless to save the high duties which since the enactment of the Dingley Law had enhanced the power of wealth and privilege.

Not all the rebels had such profound reasons for opposing Cannon. Fowler, whose bull-face was made grotesquely mild by a curl that hung over his forehead, was driven to join them by his realization that there would be no suitable currency legislation as long as Cannon's will was law in America. The great eastern city bankers on whose behalf Fowler rebelled against Cannon actually represented the very privilege that LaFollette loathed. Yet whatever his reasons for dissidence, dissident Fowler was useful to the dissident insurgents. Gussie Gardner had a rich man's enthusiasm for "good government." George A. Pearre hoped that a change in the Speakership would clear the way for his injunction bill.

A number of rebels were motivated simply by intellectual scruples against the authoritarian rules. The leader of that faction was Hepburn of Iowa. He was neither progressive nor conservative, a hot-head in debate but temperate in his conceptions, for change but only if it came gradually, not persuaded that the United States was divided between the privileged and the oppressed but ready always to believe that the country suffered from some superficial social and economic dislocations which it was the business of government to remedy. His political science called for frequent applications of iodine to the wounds of the nation but not for fundamental "progressive" surgery. Yet the rules had displeased him ever since he reached the House in 1893. In his first address as a Congressman he asked his colleagues to amend the Reed Rules. When the House first elected Cannon Speaker (with his assistance) Hepburn made a motion for a revision of the rules. Nobody heeded him. But in the autumn of 1908 rebels gathered around him. He drew them all together. They met for their plotting in his office, which was large and comfortable because he was chairman of the Committee on Interstate and Foreign Commerce. The office was furnished with a long table of dark oak around which all the rebels could sit and thresh out their program. These conferences were just a bit vexing for Old Pete. He had declined to run for re-election in 1908, and therefore he would be out of office when the Sixty-first Congress met. He would not be able to share directly in the rebellion which he was helping to plan.

As knowledge of the rebels' purpose seeped abroad, they were nicknamed the "insurgents." They were rising up. They had strong backing in the Senate, where Cummins joined LaFollette and Jonathan Dolliver of Iowa as the leaders of the midcontinent progressives when the final session of the Sixtieth Congress convened in December. The question of the fate of Cannon so preoccupied everyone's attention that scarcely any member of House or Senate took an interest in legislation during that session.

The insurgents had the center of the stage for three months, and they began to chafe uneasily. They began to quarrel over tactics. Would it be wiser after all to leave Cannon in office weakened by a revision of the rules, or must he and rules go together? Norris, despite his having taken the Rosewater pledge, began to argue that their target should be only the rules and not the Speaker. They must base their insurgency on principle, not on personality. He knew that Cannon was yet a hero to millions, and to abase him might harm the progressives more than it would help them. Murdock damned this sense of compromise. It was time to get rid of all the personnel and symbols of dictatorship, he said. He carried weight in the councils, but the view of Norris began to prevail after the insurgents learned that Taft by accident agreed with him. Agents of the incoming Administration spoke sweetly with the insurgents. They would only hurt their own interests if they overthrew Cannon, for they would thereby precipitate a long contention in the House and delay indefinitely the attainment of the prize which the progressives sought—revision of the tariff. That suggestion was potent. It discouraged the insurgents from campaigning for the removal of Cannon. Thereafter most of them dared not spread the word abroad that they intended to shake the person of Uncle Joe.

They concentrated on their effort to win support for a change in the rules. Early in February 1909 the insurgents sent a circular letter to all Democratic members of the House, saying:

So far as is known, there is but one opportunity during the life of a Congress for amending these rules. This opportunity comes at the beginning of each Congress. Hitherto it has been the custom to shut off this opportunity by the adoption of the previous question or some other secondary motion, the effect of which does not appear to the public. If these secondary motions are voted down, there is then opportunity to debate and amend the rules. . . .

We should be glad to receive any suggestions that you may care to make and to hear from you as to whether we may have your assistance at the beginning of the Sixty First Congress in amending the rules.

William Howard Taft on March 4 took the oath of president in a driving snowstorm, and he at once appointed March 15 as the day on which the special session should begin for consideration of the tariff. For the city of Washington it was a time of physical change. The mall that stretched toward the Potomac at the bottom of Capitol Hill, beneath the windows in the Speaker's rooms, was at last becoming green and beautified. The railroad tracks that disfigured it until 1908 had been removed, and the sluggish Tiber Creek, a noisome mosquito nest that crossed the mall, had been covered over. All trains now conveniently halted at the handsome new Union Station, a quarter mile north of the Capitol across a new parkway. The city was growing. A new bridge was a-building over the steep, wide Rock Creek ravine which for a century had halted the advance of Washington northward beyond Florida Avenue, or Boundary Street as it was named for years. The noble plan of Pierre L'Enfant for the capital city was at last being realized a century late. The dust and "magnificent distances" that Cannon had known as Washington for years after he and Molly arrived there in 1873 were giving way to hard paving and magnificent vistas. This activity in municipal development symbolized the restless longing of the the progressives among the insurgents for political change and modernization, but it did not deflect Uncle Joe from the course he had selected.

Letters from men with whom Cannon had established himself as hero sustained him while the insurgents were making ready for their victory dance. "What do these fool insurgents and those skunk Democrats mean to do?" Frank A. Mehling, the vice president of the Northern Ohio Blanket Mills in Cleveland, asked him. "Don't they know that your little way of chloroforming them and keeping them in a state of coma as long as they are in Congress is the best that could happen to them, and the country, too, for that matter?" James Wilson of Tama, Iowa, who was still Secretary of Agriculture twelve years after his appointment by President McKinley, assured Cannon that the insurgents were cowards like the rabble who dug up the bones of Oliver Cromwell after the Restoration and played football with his skull. "These hounds would not think of meeting you on a fair field," wrote Tama Jim. J. Sloat Fassett, whose loyalty to party suddenly turned him into a partisan of Uncle Joe, recalled the observation of Roscoe Conkling about his detractors: "I have noticed that a dried-up grasshopper in the corner of a fence can make more noise than the cattle grazing on a thousand hills." "It is fair to presume," wrote Fassett, "that most of the objectors to the rules have never read them; that if they had, they could not understand them. . . . It must be remembered that by far an overwhelming majority of the Republicans of the House are loyal to the rules, and to the Speaker, and only by impeaching their intelligence could any one accept the criticisms . . . as well founded. I just drop you this letter to hearten you up a bit, for I have felt once or twice lately that you were perhaps giving too much weight to the people who have been criticizing you." Uncle Joe himself traced his troubles to the print paper and pulp tariff. He wrote to a financial writer, W. G. Nicholas, in New York City:

So far as the attacks upon me as an individual and Speaker of the House are concerned, they had their genesis in the First Session of the Sixtieth Congress when Mr. Herman Ridder, who was the head of the publishers' organization, demanded in the name of that organization that I recognize then Representative John Sharp Williams or some other member of the House to move to suspend the rules and pass a bill putting wood pulp and print paper on the free list.

He needed heartening. He despised his critics, but he gloomily gave them a chance of victory. He kept a good face in public, appearing calm, his head up, the cigar-end ever in process of maceration between his molars, speaking softly and slowly without showing anxiety or irritation. But he lacked fire. When the Republicans met in caucus the night of March 14, Cannon addressed them without his old mannerisms. His left arm hung by his side. He never once bobbed his head. He spoke as though he thought defeat was imminent:

You cannot talk back from that chair [the Speaker's]. I am glad to have occupied that position. I have had it for six years, but I should not heave a sigh if the Republican Party, acting together, should select some other one of our colleagues to preside. I would cheerfully take my seat upon the floor and make my best contribution for the common weal. Legislate on facts. You cannot legislate nor accomplish results according to the declarations of either ignorant or vicious people. 'The shallows murmur while the deeps are dumb.' Uninformed people thunder.

Rejecting his forebodings, the caucus unanimously nominated him for a fourth term. But not all the Republicans took part in the caucus. On LaFollette's advice, the insurgents remained absent, to enable them to keep their independence. Despite this act of separation, they were not absolutely free. Vague uncertainties haunted them. Taft's vigorous support of Cannon confused them. "Nothing better could happen for the progressive movement than a contest between the Speaker and the President," John Mandt Nelson wrote in the new magazine, *LaFollette's Weekly*, in January. "Such a contest seems to be inevitable, notwithstanding rumors of peace and harmony. . . . Without the President's aid, the members of the House will remain handcuffed, manacled, and gagged by the Speaker." But Taft implacably refused to help them. The rebels could not believe that Taft meant it when he first signified that he was on Cannon's side. Even LaFollette expected that at the propitious eleventh hour he would stand up for his own interests as President and guide the insurgents toward Cannon's overthrow in order at one stroke to establish himself as the party leader and the captain-general of reform. But the contest Nelson longed for did not occur.

Accordingly the insurgents were uncertain how to use their own strength when the House convened at noon on March fifteenth, with Cannon in the chair. The first business before it in the new Congress was the election of the Speaker. The insurgents, now thoroughly disappointed by Taft, had no focus of leadership. In their confusion the bold step of moving over to the Democrats was beyond them, and the progressives remained bound by the party ties which intellectually they wanted to reject. None of the insurgents cast his vote for Champ Clark, the Democratic nominee. Eight voted for Hal Cooper, two for Norris, and one for John Esch of Wisconsin. As a tribute to Hepburn's famous independence, Lindbergh voted for Hepburn as Speaker, although Pete was no longer a member of the House. Rosewater-pledges notwithstanding, Norris and Kinkaid of Nebraska as well as Ellis and Hayes voted for Cannon. So did Gardner, Pearre, and Fowler, whom nobody wanted for Speaker. Once more the House chose wicked old Uncle Joe.

But was Cannon destined hereafter to be a Speaker without power, a judicial presiding officer instead of a political manager? When the vote was finished, little Dalzell pranced to the well of the House and offered his standard resolution to adopt the rules of the previous Congress. The resolution had passed in 1903 and 1905 and 1907. But in 1909 it was defeated. The insurgents in alliance with the Democrats carried the day. Cannon's rules went down, 193 to 189. Good Scandinavians helped bear Uncle Joe to the ground—Steenerson, Haugen, Lindbergh, Nelson, and Lenroot, who on that exciting day was beginning his career as a member of Congress. Norris, Murdock, Gardner, and Fowler voted against the rules. As Norris had promised Clark in November, the insurgents all told numbered thirty, and Clark, taking heart from this proof of his new allies' reliability, arose and offered a resolution to amend the rules. It was a knife to make a eunuch of the Speaker. It would increase the Rules Committee from the tight little company of five appointed by the Speaker to a group of fifteen to be elected by the House membership. The Speaker would not be a member, and the Speaker would keep the privilege of appointing only five committees instead of all committees—Ways and Means, Printing, Accounts, Mileage, and Enrolled Bills. The resolution was curiously timid. Cannon had been authority so long that Clark could not imagine cleanly cutting him off from all his sources of extraordinary power. Why authorize him to appoint any committees? But the vestiges of power which Clark would leave him were few, and the insurgents voted for the resolution.

Cannon stood at the edge of doom. The history of the Speaker as a figure of supreme importance in American government seemed to be ending.

But Cannon had a keen eye for a man's weakness, and he had been putting that trait to good use. As a result, he knew things about which the insurgents were ignorant. The insurgents should have acquainted themselves better with John Joseph Fitzgerald of Brooklyn, New York. Representative Fitzgerald was a Democrat, but he gave his first loyalty not to the Democratic organization of the House but to the Democratic organization of Greater New York, Tammany Hall. There was some talk going around that the tariff revisionists on the Ways and Means Committee intended to raise the federal excise tax on beer, and the heads of Tammany considered the tax on the poor man's drink already high enough. In such a situation Cannon might be of help to Tammany, and Tammany might be of help to Cannon. Cannon could keep the beer tax as it was, and Tammany's Representatives in Washington, twelve in number, could help Cannon in the struggle over the rules. The Democratic Representatives from Georgia and Florida had a weakness, too. Their interest in protecting the lumber industry in their states compromised their support for the traditional Democratic doctrine of a tariff for revenue only. It was possible that Cannon could hold the lumber tariff at a good protective level, provided Georgia and Florida made it possible for Cannon to keep on controlling affairs in the House. Rural Louisiana, too, was overrun with that political push-me-pull-you, the Democratic protectionist. The Louisianans needed defense against foreign sugar.

As the clerk called the roll on Clark's resolution for amending the rules, Fitzgerald and ten of his eleven Tammany colleagues; Robert F. Broussard of New Iberia, Louisiana; six Georgians, six Floridians, and Democrats from Massachusetts and Illinois voted against Clark. Cannon had but one means for outwitting the insurgents, and that was to balance the insurgent Republicans moving to Clark's side with insurgent Democrats moving to his side. The trade was about even. Clark had thirty Republicans and Cannon had twenty-two Democrats. Cannon not only obtained the necessary votes, but his new allies baited the astounded insurgents and regular Democrats with salty witticisms. "The reason the Democrats have not been legislating since I have been here has

not been due to too many rules but to too many Republicans," said
William G. Brantley, a lumber Democrat from Brunswick, Georgia.
Cannon was not emasculated. The final vote in his favor was 203
to 180. Within a week Cannon appointed Fitzgerald to the Rules
Committee and Broussard to Ways and Means. LaFollette wrote
in his *Weekly*:

It was not the Speaker who gained a victory in the House of Representatives on Monday March the fifteenth. It was Special Privilege.
That victory means hundred of millions of profit to privilege. It was
not the little band of courageous and independent Republicans who
were beaten. It was ninety millions of people. They lost all that Special
Privilege gained that day.

Test of Honor

WHILE THE insurgents were spending the winter hopefully form-
ing their useless plans for discomforting Cannon, one of the stalwart supporters of the object of their gripe, Chairman Sereno
Elisha Payne of the Ways and Means Committee, was concentrat-
ing his attention on the principal matter which inspired the progressives among the insurgents to launch their vain rebellion—the
tariff. Payne had called his committee together in November, immediately after the elections, for hearings on a new tariff, and a
final draft of his bill was almost ready for submission to the House
when the Sixty-first Congress opened with its hullabaloo over tyranny and czarism.

The tariff was an issue of honor in 1909. The question was
whether the Republican Party would make good the promise implied in the platform of the Chicago convention for revision downward. The Republicans who actually wanted lower schedules felt
that their personal integrity was at stake in the decision to be
made. The enactment of higher duties, or the failure to depress
the duties to a marked degree, would humiliate them by depriv-
ing the party to which they belonged of its reputation for trust-
worthiness. Nobody could put faith in an organization whose candidates sought office on a tariff-revision program and, after gaining
office, ignored the political bond so plighted. Not only the insurgents but most Americans saw the question in that unusual light,

and they thus vested the issue with a high meaning and solemnity seldom found in legislative matters.

The question of honor took precedence over issues of economics, although, of course, one's interpretation of what the Republicans had actually promised at Chicago depended pretty much on one's economic opinions. The tide of opinion was changing. Whereas the manufacturer and miner stood at the center of the protectionists' economic philosophy in the nineteenth century, the consumer had become the focus of economic interest for the progressives and also for the National Association of Manufacturers and millions of other Americans of mild protectionist leanings who favored downward revision. Senator Cummins contended that protective schedules stifled competition in the United States when they were higher than absolutely necessary to save American producers from foreign competition. Only in an energetically competitive society could the consumer derive the greatest advantage in ease and standard of living, for competition drove down prices and thereby increased the value of the consumer's income.

The consumer was any purchaser of goods, whether a housewife in Madison buying protected woolen cloth from which to make herself a dress or a publisher buying protected newsprint essential to his business. But the progressives in the main thought of the consumer as an individual, not a manufacturer, and the ability of the individual consumer to stretch his dollar had been declining steadily in the years since the enactment of the Dingley Law. Ida M. Tarbell reported in her study of the tariff (serialized in the *American Magazine* in 1909) that the annual per capita cost of necessaries went up from $74.31 in 1896 to $107.26 in 1906; prices rose 35 per cent, and wages (based on inquiries among 334,000 wage-earners) rose 19.1 per cent. The United States Steel Corporation paid an average wage of $775 a year, and the cotton textile industry averaged $416. The high prices widened the gulf between the condition of the poor and the condition of the rich, for the poor, like the rich, had to buy clothing and food, and the tariff raised the price of both. Dingley's tariff on tinplate started a progressive rise in the cost of canned foods. Shoes cost more because of Dingley. His law was the first American tariff that imposed a duty on hides; Dingley also raised the tariff on leather and on flax, from which was made the thread used in manufacturing shoes.

Miss Tarbell explained how the trusts and overprotected industries intertwined. The United Shoe Machinery Company controlled
the sale and renting of all machines used by shoe manufacturers for
welting, lasting, heeling, and pegging shoes; therefore, the machinery company had the power to designate those who might and
those who might not make shoes in America behind the tariff wall.
As a result price competition in the protected shoe business was
rare. The combination of the Dingley duty on thread and the op-
eration of the Coats thread trust increased the cost of dresses and
overalls made at home. The housewife felt the pinch of the tariff
even at the washtub, for Dingley protected starch and many Americans grumbled that the starch monopolists—the "glucose trust"
as the Corn Products Company was nicknamed—held the price
above the protected level. Besides those specific items of particular interest to poor Americans in the city and on the farm, the
tariff worked to keep high the whole general level of prices, and
the progressives blamed that fact for the dearness of all living.

As protectors of the consumer, the progressives interpreted the
Chicago resolution to mean that the Republican Party was committed to lowering tariffs. The progressives had reason to assume
that Taft agreed with them. He was never a tariff crusader, but
in his speech in Cincinnati accepting the presidential nomination
in 1908 he acknowledged the presence of flaws in existing schedules. In the protectionist tradition he recommended that the duty
on every imported article should be sufficient to cover the difference in the cost of production at home and abroad, including the
difference in wages, and sufficient also to give a reasonable profit
to the American producer. "The tariff in a number of schedules
now exceeds the difference between the cost of production of such
articles abroad and at home," Taft said. "The excess over that difference offers a temptation to those who would monopolize the production and sale of such articles in this country, to profit by the
excessive rate. On the other hand there are some few other schedules in which the tariff is not sufficiently high to give the measure
of protection which they should receive upon republican principles, and as to those the tariff should be raised." Taft's thriftiness
gave him the consumer's point of view about the tariff. As Secretary of War he recommended that the Panama Canal Commission
buy steel rails in England at two-thirds of the price they could be

bought for in protected Pennsylvania. Taft told Henry Riesenberg, chairman of the National Tariff Commission Convention, which met in Indianapolis on February 16, that he favored the establishment of "some such body" as the commission, but he did not promise to recommend its inclusion in the new bill.

The progressives, however, could not add Taft up to a neat sum. His running mate, Jim Sherman, sent shivers down the spines of the sincere revisionists and of officers of the National Association of Manufacturers. "I am a protectionist," he announced in his speech of acceptance, delivered in Utica while the bells rang in churches and town halls up and down the Mohawk Valley from Little Falls on the east to Rome on the west, and he said little more about the tariff. Taft's reiteration of the old cost-of-production formula played into the hands of those who wanted to keep the walls of protection higher than necessary. Acting at the orders of the State Department, the consuls abroad tried but failed to obtain the statistical information necessary for the drafting of a tariff law on that basis. In the end Congress had to rely on the manufacturers and miners seeking tariff protection to tell them what the protective duty should be. In his Inaugural Address on March 4, Taft repeated what he had said in his acceptance speech, and he suggested also the enactment of a maximum and minimum schedule as a device by which the United States could slap back at foreign countries discriminating against American goods. That coincided with Cannon's opinion.

By the time Congress convened, the progressives suspected that Cannon and the men in charge of the work of writing the new tariff bills were aiming at higher and not lower schedules. Senator Julius Caesar Burrows, chairman of the tariff sub-committee of the Finance Committee, had been in Washington since August, 1908, for the arduous and cumbersome task of preparing a bill to take the place of Dingley's law. He was a standpatter, and none who sincerely favored revision downward relished the fact that he had influence in the matter. Stout Chairman Payne was a high protectionist of long standing who had considered low duties a source of danger to his country ever since the enactment of the tariff-for-revenue-only Wilson Law in 1894, which was followed by panic, by a fall in the value of railroad stocks to 12 per cent of par, by unemployment, and by widespread destitution. He had kept a discreet silence about his tariff philosophy since the Chicago convention, and he had cheered the downward revisionists by opening his hearings with witnesses representing the consumers. In his mahogany and gilt committee rooms down the corridor of the Capitol from the Speaker's quarters, he listened to testimony for two months while he made almost a public function of the task of rewriting the law. That procedure contrasted sharply with the manner of preparation of the Dingley Tariff, which Dingley and Payne and the other Republican members of the Ways and Means Committee of that day had worked out in an obscure room of the Cochran Hotel, far from the public gaze, in three weeks' time.

As the Congressional session opened, Payne reported to the Speaker that his committee had drafted a bill which, honoring the general sentiment and the common understanding of what the Republican platform meant, severely reduced many duties. It was not to Payne's liking to forsake Republican tradition in that way. But the intensity of the national yearning for relief from the high cost of living had so impressed most of Payne's colleagues that they insisted upon a sweeping repudiation of Dingley. Foreign lumber was to enter the country free. Zinc ore was to remain free. Hides, from which shoe-leather was made, were to be free. Petroleum and petroleum products were to be free. Upon receiving that information, Cannon took over Payne's prerogatives as Chairman of Ways and Means. He instructed Payne to inform his colleagues that they must change their draft.

Accepting the comment of the Speaker as a ukase, the colleagues obliged, and Payne on March 17 reported to the House a bill that would pinch the consumer harder than Dingley ever dared to pinch him.

To be sure it pleased the conservationists and the publishers. In the course of the investigation which Cannon had directed him to make in order to shut up Ridder, Mann concluded that the spruce trees in the United States would last only fourteen more years if the country relied on domestic woods as a source of its newsprint. To save our forests, he recommended that woodpulp enter America free and that Congress drop the import tax on newsprint from six dollars to two dollars a ton. Payne accepted Mann's suggestions, and included them in the bill which he presented to the House. And the bill offered a novelty (which Taft had recommended in his Inaugural Address) in a federal inheritance tax, imposing a levy of 1 per cent on estates above $10,000 when assigned to direct heirs and 5 per cent when assigned to collateral heirs. The provision was modeled after the state law in Payne's own New York. Its inclusion in a bill put together under the direction of standpatters bore witness to the intensifying national distrust of wealth.

On Cannon's behalf, however, Payne squeezed the home-builder in the revised draft by taxing imported lumber at one dollar a thousand feet.

In recognition of Democratic Louisiana's friendly attitude toward the Republican Speaker, the bill further squeezed the wage-earner and house-wife by continuing the tariff on sugar. A forecast that clothing and food would be dearer was contained also in proposals for higher tariffs on cotton, chocolate, cocoa, fruits, vegetables, and nuts. Sharing Cannon's regard for the welfare of glove-maker Littauer, the retired member of the Speaker's court, Payne asked Congress to raise the duty on ladies' gloves. The tariff of 1897 had already given Littauer and his fellow American manufacturers a monopoly of the American market in men's gloves. Payne's bill increased the tariff on hosiery by 30 per cent, "a cruel outrage on men, women, and children," complained Champ Clark. Cannon's district was producing more oil than any area east of Illinois, and Payne proposed the retention of the Dingley duties on petroleum and petroleum products. Payne redeemed Cannon's pledge to Missouri by recommending a tax of one cent a pound on zinc ore. Pleasing to Cannon's supporters in Tammany was the fact that the bill did not bear out rumors that the federal excise tax on beer was to go up from one dollar to one dollar and fifty cents.

The tariff which Payne reported after conference with Cannon dealt with four thousand articles of commerce and reduced the duties on only four hundred. It recommended increases in seventy-five articles, and it subjected many of the reduced articles to eventual increase by the application of the maximum and minimum provision, since most foreign countries discriminated against American goods by some statutory or administrative device. The bill depressed people who had continued to take seriously the optimists' interpretation of the Republican platform. It was written to suit Cannon.

"Amusing indeed were the ponderous assurances of Mr. Taft that the Republican Party would revise the tariff downward," Representative Oscar Underwood of Alabama remarked to his colleagues in the House. "I say to you that there is more real power in one five-cent cigar between the iron lips of Joseph G. Cannon than in the big sticks of a whole regiment of Roosevelts and Tafts."

A delegation of women from Chicago called at the Capitol bearing a petition which, had all the sheets of paper comprising it been pasted together, would have reached three miles. It bore the signatures of two hundred thousand opponents of the suggested tariffs on gloves, both short and long (for Payne's bill proposed a higher duty on gloves over fourteen inches in length than on those which ended at the wrist). But Mann, in his capacity of majority leader, refused to make arrangements for the women's reception, and they had to carry their bundle of signatures back to Chicago. The House did not disturb Payne's recommendations for gloves or hosiery. The only important change which the House made in the bill as Payne reported it affected petroleum. In spite of a fervid, arm-swinging argument by Cannon for continuation of the Dingley oil tariff, the Representatives, led by Norris, voted to admit petroleum and its products without duty. On the whole, however, the bill promised revision upward, and what Cannon had lost in the House he had a chance to recover in the Senate.

The Senate looked like a free institution. No Iron Duke in the pattern of Cannon directed its functioning. Its rules explicitly upheld the principle of absolute equality among members. Each of the ninety-two Senators had the right to speak for as long as he wished on whatever topics interested him. The committees could not be repressed. The long term of office, six years in contrast with the Representatives' two, ostensibly encouraged independence in every Senator.

Yet the appearance of absolute freedom was misleading. Almost all the Senators, excepting only a few from states which chose theirs through primaries and elections, owed allegiance to some particular group of men representing a special economic interest and social orientation, because, as the Constitution provided, they were elected by the state legislatures; and the legislatures were dominated in most cases by owners and managers of the greatest enterprises in the state. One could only say that each Senator was completely free to represent his sponsors to the best of his ability. In Massachusetts the makers, not the consumers, of cotton textiles and boots and shoes called the tune when the legislature chose its Senators. In Montana the senatorial kingpins were the owners of the mines, not the laborers in them. So the majority of Republican Senators in 1909 had a natural sympathy for the enterprisers who profited from the existence of a high protective tariff.

Most sympathetic of all was Nelson Aldrich, an urbane little gentleman of sixty-eight from Rhode Island, where he had made a fortune in traction. Aldrich, who had been in the Senate for twenty-eight years, was chairman of the Finance Committee, the counterpart of Ways and Means. He was a shameless standpatter. Working independently of Payne, he and Burrows drafted a bill so offensive to the consumer that LaFollette in his *Weekly* cried, "Take Aldrichism to the primaries," and exhorted his readers:

For the Senators of other states in which the people are supposed to rule to bow to the Aldrich power and accept the Aldrich dictation should be the signal for such an uprising of the voters in those states as shall forever put an end to the Aldrich rule in the United States Senate, by retiring the Senators who support that rulership.

LaFollette and six other Senators who owed no fealty to special interests or inflexible personal prejudice spent hours on the Senate floor, denouncing Aldrich's tariff on iron ore and iron scrap, on cotton, on lumber, on wool. They were LaFollette, Beveridge of Indiana, Cummins and Dolliver of Iowa, and Minnesota's Moses Clapp and Knute Nelson, the old Norwegian who had moved away from his countrymen in Dane County in order to keep his independence. But every amendment which they offered on behalf of the consumer the Senate voted down. They blamed Democrats who supported Aldrich for their defeats, but they would have lost had all the Democrats been on their side. The standpatters worked their will. They slipped a joker into Mann's provision for free wood pulp; it would not enter free, the Senate agreed, from countries which imposed export duties on pulp. Canada, the chief foreign source of pulp, did impose such duties. The Senate also raised Mann's duty on newsprint from $2.00 to $3.75 a ton.

The standpatters usually kept silent, while the seven progressives spoke at length. The protesting Republicans had all the time they wished for criticizing Aldrich's bill, although none could offer more than five amendments to it. They excited the country, but they did not influence their colleagues. When the Senate approved the bill on July 8, the seven steadfast progressives voted nay, but the standpatters outnumbered them. In the Senate they could not say that Czarism had beaten them.

The confident Cannon assumed that the standpatters would outnumber the progressives forever. Perhaps they would have done so if Cannon had given the progressives a free chance to show their strength or weakness in the House.

But the Aldrich bill only prodded Cannon to make a new display of despotism, and each act of despotism now won new allies to the progressives. He was harassed by uncertainty. Aldrich had shown that the progressives controlled only a small fraction of the votes in the Senate, and it seemed incredible to the Speaker that the discontent blowing east from the plains would be taken seriously by a majority of members of the House. At the same time a tiny shred of gnawing doubt that the progressives were as weak in the House as they were in the Senate began to pick at him.

The Representatives were growing restive by July because many of them had spent at home the seventy days which it took the Senate to act upon the bill, and they had discovered that their constituents were losing faith in the Republican Party out of disgust with the Congressional performance. The Speaker had resources for ascertaining the national sentiment without leaving Washington. "There isn't a publication of note anywhere that has a kind word to say for the measure (the tariff bill) in its present form," the *Washington Post* said in an editorial. "A newspaper? A ton of paper, a barrel of ink, and a typesetting machine, and that's all," said Cannon. "The publisher of a great newspaper," he said elsewhere, "may have thousands of readers, but he cannot destroy their political convictions or deliver their votes in the ballot box." He did not want to believe that the nation would ever turn away from the Republicans as long as the Republicans honored protection.

To make positively sure that traditional Republican principles survived, Cannon chose the six most thoroughly stand-pat members of the Ways and Means Committee to work out a compromise of the House and Senate differences with Aldrich, Burrows, and other Senators in the conference. In the group he included Joseph Fordney of Michigan, who had exclaimed in the spring, "I sweat blood every time they reduce a schedule." "If I had my way about it," Fordney also had said, "I would not make a change in the Dingley Law." The selection of Fordney was criticized because he stood well down in the list of membership of the Ways and Means Committee. So did William Alexander Calderhead of Marysville, Kansas, whom Cannon designated as one of Fordney's colleagues on the conference committee. Other Representatives whom Cannon did not name had served longer on Ways and Means. But the Speaker could take no chances of appointing some member who might at the wrong moment surrender to the clamor for revision in his home district and attempt to cut the duties.

Cannon's audacity in selecting House conferees for the sake of upholding the Senate bill bothered Taft. "I don't think that Cannon played square," he wrote to his brother Horace. The President had been napping through almost the whole long episode of the tariff debate in Congress. He trusted the leaders of Senate and House to carry out the promise which he had made for downward revision. When Aldrich was well along with his assignment of building a newer and higher tower of protection, Secretary of the Treasury Franklin MacVeagh, speaking on behalf of the President in Chicago, said that the tariff would be revised to suit the public taste, especially the taste of the Middle West. Not until the bill went to conference did Taft awake to the danger that a bill was being passed which would fill the Middle West with revolt. Then he showed a far greater capacity than Roosevelt ever had for persuading Uncle Joe Cannon to do what he did not want to do.

Taft insisted that the glove duty come down. Cannon said that he would defeat the bill unless the glove duty remained at the Littauer level, which the House had accepted. When Aldrich supported Taft, Cannon gave in. Taft said that the lumber tariff should not exceed $1.25 a thousand. The Senate bill taxed lumber at $2.00, and Cannon threatened to adjourn the House of Representatives without acting on the bill unless $2-lumber remained. Aldrich urged Taft to surrender, but Taft said that he would call Congress back into a new special session at once if the first special session failed to enact a satisfactory tariff. Again Cannon the invincible surrendered to the President.

But it was too late to change the bill in any fundamental way. Taft had slept over long. And after he exacted two concessions from the Speaker, he sought no more. He could not drive himself to fight. What a different world we might live in had Taft continued thereafter to assert himself with such skill and vigor! The tariff was revised upward. It was not Dingley all over again; it was more than Dingley. Instead of establishing a permanent tariff commission, the bill authorized the President to appoint a board of experts to help him administer the tariff, especially to help him apply that device beloved by the high protectionists, the maximum and the minimum. It did remove the duty from petroleum to Danville's woe. And it contained a novelty which, in an earlier year, Cannon might have had expunged. That was a tax of 1 per cent on the net incomes of corporations, which, at the request of Taft, Aldrich had inserted after the Finance Committee had deleted Payne's inheritance tax. Incidental to the tariff discussion, the House and Senate had approved (also at Taft's request) a resolution calling upon the states to amend the Constitution by authorizing the federal government to collect an income tax from individuals. That was the same year in which the British parliament approved Lloyd George's sensational budget, inaugurating a tax of seventeen pence to the pound on unearned wealth and on incomes exceeding fifteen thousand pounds a year, to help the government pay for the "pressing needs of social reform." The new tide which has reached its flood in our day was then beginning to run in the world.

Taft's tax policy was certainly a step in a new direction, but, with his bumbling genius for doing a good thing in a bad way, for striking when the iron was cold, he pleased neither the progressives nor the men of property. Believing that the tariff duties constituted a heavy tax on the poor, the progressives ardently wanted the enactment of an income tax law in 1909 in order to tax the rich. They grumbled that the President had proposed the corporation tax and a constitutional amendment that would authorize the imposition of an income tax at some future day only in order to prevent Congress from imposing an income tax immediately. "President Taft's host of admirers can drink to him no more gracefully than to express the wish that he may live until he gets the constitution amended," was one sarcastic progressive comment. While LaFollette complained that the corporations would simply force the consumers to pay the tax by charging higher prices for the goods which the corporations sold, Elbert Gary, president of the United States Steel Corporation, speaking as an inside authority on corporations, complained that the corporation tax was "extreme" and would encourage extravagance in government. Justice David J. Brewer of the United States Supreme Court, whose decisions showed his sympathy for corporate pleaders, remarked, with considerable prescience, that "if once you give the power to the nation to tax all incomes, you give it the power to tax the states, not out of their existence, but out of their vitality."

On the whole the discontented found little to praise in Cannon's tariff, which was known formally as the Payne-Aldrich Tariff. It was "a most unwarrantable re-enactment of special favors" and a "bare-faced violation of party pledges." In bitter disillusionment, some called it a swindle.

So Cannon triumphed again. The seven bitter-enders among the Senate Republicans voted against the bill in its final form—Beveridge, Bristow, Clapp, Cummins, Dolliver, LaFollette, Nelson—and twenty Republicans in the House voted against it. Offended by the refusal of the Senate and the conferees to follow his recommendations on pulp and newsprint, Jim Mann, the Speaker's faithful supporter, joined the Republicans on the nay side. Once more, however, Cannon was saved by the mystic sense of fealty which party membership imparts even to the most restless. A shift in six votes would have beaten the tariff in the House. Yet many progressives and insurgents who had opposed Cannon on the rules in March helped him on the tariff in August. They lost their nerve when they contemplated an action which might harm the party. The failure to pass the bill would be a fiasco for all Republicans, standpat and insurgent. Norris and Hal Cooper voted as Cannon voted—aye.

But Norris and Cooper paid for the sins they had committed in the spring. In the flush of victory Cannon drove his advantage home in the House by dismissing the most obstreperous progressives and other insurgents from the committees where they could do him harm. Cooper lost his chairmanship of Insular Affairs, and Norris lost his membership on Public Buildings and Grounds. Cannon removed Fowler as chairman of Banking and Currency, and he dropped Lindbergh from Indian Affairs. He put Lenroot to one side by assigning him to the inane Committee on Ventilation and Acoustics. He mixed rewards with punishment, always with an eye to defending his traditional principles from the onslaughts of discontent. He gave Fowler's place to the faithful Vreeland, and Mann, forgiven for his vote against the tariff, he named chairman of Interstate and Foreign Commerce. To confound the advocates of postal savings, he named John Weeks, a reliable young standpatter from Massachusetts, as chairman of the Post Office and Post Roads Committee. Cannon tried to grant the deserving members what they wanted. He appointed James Breck Perkins of New York chairman of Foreign Affairs, the very post which Fassett had requested for him the previous autumn in that letter which revealed the confidence of both Fasset and Perkins that Cannon would rout his enemies and maintain his privilege of naming the committees. Such faith deserved reward.

The momentum of victory now swept Cannon to heights of power which few Americans ever enjoyed. He became master of President and party. Where hitherto he had dictated what could not be done, now he determined what would be done. Taft perforce bowed to the Speaker's influence when he signed Cannon's tariff on August 5, 1909. That was the signal that the Republicans had failed the test of honor. The party's pledges meant what Cannon wished them to.

Taft was "a large good-natured body entirely surrounded by people who know exactly what they want," said Dolliver. Of all those knowing people Taft liked Cannon least and heeded him the most. Cannon will be the "incubus" of the Congressional election campaign in 1910, the President complained to his wife. He loathed Cannon as "vulgar," but Aldrich charmed him, and to repudiate Cannon on the tariff would mean repudiating Aldrich.

Cannon never became refined. When he arose to speak at the

banquet marking James Cardinal Gibbons' golden jubilee as a priest and silver jubilee as cardinal, he tossed the pages of his prepared address through the air in a kind of snowfall over the heads of the diners and then spoke half an hour ex tempore while he shook his left arm and pirouetted on his toes. At the White House one evening as a guest at dinner for Prince Chi Tao, brother of the regent of China, Cannon embarrassed Taft twice—first, when, upon being asked to walk over to the prince, in a distant corner of the drawing room, to be introduced, he said in a clear, carrying tone, "It goes against my pride for an American free-born citizen to cross a room to meet a heathen Chinee," and second, after dinner, when he sat with one arm about the prince's shoulder while he told amusing anecdotes about American politics and punctuated the stories with sharp digs of his left thumb into the royal ribs. Cannon's presence was "enough to ruin an evening" for Taft, but Taft, to put the progressives in their place, entertained Cannon with more formality in the evening than Roosevelt had.

That strange influence of party orthodoxy kept Taft in Cannon's thrall. The President found greater intellectual comfort in going along with the crowd, composed of the majority of the party office-holders who perfectly sympathized with Cannon and Aldrich, than in striking out boldly and alone to defend the proposition by which he had attracted enough votes to win the presidency —revision downward. Taft was not a man to seek glory in splendid solitude. The party irregulars led by LaFollette he damned as "yellow dogs." Cannon mastered Taft because Cannon's vigor and determination enabled him to define party orthodoxy. From time to time Uncle Joe was compared to Speaker Tom Reed, who ever served as Cannon's model as a parliamentarian. But Reed had used his sway over the House to bring about the realization of his party's platforms, principles, and pledges as approved by the people in the voting booth. Cannon used his authority to impose his own peculiar conception of Republican principles upon the party. Those principles Taft accepted because he dared not challenge Cannon for party leadership.

Taft was an honest man. He candidly told the public that he had put the party above his promise. In the middle of September he made a speaking tour that took him to the Pacific Coast. On the seventeenth he stopped in Winona, to say a good word for

Tawney, whose constituents, living in the midst of the region of discontent, were questioning his vote for the tariff. The new law is the "best tariff" which the country ever had, the President said. But he knew that where tariff laws were concerned, the "best" by no means necessarily meant "good." He explained that the principle of party fealty had prevented the "best" law from being a better law:

I believe that the interests of the country, the interests of the party, required me to sacrifice the accomplishment of certain things in the revision of the tariff which I had hoped for, in order to maintain party solidarity, which I believe to be much more important than the reduction of rates in one or two schedules of the tariff.

The speech electrified Cannon, for it opened his eyes to the possibility of reorganizing the Republican party without the progressives. Let his enemies identify themselves with the Democrats, and then he need no longer fear assault from party colleagues upon his position in the House or upon his principles in the country. In a letter which he wrote to Tawney the day after Taft's speech there he gave an inkling to what was on his mind:

I read with pleasure Taft's speech at Winona. It seems to me it was a very politic, forceful, square speech, and it ought to have the effect of strengthening the Republican Party all over the country. Of course, the Bryan party and the assistants of that organization will denounce it, and those who claim to be Republicans but constantly seek to betray the party will, it seems to me, be driven to forsake their position heretofore taken or to openly join the enemy.

The need for driving the progressives from the party was growing pressing. They refused to accept their defeats on the reorganization of the House and on the contents of the tariff bill. To save the good name of the party, they were planning in the primaries of 1910 to sweep the party clean of standpatters who had dishonored what they considered the promise of Chicago. It grew clear to the Speaker that he and his faction of the party faced a new struggle for survival. Victory had brought no rest. A few days after he wrote to Tawney, he talked with McKinley. Those two defenders of the nineteenth century decided that Taft had provided them with their best possible weapon against the progressives in his Winona speech, and McKinley wrote to Loudenslager, as secretary of the Republican Congressional Campaign Committee, an earnest exhortation to circulate a huge edition of the speech. "I want to impress on you," McKinley said, "that a policy of sitting down and waiting until the progressives have licked out all the stalwarts in the primary campaigns will not appeal very much to us in the central west. . . . If the Congressional Committee sits with their hands folded until October 1910, they will certainly have an opportunity in Kansas, Nebraska, Iowa, Minnesota, and Wisconsin of choosing between the LaFollette and Cummins nominees or the Democratic nominees."

In the safety of his own district Cannon could not consider the progressives a menace. "The kicker has his place," he told his constituents in Kankakee at the laying of the cornerstone for the new courthouse there on October 3. "He puts the men who are pulling the load on their good behavior. The kickers are like the wife in the story told by Lincoln. Her husband was a great big man and she a little bit of wife who was a vixen. She would hit him and scratch him and pound him and scold him. Somebody said, 'Jim, why do you let that little woman impose on you? Why don't you stop her? You could crush her with your hand.' 'Oh,' said Jim, 'never mind. It seems to give her comfort and it don't hurt me.' "

But he knew that he could not treat the western defection lightly. After the pleasant day at Kankakee, he visited the prairie states west of the Mississippi River to gauge the temper at first hand. He heard and read much criticism of himself as the embodiment of evil. The harsh words did not chasten him. He was proud of his independence. He was loyal to his principles. When he addressed the Association of Illinois Mayors at Elgin on October 19, he pulled back his coat and cried:

"Behold, Mr. Cannon, the Beelzebub of Congress. Gaze on this noble, manly form—me, Beelzebub, me, the Czar."

He then took up the party question:

I was over in Iowa last week and found that it is an open secret there that Senator Cummins not only proposes to join hands with Bryan, but he says the agitation will not stop and he will appeal to the people until the tariff is revised according to his notion. It is well known that Senator Cummins is out to defeat every member of Congress in Iowa who voted for the bill. In this campaign to be waged by Senator Cummins the issue appears to be whether the seven Senators and twenty members of the House who voted against the tariff bill constitute the Republican Party or whether the majority of Republican members of Congress and the President who signed the bill made up the Republican Party.

These people under the leadership of Senator Cummins and Senator LaFollette call themselves Republicans. But if they are, then I am something else.

He pursued the progressives into the heart of their domain. In November he addressed the Knife and Fork Club in Kansas City. "When Senators Cummins, LaFollette, and Bristow and their so-called 'progressive' following join hands with Mr. Bryan in making war upon the members of Congress who passed the tariff bill and upon the President who signed it, in that contest I know of but one way to treat them, and that is to fight them just as we fight Bryan and his following," he said. He denied that he had read anybody out of the party. But he recalled Republicans who "read themselves out" by supporting George B. McClellan against Lincoln in 1864, Horace Greeley and his Liberal Republicans against General Grant in 1872, Grover Cleveland against James G. Blaine in 1884, and William Jennings Bryan against McKinley in 1896. "Lucifers," he branded the progressives. He was the Angel Gabriel to whom they must answer.

Decline and Fall

THE CANNON who threatened to throw the progressives "over the battlements" of the Republican heaven was a desperate man. The signs were multiplying that in his policy toward the tariff he had gone at last too far. He was finally in danger of losing that power in his person which had enabled him to tyrannize through the rules and to take control of President Taft. He drew the power from two sources—his unwavering certainty that his policies furthered the interests of his country, and confidence that the conservatives who shared his opinions would always outnumber the progressives. Now, however, leading conservatives who had profited from Cannon's tyranny in the past were coming to the conclusion that the Speaker was a liability weakening their cause, which for years he had helped. From the tariff struggle he had emerged as the enemy of the very people themselves, in contrast to his earlier experiences in czarism, which seemed to pit him primarily against President Roosevelt and special groups rather than the public as a whole. Before the autumn of 1909 only a few of Uncle Joe's detractors had felt his heels directly on their necks. His manner in bludgeoning the dear tariff hopes of millions of Americans who until then had no intention of attaching themselves to LaFollette and Company planted the fear in the most determined enemies of LaFollette that Cannon was driving many mild supporters of conservatism over to the progressives, if not to the Democrats. He was giving conservatism a bad name. For that reason the conservatives began to hound the Speaker by forecasting disaster for political traditionalism if he, the symbol of traditionalism, continued in office. They had come to long even more poignantly than LaFollette for his abdication or removal from the chair.

The conservative drum-beat against Cannon began in *Harper's Weekly*, edited by George Harvey, immediately after enactment of the new tariff bill. Harvey, who loathed Theodore Roosevelt as a grand-standing usurper of the rights and privileges which the Constitution had bestowed on Congress and the Supreme Court, stood for property. In holding off Roosevelt, Cannon had served Harvey's interests, but the indignation which the Speaker aroused by his effort to help his friend Littauer and by his packing of the conference committee blinded Harvey to Cannon's usefulness. "If he would like to round out his career by conferring a special favor upon the country," Harvey wrote in his weekly magazine, "he can do so most easily by withdrawing entirely from public life." The *Wall Street Journal* joined in the conservative outcry: "The clock has struck for Uncle Joe. He is out of date, not because he is no longer young, but because he has ceased to be representative. He has stood between the people and too many things that they wanted and ought to have, and the fact that he has stood off some things that they ought not to have won't save him." Up on Lake Champlain an old conservative friend was having second thoughts. Representative Dave Foster of Vermont heard his constituents demanding a change in the Speakership, and his enthusiasm for Cannon, which he had expressed in verse two years earlier, dried up. "The moderate members [of the House] have consulted together as to the means of bringing about this change with the least friction and a minimum of peril to the party," the Burlington *Free Press*, leading paper in Foster's district, reported. Senator Lodge, a philosophical brother of Cannon and a strong supporter of Aldrich in guiding the high-protection bill through the Senate, heard the murmur against the Speaker and wrote Roosevelt: "It would be impossible in my judgment to elect a House if it was known that Cannon was again to be the Speaker if the Republicans won." Even Cannon's unwavering friends were saying, "The Old Man is losing his grip."

The Old Man continued to fight, privately and in public, for the perpetuation of the way of life he thought best, as though he did not read or hear the predictions of defeat. His slogan was, "No compromise." He refused to compromise even with the conservatives, including those who still upheld him, when they pressed views that he disliked, any more than he would curry favor from the progessives. Tawney entreated him to visit Winona and speak up for inland waterway development before the Upper Mississippi River Improvement Association, so that Tawney's constituents would find out that there was something on which they and the Speaker agreed. Cannon had always opposed the waterways, and he opposed them now, when to pretend that he supported them would have done him good. "I am hardly in favor with the policy of mortgaging the future for wholesale waterway developments," the Speaker wrote his old friend, who was hard-pressed in Minnesota. When the Minnesota Republican Congressmen returned home after the special session, the St. Paul *Pioneer Press* had given a monster reception to all of them but Tawney, who was not invited.

If he would not cross his principles to save Tawney, he might at least have solicited the help of the bankers, most of whom were rocks of conservatism, in overcoming the conservative timid souls who wanted to jettison him. Aldrich now favored the establishment of a central bank, under government supervision, which the city bankers themselves wanted. But not Cannon, and he told the bankers so straight out when he addressed the convention of the American Bankers Association in Chicago in September 1909. He announced that he was opposed to radical changes in existing currency laws and declared that there would be no possibility of Congress' revising the Vreeland-Aldrich Act at the forthcoming session. In passing, he reminded the three thousand five hundred bankers present that they were but a spoke in the immense wheel of the nation.

"Just exactly how it was possible for Mr. Joseph G. Cannon . . . to stand before the several thousand bankers of the country holding and expounding the arguments which he did is incomprehensible," the *American Banker* commented. "That he should declare there would be no action on the part of Congress toward currency reform was an affront not to the bankers, nor alone to the advocates of so necessary a movement, but to the whole of the people of the country. That he should proclaim the present bond-secured method satisfactory for the nation shows either supreme ignorance of the first principles of a circulating medium, or interests devoted to other than the advancement of the legitimate business of the nation." Few bankers cared thereafter whether bad luck befell Cannon.

Many newspapers and magazines of large circulation managed by essentially conservative men continued to follow the anti-Cannon line which they had inaugurated in the controversy over the tariff on pulp and paper and which, for some of them, had broadened out into a general interest in reform. The pulp and news-print schedules in Cannon's tariff failed to soothe them. The province of Quebec, the chief Canadian source of pulp for newsprint made in the United States, in September 1909 forebade the export of pulp. Ridder protested vainly to Taft. Already the *Saturday Evening Post,* the *American Magazine, Everybody's* and *Cosmopolitan* were hammering the Speaker and praising the idea that the nation could progress through legislative action. *Collier's* weekly magazine assigned its progressive correspondent in Washington, Mark Sullivan, to the task of conducting polls to prove that the country did not want Cannon. The Speaker's tariff policy killed all possibility of Lawyer Beale's again browbeating Medill McCormick into supporting Cannon with the Chicago *Tribune.* The *Tribune* foresaw a sectional struggle between the states of the upper Mississippi and Missouri Valleys on the one hand and the mill owners' New England and the bankers' New York on the other. New England and New York, it claimed, imposed the tariff on Congress and nation, although Cannon asserted that the trans-Allegheny states had more industry and received greater benefits from the tariff law than did New England. How reminiscent of complaints against New England made by the free trade South in another sectional despute! "The tariff can be revised and revised properly," the *Tribune* said, "and this may be accomplished in the next Congress by retiring standpatters and electing in their stead men of progressive tendencies." The greatest paper in the West belonged to Cannon's enemies, and so did most of the lesser papers.

A charge of corruption against Cannon made by a member of the

House qualified to succeed Cannon as Speaker, Herbert Parsons of New York, fed the editorial attacks on the Old Man. Parsons on October 2 attributed the pro-Cannon votes by Fitzgerald and his Tammany colleagues during the rules fight in March to a deal made in Albany, New York, between the leaders there of the state Republican and Democratic organizations. He said that the Republicans, in payment for Democratic support of Cannon, agreed to prevent enactment by the state legislature of pending bills for increasing the penalties in cases of election fraud and for subjecting the telegraph and telephone companies to the control of the state government. The New York *Post* embroidered Parsons' charges with a hint that any deals in Albany affecting Washington might have been arranged through Lucius Littauer, who remained a strong figure among New York Republicans, with an eye to his glove tariff. The charges were never proved. "I don't like to make a hullabaloo about it," Cannon said when he heard what Parsons had said. "When I first used to go hunting as a boy along the Wabash, I saw one kind of animal that I never had seen before, and kicked at it. I was weeks in recovering, and since that time I have never kicked at that kind of animal in private life or politics." But the progressives and their cheer leaders used Parsons as a new club for lambasting Cannon. William Allen White, the editor from Emporia, Kansas, announced that he believed the accusation. "The people are tired of Cannon," he said. "They are going to retire him from public life. Before the end of the Taft Administration the progressive element of the Republican Party will be in control."

The progressives gave promise of bearing out White's predictions and the conservatives' fears by fattening on Cannon's denunciations of them. In August and September the progressives had been blaming Aldrich about as much as they blamed the Speaker for the repudiation of the tariff promise. But Cannon stood out alone as the supreme enemy of the discontented, without peer, as soon as he undertook to excommunicate the few Republicans who voted nay on the tariff. In the speeches at Elgin and Kansas City, supplemented by others in the same bold vein at Des Moines and Oak Park, Illinois, Cannon confirmed for many Americans the reports that he was a despot by nature. He seemed to be flaunting his villainy. It was arrogant in Cannon to set himself up as the censor of the party, not so much because he lacked formal title to the position but because it violated American custom. In the United States every man was free to join and speak up for whatever party he wanted. The two great parties were great because they had room in them for all sorts of men who disagreed on principles. The problem of the American political leader was then and is now not to eject his unsympathetic party colleagues but to tie together all the quarreling cats and dogs and drakes and foxes who wear the same party costume. If the political leader cannot tie them together by dominating them all, he has to try to do it by compromises with them all.

Cannon had squandered so much of the good feeling which Congress and the country lavished on him at his seventieth birthday party that he could not possibly dominate all the factions in the party, and his crusade for Republican fundamentalism made it unthinkable that he would attempt to compromise with the anti-fundamentalists. So the shout of "Lucifers!" sounded like the defiant cry of a cornered man, and the leaders of the progressives welcomed the speeches as signs of Cannon's decline. LaFollette wrote in his *Weekly* that the Speaker's remarks were the "snarlings of a grim old wolf who hears the beaters in the woods and scents them closing in." Charges that they were disloyal to the party invigorated the westerners instead of unnerving them, because they aimed by their rebellion to liberate party members from the custom of denying their dictates of conscience in order to follow a party leader. "Western Republicans . . . are not as deeply concerned as President Taft declares himself to be about party solidarity," the St. Paul *Pioneer Press* said. "One of the fundamental principles of insurgentism . . . is that each Representative is responsible to his constituents for his actions in Congress and not to any party organization," said Representative Gronna of North Dakota. Instead of frightening the progressives into seeking peace with the standpatters, Cannon only pricked them into flaunting their independence. Cummins, addressing the Marquette Club in Chicago on November 6, 1909, gave the Lucifers' reply to Cannon:

Let it be understood once and for all that we accept the challenge and are ready for the fight. Our struggle will not be to exclude anybody from the Republican Party, but upon the principle involved we ask no quarter and shall give none. The day has come for an inquiry into the qualifications of a Republican. I am willing to accept an arbiter, but it will not be Aldrich, it will not be Payne, it will not be Cannon. The Republicans in sympathy with the course pursued by the insurgents intend to take away from these men some of the power which they now exercise, and intend to reduce their influence to that point at which they will feel it necessary to consult rather than to command.

The Iowan stated his text at the Marquette Club in the form of a question: "Are Aldrich and Payne with their associates . . . the Republican Party, or are the insurgents the Republican Party?" He then defined the progressives' attitude toward both party and the tariff: "I am astounded to hear so modest a man as the Speaker of the House claim that the leaders who constructed the tariff bill and the majority who passed it constitute the Republican Party. . . . I am sure that this is the first time they have become so intoxicated with their power as to imagine that they constitute the Republican Party. If Mr. Cannon and his allies shall be successful in putting every man out of the Republican Party who would not have voted for the tariff bill had he been a member of Congress, he will have eliminated a majority of the Republicans in every northern state from Ohio to the Rocky Mountains. The mere fact that the duties of the Dingley Law had become excessive would not have been a sufficient reason for a revision of the tariff, unless there had been coupled with it another vital fact, namely, that in many of the most important fields of industry, domestic production had been wholly suppressed or substantially impaired, so that the prices were fixed not by the ordinary forces of trade, but by the arbitrary will of one producer or a combination of producers. To say that the tariff bill just adopted is not a fulfillment of the Republican platform is only the truth. . . . The Republicans who insist that import duties shall not furnish monopolies and combinations an opportunity to exact unfair prices are the best and truest friends that the policy of protection has among the people of the United States. In my judgment, when competition goes, our form of government will go with it. The protection which rivalry in business gives to the people is the one barrier that socialism cannot cross."

The voice and the words were Cummins', but the intrepid con-

fidence of the progressives in taking advantage of Cannon's attacks on them represented a triumph above all for LaFollette.
The organization of the discontent into a coherent political movement was his work. Years before Cummins left Iowa for Washington, LaFollette was standing bravely alone in the federal
Senate as the national symbol of New Idea Republicanism. Then
his fellow Senators seldom voted with him, and few of them respected him. Again and again he interrupted his speeches at the
Capitol to glower at the contemptuous conservatives who
whispered and laughed while he spoke. But he was patient, and
now he had six allies in the Senate and perhaps thirty in the House.
By his Chautauqua lectures and campaigning through all the
West, LaFollette encouraged the bashful yearners for reform to
come forth boldly and state their cause. Without him the country
would indeed have been riven with discontent, but the discontent might never have found a focus if he had followed all his
life the moderate course which marked his early career. By planting a sense of unity of interest in the West from Lake Michigan
to the Black Hills (and even to the Cascades) and from Lake
Superior to southern Kansas, he made possible the insurgent alliance in the House and the Senate. He not only exhorted the
western voters to send independent Republicans to Congress, but
from his Senate rooms he guided those western independents in
their rebellion in the House against Cannon.

While the rebels so far had failed to remove or curb the Speaker,
LaFollette methodically continued to win new supporters in the
West for the ideas which the Speaker opposed and from which
the rebellion drew its strength. The summer's tariff defeat at the
hands of Aldrich, Payne, and Cannon only sharpened his hunger
for victory. He was as unyielding and indomitable as Cannon himself. This man of iron never gave way to the Speaker's push like
Roosevelt. He was the evangelist of discontent. After the Senate
adjourned in August, he went about the country preaching the
iniquity of Cannon's tariff and calling upon Republicans to vote
the conservatives out of office. He was a stern-faced and tight-
lipped and coldly righteous character, but his oratory was warm
and beautiful, and it drove home. His visit to Spokane in the
autumn of 1909 to speak in the Hall of Doges and the First Methodist Church at the invitation of Representative Poindexter was

the signal for the editors of small dailies in eastern Washington to establish the Progressive Republican League in formal defiance of the traditional Republican tendencies. "This is a great national movement that is rapidly crystallizing, and this organization is only an evidence of the way the movement is taking shape," Rufus Woods, editor of the Wenatchee *World* and president of the League, said.

Cannon made possible the crystallization. Ideologically LaFollette never had many true-hearted followers. Even in Wisconsin it was always touch and go. But he brilliantly exploited the disgust with the Speaker. The growth of LaFollette's following proved the soundness of Dave Foster and other conservatives in fearing that Cannon was driving Americans to progressivism. The gradual transformation of the public conception of the Speaker from a likable frontiersman who symbolized the great American tradition to a harsh despot who stood for evil brought together a host of Americans who became anti-conservatives, and at least temporarily progressives, because they were anti-Cannonites. Such are the positive uses of villainy. The newspaper publishers and magazine editors were more responsible than LaFollette for the revulsion against the Speaker. But LaFollette's progressivism gave the antis an affirmative interest when they did not know where to turn as they recoiled from the standard-bearer of tradition, and this sense of affirmation made them a force to be reckoned with. Thus LaFollette and Cannon together pointed the way to America's future.

The long pursuit of Cannon by LaFollette and others seemed to be nearing its end when the second session of the Sixty-first Congress convened in December. Only custom stood between the insurgents and their quarry. It was the custom not to remove the Speaker or to change the rules once the House was organized for the two-year term. Yet observance of that custom in 1909 would leave things as they were until March 1911, or perhaps December 1911, when the next Congress would meet for the first time, and the popular reaction to the tariff and the rapid decline of Cannon's personal power made some leaders of the insurgents impatient to close out the whole business. The St. Paul *Pioneer Press* early in November had given the needle to progressives immobilized by custom. "Very likely a great many of the members, if not nearly all, will try to tell us that Cannon cannot be ousted now, but must serve the term for which he has been elected, but that will depend upon how many want to get rid of him," the paper said. "We do not believe there is anything impossible about it. If there is, so much the worse for the important majority when the voting time comes." Murdock of Kansas, the "chief insurgent" in the House, agreed with the *Pioneer Press*. "If the Constitution of the United States had said that Congress should consist of the Senate and the Speaker, it would never have been ratified," said Murdock. He returned to Washington from Wichita after Thanksgiving with a petition calling on Uncle Joe to resign the Speakership. If he could get the signatures of a majority of the members of the House on his petition, he was sure that Cannon would quit the chair for good. But the custom slowed down the collection of names. And some men who had long served under the Speaker still feared him, while others who hated the tyranny loved the tyrant for his stout heart.

The insurgents themselves disagreed, moreover, about the best means for achieving their aims. Murdock insisted that they could get rid of Cannonism and remove the barricade to progressive legislation only by getting rid of Cannon. He wanted a new Speaker in order to liberate the members of the House from their "pitiable" condition as "advisers and petitioners" to Cannon. LaFollette agreed with him.

Norris of Nebraska, on the other hand, argued that it would be enough to amend the rules to remove the Speaker's control over the Rules Committee and to deprive him of the privilege of appointing the membership of all committees. Gussie Gardner hemmed and hawed in doubt about the wisdom of doing anything at all about Cannonism in 1909 or 1910. He was caught by the dilemma of the non-progressive insurgent. His bitter memories of the immigration bill and his concern for the survival of real representative processes disposed him to fight for Cannon's removal. But his disapproval of the radical ideas that were popular in the West disposed him to flee from the progressives. He especially feared the notion, supported by LaFollette, of the initiative and referendum, because it might "destroy representative government." He wanted at the most to hold the door open for the Speaker to withdraw quietly under his own steam, to save the party from the dangerous fight that would be necessary to drive the Old Man from his chair. "I told Norris . . . that he could depend on me to support him in matters of the rules at any time he notified me," Gardner wrote his friend E. E. Gaylord, "although . . . I personally would prefer a truce for the present."

By December the insurgents abandoned what shreds were left of their illusion that Taft, whom in midsummer they had still considered a good-hearted progressive, had not succumbed to Cannonism. The Speaker and the President in the autumn had traveled down the Mississippi River together in a show of genial camaraderie, and both had made speeches that discouraged the waterway people. Taft often puzzled Cannon at the tag end of his presidential term, when Taft became less and less of a regular party man. Taft appointed Edward D. White, a Democrat from Louisiana as Chief Justice, and Cannon remarked: "If Taft were Pope, he would name some Protestants to the College of Cardinals." But he spoke well of Taft in 1909 and 1910. "Here's a toast to Taft," he wrote to J. Van Vechten Olcott of New York. "May he continue to disappoint both extremes, and, in patience and soberness, work out the policies of the great majority of the people who placed the responsibility on him, heeding neither the demands of those who want to blow up the engine, nor the fears of those who would have the fires under the boiler put out. And I have confidence in his ability to do it."

When the House reformers sought an audience with the President to discuss the Speakership, he rebuked them. Lenroot, Norris, and Clarence Miller of Minnesota complained that the President was withholding patronage from them, although Murdock had no such trouble. Jim Sherman continued to pay through Taft his debt to Cannon for the vice presidential nomination. Taft was making a personal companion of Sherman, who remained a standpatter.

The progressives as a result did not give the President credit for being serious when at the opening of the new Congressional session he recommended a legislative program that Cannon could not swallow—government regulation of corporations, physical valuation of the railroads, postal savings, conservation, and restriction of the issuance of injunctions in labor cases. He still wanted a permanent tariff commission. What was not "socialism" for Cannon in that list was "populism," and the committees as Cannon had organized them would never approve the proposition while Cannon had his power. But Taft would not repudiate Cannon. The President was caught in a strong web. Because he had told Theodore Roosevelt that he would do both, he simultaneously advocated reform and placated the great enemy of reform, Speaker Cannon.

Discouraged by Taft, the insurgents decided to go it alone. As long as no opportunity to oust the Speaker presented itself, no disagreement between Murdock and Norris shook their united front. The rules still prevented them from initiating action in the House, but they waited for a chance to trip the Speaker if he should try to take the initiative in any matter. They wanted to prove their strength.

The chance came on January 7, 1910, when the House authorized an investigation of the Department of the Interior and the Forest Service. It was the perfect issue on which Cannon and the insurgents could divide, for at stake was the question of conservation, on which the non-progressive and progressive insurgents stood together. Cannon was as thoroughly opposed to the establishment of federal land and forest reserves in 1910 as he had been in 1908. Since the time he denied Roosevelt's requests for authority to establish the Appalachian and White Mountain national forests under federal aegis, Cannon had had Tawney put another crimp in the conservation movement by forbidding any government bureau, office, division, or department to lend its employes to the Conservation Commission—which the governors' conference on conservation at the White House in May 1908 had founded. He thus prevented the commission from functioning.

Roosevelt in January 1909 had got around Cannon's antipathy for conservation laws by letting James R. Garfield, his Secretary of the Interior, remove about one million five hundred thousand acres from the roster of public lands available for private purchase. This western acreage embraced many water sites in which electric power companies were interested. Richard Ballinger of Seattle, whom Taft in March 1909 appointed to be Garfield's successor, restored the acres to the lists of land subject to private pur-

chase, and thereby precipitated a row with Gifford Pinchot, the
Forester. Ballinger said that there was no law to sanction Garfield's action, but the outcry of the conservationists prompted him
to reverse himself. Ballinger and Pinchot buffeted one another
again in August, when they spoke on successive days at the National Irrigation Congress in Spokane. Pinchot ardently recommended that the western lands be kept out of the possession of
great capitalistic proprietors. "There could be no better illustra-
tion of the eager, rapid, unwearied absorption by capital of the
rights which belong to all the people than the water power trust,
not yet formed but in rapid process of formation," said Pinchot.
The control of water power meant the control of irrigation as well
as control of sources of electricity. On the other hand, said Ballinger: "It is not the policy of the national government to hinder
or interfere with the investment of private capital in the construction of irrigation works, but rather to lend it encouragement." The
two men completely disagreed, but Ballinger's statement struck
a sweet chord for Cannon. Mormon settlers had once called Joe
"Slasher Cannon" because he refused to approve a federal grant
for irrigation in Utah.

The differences between Pinchot and Ballinger grew critical
when Louis R. Glavis, special agent in the Land Office in Seattle,
accused Ballinger of issuing with unseemly haste patents on coal
lands in Alaska the owners of which had employed Ballinger as
counsel. Ballinger denied that he had been dishonest, and Pinchot
backed Glavis. Taft in September exonerated Ballinger. Pinchot
in December wrote Senator Dolliver a letter in defense of Glavis.
When Dolliver read the letter on the Senate floor, Taft fired Pinchot as Forester. This row in the Taft official family prompted the
introduction in the House of a resolution calling for an investigation by the House and Senate of both Ballinger's Interior Department and Pinchot's Forest Service, and the House approved it.

The insurgents stood by Pinchot. They expected that Cannon,
given a free hand, would assist Ballinger. Pinchot, "the millionaire with a mission," whose interest in protecting the out-of-doors
grew from his passion for fishing in streams and ponds in the
woods and from his father's admiring comments on the forestation
of northern France by Louis XIV, spoke the progressive language.

"Rigid construction of the law works, and must work, in the vast majority of cases, for the men who can hire the best lawyers and who have the sources of influence in lawmaking at their command," he said in comment on Ballinger's reluctance to act without statutory authority. "Strict construction necessarily favors the great interests as against the people, and in the long run cannot do otherwise. Wise execution of the law must consider what the law ought to accomplish for the general good."

Cannon and the insurgents collided in the Pinchot case over the selection of the members of the committee of the investigation. By custom Cannon would appoint the House members. But the insurgents feared that he would name men predisposed to exonerate Ballinger and damn Pinchot. To thwart such a possibility, Norris offered an amendment to the resolution for investigation that would direct the House to elect, and not the Speaker to select, the committee. Cannon was absent when Norris rose, and Walter I. Smith of Iowa, Sherman's successor on the Rules Committee, a pleasant but not alert standpatter, recognized him without sensing danger. More than thirty of Cannon's reliable Republicans were absent. Norris and twenty-five other insurgents joined the Democrats present in voting for the amendment, which carried with three votes to spare. Thus the Speaker suffered his first notable defeat, (but the committee of Senators and Representatives exonerated Ballinger of misconduct).

Spirited by that success, Norris prepared himself to meet the greater opportunity, which he hoped would arise some day, for a direct onslaught against the Speaker's powers. Norris had suffered much ill-treatment at Cannon's hand. When he asked the Speaker for membership on the Judiciary Committee, the Speaker told him to "get a reputation." Cannon cut him dead whenever they met, even when they rode together in one of the Capitol's tiny elevators. In 1908 the Republican Congressional Campaign Committee declined to help him in his campaign for re-election. Nevertheless, he held to his position that the quarrel over the Speakership was a quarrel about rules and not about Cannon as a person. For two years he had carried in the pocket of whatever suit he was wearing a resolution to amend the rules. It read:

The Committee on Rules shall consist of fifteen members, nine of whom shall be members of the majority party and six of whom shall be members of the minority party, to be selected as follows:

The states of the Union shall be divided by a committee of three, elected by the House for that purpose, into nine groups, each group containing, as near as may be, an equal number of members belonging to the majority party. The states of the Union shall likewise be divided into six groups, each group containing, as near as may be, an equal number of members belonging to the minority party [with one Rules Committee member to be chosen from each group]. . . .

The Committee on Rules shall elect its own chairman.

The Speaker shall not be eligible to membership on said Committee.

All rules or parts thereof inconsistent with the foregoing resolution are hereby repealed.

From January onward Norris made it a point to attend every meeting of the House in wait for the moment when he could present his resolution. The weeks went by, and no chance arose. Cannon managed the House as firmly as ever, and he repented nothing. On March 15 he wrote a letter to George C. Rankin, president of the Illinois Republican Editorial Association, praising the tariff of 1909.

On the following day Norris thought for a moment that at last his chance had come. It was Wednesday, the day which, by Rule XXIV, was reserved for consideration of legislation on committee calendars. Judge Edgar Crumpacker of Indiana, the stand-pat chairman of the Census Committee, seemed to violate the rule by asking consideration of a resolution permitting the classification in the census of foreign-born Americans by their mother tongues as well as by country of origin. It would enable a Polish-American to identify himself to the census-taker as a Pole and not as a Russian, and the Irish-American could call himself Irish instead of British. The merit of the bill, however, did not interest the House. Its presentation on Wednesday jeopardized the one chance the members had of dragging bills forth from their tombs in the committees, and they wanted no other business to come before them.

With Norris listening, Cannon said that it was proper for Crumpacker to present his resolution, because it involved a "higher question than the rules—the Constitution." The Constitution directed the federal government to enumerate the inhabitants, and, said Cannon, "the fixed law of the land—the Constitution—of course overrides any rule that the House might make for its procedure although it is true that the Constitution empowers the House to make rules for the conduct of its business." Cannon had precedents for his ruling, but the House rejected them and refused 112 to 163 to consider Crumpacker's resolution on Calendar Wednesday. When the vote was completed, Norris put a question to Representative Marlin E. Olmsted of Pennsylvania, a stand-patter to whom Cannon had given Hal Cooper's old place as chairman of Insular Affairs.

"I want to ask the gentleman on the constitutional proposition, if his theory is right, would it not follow that this would be in order even though there was no report of a committee on the resolution?" Norris asked.

Blithe Olmsted, sensing no trap, replied:

"It has been so held in election cases as to the right of a member. It was so ruled by Speaker Reed."

"Any member could come in with a bill," Norris continued, "that had not even been printed and take up the time of the House on the ground that it was an amendment to the census?"

Growing wary, Olmsted replied that the member would have to bring the matter up in a regular way, and that the resolution should have the approval of a committee.

The next day was the Feast of St. Patrick. When the clerk called the roll, more than one hundred members were absent. They had left for home to enjoy the long week end; many of them, indeed, had been gone all week. Most of the absentees were Republicans, and Cannon, Tawney, Dalzell, Payne, Mann, Olmsted, and Walter Smith had been discussing the invocation of an old rule to fine absentees. The Democrats and insurgents had been able to send the legislative appropriation bill back to the committee for improvements because too few regular Republicans had been present to defeat the action.

The stand-pat leaders were still turning this problem over in their minds when the bells rang at noon for the convening of the day's session. Crumpacker opened the proceedings of Thursday by presenting the census bill that the House had refused to consider on Wednesday. Again Cannon stated that the bill was privileged, "notwithstanding the rules of the House," because it would carry out a requirement of the Constitution. The Speaker's ruling decreed that measures privileged under the Constitution could be called up at any time. The House upheld the Speaker, 201 to 72.

Norris voted against the ruling. Then, while the clerk continued through the alphabet in the call of the roll, he wrote out on the back and front of an old envelope the resolution which he had nursed for two years. At last his day was here. When the Speaker announced that the Crumpacker resolution was adopted, Norris jumped to his feet and waved his envelope in the air.

"Mr. Speaker," he said, "I present a resolution made privileged by the Constitution."

Cannon did not recognize the voice of doom when he heard it.

"If it is a resolution made privileged by the Constitution," he said, "the gentleman will present it."

The clerk read the fateful words that foretold, if the House approved them, the end of the strangest tyranny in American history —tyranny conducted by due process.

Cannon looked as calm as though he had heard a motion to adjourn on a dull day. The members present sat in absolute quiet, stunned, except Dalzell, the keeper of the rules.

"I make the point of order that it is not in order," said Dalzell. "It is not privileged."

"We have just decided by a vote of the House a census bill coming under the Constitution," Norris said. "It is a privileged question, and it is entitled to consideration, notwithstanding that it conflicts with the rules of the House.

"Now Article I, Section 5, Paragraph 2 of the Constitution reads as follows:

"'Each House may determine the rules of its proceedings.'

"I submit, Mr. Speaker, if the action of the House makes a census bill privileged because of the Constitution, then any proposal to amend the rules must be privileged by virtue of the same instrument."

The situation had become clear to all by the time Norris concluded. Those present stood at Armageddon. The war against Cannonism, long suppressed first by the popularity and then by the skill of the Speaker, was in progress, and Oscar Underwood of Alabama, the Democratic floor leader, cried out for blood.

"The time has come, gentlemen," he said, "if you propose to

amend these rules, to vote to make a proposition to amend them in order. . . . I do not believe in allowing a set of rules to bind my hands when that set of rules is no longer of benefit to my constituency and the American people."

The debate on the nominally great question of constitutionality which followed was idle and lifeless. Everybody knew that the quality of the arguments would have no effect on the decision. Numbers would determine the outcome. Cannon certainly would uphold Dalzell, Norris would appeal to the members to overturn the ruling, and whether Cannon or Norris emerged the victor would depend on who outnumbered whom at the moment the question was put to the vote—the regulars or the combination of insurgents and Democrats. So instead of heeding the remarks issuing from their colleagues, the members speculated whether Cannon would be able to lure back to Washington enough holiday-minded regulars to sustain him in this dark hour.

The Republican supporters of Norris continually marveled at their own daring and devoted large portions of their speeches to bucking up one another. "We have no cause to fear," said John Mandt Nelson. "The people are with us. The House machine is not the Republican party." By then the sun was setting, and when Nelson had spoken, Cannon turned the chair over to Dalzell. The old Speaker hitched down the lobby to his rooms to assess his situation. With Asher Hinds he consulted the precedents. Faithful Tawney was with him, and Payne. But had other old-timers who had helped him when he was powerful abandoned him now that he was weak? Where was Bill McKinley? Among the absent was husky Diekema, who once had fled from a committee room for Cannon's sake to kill a quorum. What of Henry Sherman Boutell, who had placed Cannon's name before the convention in 1908 for the presidency? Where was he now?

Aside from immediate surrender, the Speaker had only one course to follow. He must conduct a filibuster in order to postpone decision until he had got the stalwarts back in the capital. He had the privilege of postponing the ruling until he felt like making it. "We cannot ask the Speaker to pass on it till he is ready," said Norris.

So the struggle over the Norris resolution became a contest between the stubbornness of the Speaker and the physical fitness of his followers. The Democrats and insurgents tried to exhaust the standpatters by keeping the House in continuous session while the Speaker waited for his reinforcements to arrive from the States.

At dinnertime Tawney made a motion to recess until eleven o'clock the following morning. He was defeated, 147 to 142. At 10 P.M. the filibuster was eight hours old. Dalzell, ever prim, sat in the chair as straight and neat as a nun in her school room. Champ Clark twitted him:

"Mr. Speaker, it seems to me, with all due deference to the chair, that the chair must have information by this time of night to rule on this question. If the chair has not received enough parliamentary information to rule on this question, he has picked up a great deal of valuable information on other subjects."

The House chamber took on the appearance of a luxurious flop house. Snoring members slumped in their seats. A few Democrats and insurgents who kept their eyes open ate sandwiches. The stenographic reporters relieved one another in endless relay to take down the mumbled irrelevant observations of a succession of sleepy debaters.

At 1:30 A.M. Tawney moved that the House recess until 11:55. Again he was beaten, 141 to 134. With that roll call finished, Republicans began quietly to drift through the doors. Ten minutes later twenty-five of them had departed. Tawney made the point that the House lacked a quorum.

Dalzell counted one hundred and fifty-four members present, which meant less than a quorum. But Underwood foiled Tawney's hopes that the absence of a quorum would force a recess and enable all to sleep. The Democrats intended to stretch the standpatters to the breaking point. Underwood moved that the sergeant-at-arms be instructed to arrest the absentees and bring them to the bar of the House, and the House approved the motion.

In his rooms across the corridor from the chamber Cannon reclined on his red couch to sleep and strengthen himself for the contest ahead. But it was a restless night, interrupted by conferences with his courtiers. They grew timid and began to feel that the cause was hopeless. Olmsted and Smith, the newcomers in the court circle, suggested compromise. Cannon might save his own membership on the Rules Committee if he would agree at once to an enlargement of the committee. The Speaker's God-damns filled the air, and talk of compromise ceased.

Tawney, Payne, Mann, and Dalzell alone stood by him in absolute sympathy. Having alienated Cannon's enemies in the House, President Taft refused to help the Speaker thwart those enemies. Taft was in Erie, Pennsylvania, when he received the news of the struggle in the House.

"Even if they don't beat him this time," he said to Archie Butt, his military aide, "it indicates one thing: That the Old Man has got to go and that he can never be elected to the Speakership again, if indeed he can retain his seat in Congress. . . .

"But it is fine to see how he is fighting. That is the quality I admire most in Uncle Joe. He does put up a good fight."

The insurgents and Democrats wasted the night in carping at the standpatters and in upbraiding Casson, the sergeant-at-arms, because his deputies failed to bring in the missing with satisfactory speed. They could have served their own interests better during that ghostly time by discussing their next step if they should carry the Norris resolution.

The problem turned on the person of Cannon. Did they want him to continue as Speaker or not? Norris held to his purpose of opposing the Speaker only on the highest and most impersonal plane. Murdock, however, saw clearly that the anti-Cannon voters would blame progressive as well as standpat Republicans if Cannon remained in the chair. Haugen of Iowa feared that the ousting of Cannon would harm the progressives by creating sympathy for the Speaker, as Cannon's constituents had rallied around him in 1908 when they concluded that the drys were treating him unjustly. The incensed Democrat, Burleson, who had been fuming inwardly for two years at the unfairness of the Speaker, longed for the chance to unseat him. Democrat Clark wisely understood that his party needed Cannon in the chair, where he would continue to represent Republicanism and overshadow those men among his party colleagues who, by the progressive standards of the time, deserved national support.

"He is our most valuable asset in the impending campaign," said Clark of Cannon. But Clark did not pass that sound opinion on to his party colleagues. He did not try to ascertain whether Murdock or Burleson intended to move for the dismissal of Cannon from the chair. They did not select a candidate for the Speakership to succeed Cannon. They all merely sat out the night in wait for Cannon's reappearance from his rooms.

The Speaker returned to the chair at 7 A.M. His grey hair was rumpled. In place of a collar and tie he wore two collars, one over the other. His shirt hung open. He had spent a few hours napping, but most of the night he had been telephoning and telegraphing the absent courtiers.

The tempers in the House were growing short. The little band of valiants who had stayed through the night were hungry and dirty. Casson's efforts to drag a quorum from bed had failed, and Underwood in irritation complained that the sergeant-at-arms was "thwarting the will of the House." He threatened to discipline the sergeant by a point of order if things did not improve.

"The gentleman does not seem to know a point of order from a hole in the ground," said Payne.

The standpat Republicans were tired and cross but not exhausted by the vigil, and at 10 A.M. the Democrats gave up the effort to break them physically. They agreed to recess until 4 P.M.

The ensuing six hours tried Cannon's spirit. Only a few friends rallied to him. McKinley and Boutell and eighteen other Republicans gave up their holiday at his request, but they were not enough. When it became plain in midafternoon that he could not get the votes, Cannon faced the fact and, upon the reconvening of the House at 4 P.M., announced:

"The Chair is prepared to rule upon the question of order made by the gentleman from Pennsylvania [Dalzell] upon the motion made by the gentleman from Nebraska [Norris]."

Tawney moved, and the House agreed, to recess until the following morning. The action suited the insurgents and Democrats because they were confident that men whom Cannon had been unable to reach that afternoon he would not reach by morning. They all needed sleep to fit them for the final test of strength that would follow the Speaker's disclosure of his ruling.

Cannon spent the night again in his rooms at the Capitol. He must remain near the scene of battle. But Neal, his servant, brought him clothes from his house, and his hair was neatly combed, his beard brushed, his coat clean and unrumpled when he walked to his chair the following morning. His voice was steady as he spoke, but he spoke without those strange yet familiar contortions of the body with which he punctuated most of his public addresses. He was calm only when he was nervously determined to prove that he was at ease.

"To give all subjects [mentioned in the Constitution] constitutional privilege would be to establish chaos in the House," he began.

The identical question had arisen on December 13, 1878, and Speaker Randall had decided then that a proposition to amend the rules was not a case of constitutional privilege. (Randall was a high-tariff Democrat from Pennsylvania who treated young Congressman Cannon considerately. Cannon the red-beard was a free-trading farmer's man when he entered the House, but Randall won him to protection.)

"Planting himself on the law made for the House by Mr. Speaker Randall, appealing from the passions of this day to the just reasons of that day, the chair sustains the point of order and holds that the resolution is not in order."

Norris and two standpatters leaped to their feet. "I appeal from the decision," called Norris. At the same instant Dalzell moved that the Norris resolution be laid on the table (the equivalent of final burial). Above the voices of the two rang the words of another Cannonite, Joseph H. Gaines of West Virginia, calling for adjournment. The House roared down Gaines' motion, and it defeated Dalzell 182 to 164.

At last Norris and Cannon, the two champions, faced one another for the show-down. The history of four years hung heavy over every man in the chamber. The good humor and the courage of the Speaker still shone. But nothing could obliterate the bitter memories of Littauer and his gloves, the packed conference committee on the tariff, the dishonorable upward revision, the effrontery at Elgin, the repulse of modern ideas by the resolutions committee at Chicago, the rebuffs to the conservationists, the repression of temperance legislation, and the stony blocking of Gompers. What progressive could forget the galling humiliation visited repeatedly on their supporters? The House was not merely voting on the rules. It was about to pass judgment on an epoch.

The judgment it passed was that Cannon's opinions were outworn and that Cannon had forced his opinions on the country by repugnant methods. On the question whether the House would accept the decision of the chair respecting Norris' resolution, the members voted "nay" by 182 to 163. Norris thereupon removed from his resolution its clumsy device for the appointment of the members of the Rules Committee and amended it to provide simply for a Rules Committee of ten members, elected by the House, the Speaker not to be a member. The resolution passed. No Fitzgerald on the Democratic side helped Cannon now. Forty-two Republicans (including Gussie Gardner) joined one hundred and forty-nine Democrats in upholding Norris. Speakers had been chairmen of the Rules Committee since 1858. The tradition was ended. Cannon, the most powerful of all the Speakers, now had less formal power than any predecessor in forty years.

He retained enough power in his personality, however, to throw the House into confusion by daring the members to supplement their attack on the rules with an attack on him. Having announced the results of the roll calls that symbolized the revolution, the Old Man, deserted by friends on whom he had counted, repudiated by party colleagues, but steady of voice and arm, discomforted the rebels by saying:

Actions, not words, determine the conduct and sincerity of man in the affairs of life. This is a government by the people acting through the representatives of a majority of the people. . . .

The Speaker cannot be unmindful of the fact, as evidenced by three previous elections to the Speakership, that in the past he has enjoyed the confidence of the Republican Party of the country and the Republican members of the House, but the assault upon the Speaker of the House by the minority, supported by the efforts of the so-called insurgents, shows that the Democratic minority, aided by a number of so-called insurgents, is now in the majority, and that the Speaker of the House is not in harmony with the actual majority of the House, as evidenced by the vote just taken.

There are two courses open for the Speaker to pursue—one is to resign and permit the new combination of Democrats and insurgents to choose a Speaker in harmony with its aims and purposes. The other is for that combination to declare a vacancy in the office of Speaker and proceed to the election of a new Speaker. . . .

The Speaker, being in harmony with Republican policies and desirous of carrying them out, declines by his own motion to precipitate a contest upon the House in the election of a new Speaker, a contest that might greatly endanger the final passage of all legislation necessary to redeem Republican pledges and fulfill Republican promises.

This is one reason why the Speaker does not resign at once. And another reason is this: In the judgment of the present Speaker, a resignation is in and of itself a confession of weakness or mistakes or an apology for past actions. The Speaker is not conscious of having done anything wrong. . . .

The Speaker does believe and always has believed that this is a government through parties, and that parties can act only through majorities. . . . The Speaker has always said that under the Constitution, it is a question of the highest privilege for an actual majority at any time to choose a new Speaker, . . . and under existing conditions would welcome such action upon the part of the actual majority of the House, so that power and responsibility may rest with the Democratic and insurgent members who by the last vote evidently constitute a majority of this House. The Chair is now ready to entertain such a motion.

The unexpected declaration of the Speaker's testament of faith in himself and in party government brought hysterical applause, even from Democrats like Clark. Middle-aged men ran to the well of the House in front of the Speaker's desk and shouted to gain Cannon's attention. Above the rest Cannon caught the voice of Norris moving for adjournment, to prevent the Speaker from forcing the House to make a judgment on his person. Burleson was crying over and over, "I offer the following resolution." Suspecting Burleson's purpose, Democratic Representative Swagar Sherley of Kentucky, screamed, "I move that the House do now adjourn." "I demand the reading of my resolution," shouted Burleson, and from his seat Loudenslager, relishing the disorder in the ranks of the victors, hollered sardonically, "We have *no* rules now."

The faithful Tawney entered the fray on behalf of Cannon. "The gentleman from Texas [Burleson] has been recognized," he said. "My motion is privileged," said Sherley. The Speaker instructed the clerk to read Burleson's resolution:

Resolved, that the office of Speaker of the House of Representatives is hereby declared to be vacant, and the House of Representatives shall at once proceed to the election of a Speaker.

"The only motion before the House is the motion to adjourn," said Sherley. Like Clark, he realized that the continuation of Cannon in the chair would provide the voters with a constant reminder of Republican high-handedness that might provoke them to give the Democratic Party the control of Congress in the elections of 1910 and control of the presidency in the elections of 1912. But not many members were looking ahead with Sherley and Clark. Some wanted the Speaker ousted; others wanted to give him his chance for vindication as a human being. His bold dare to his opponents filled the members once more with that old admiration on which he had erected his despotism in the first place. Seven progressive insurgents understood the danger to their cause in leaving Cannon in the chair, and voted with Burleson and the Democrats who followed him. They were Murdock, Nelson, Hal Cooper, Gronna, Lenroot, Lindbergh, and Poindexter. The majority of the members defeated Burleson's resolution to remove Cannon from the Chair.

The House adjourned on Saturday, March 19, at 5:30 P.M., and Cannon returned to his house on Vermont Avenue for the first time since he had left it after breakfast on Thursday. He was a different man. He was Speaker, and he still had authority to name every committee but the Rules Committee. Yet now that he had been successfully defied, men would no longer take his word for a command. Henceforth he could speak only for himself and not for others. He lost his influence with the committees. Taft need no longer fear him or truckle to him. The Lucifers' right to their places in the Republican heaven was challenged no more. The events of the three days should give us confidence in our institutions. Representative government had proved its competence to act, and without resort to violence or meanness the legislators had freed the House, the President, the party, and the country from the control of a despot.

The Heritage

JOSEPH GURNEY CANNON has long since crossed over, but he is with us yet. Today government, having become the arbiter of society and the regulator of the contest between poor people and people of property, follows the course and exercises powers which the American began to thrust upon it almost forty years ago in the great reaction from the conservatism which Cannon tried to preserve. Presidents of an era long after Cannon's, Franklin D. Roosevelt and Harry S. Truman, may appear responsible for the deep intrusion of government into private lives. But they shaped their policies in moulds forged in the heat of the struggle over Cannonism, during which progressive leaders gave its modern form to the idea that the American nation as a whole, expressing itself through the federal government, is responsible for the well-being of all the separate members of the nation.

The role of Cannon was to quicken the pace and broaden the scope of the process of enlarging the government's powers by forcing upon the American voters the issue of the nature of American government as relentlessly as the southern secessionists had forced upon them the issue of the nature of the American union. It was the southerners, the pro-slavery element, and not the abolitionists who precipitated the conflict that eliminated slavery; likewise it was the conservatives, not the changers, who brought on the struggle that led to the abandonment of nineteenth century conservatism. By inciting the progressives to oppose him as a person, Cannon at the same time prodded them to explore carefully, describe, and praise the areas where Cannon had forbidden them to go.

As a stimulant to political thought Cannon has seldom had a peer. His tariff policy in 1909 provided Theodore Roosevelt with the reason or the excuse for his return to political activity, which he had abandoned upon turning the presidency over to Taft, and the return led to Roosevelt's campaigning on a platform of progressivism very closely allied, at least in its phraseology, with what in these days is commonly called liberalism. To give Taft a free rein, Roosevelt, after the inauguration of his successor, had betaken himself to Africa for hunting. There from letters he learned about Cannon's conquest of the President and about the President's widening of the breach between the progressive and conservative factions of the party. "Is President Taft leader or follower in his party?" *Success Magazine* asked its readers, and from all the answer came, "Follower."

Although Roosevelt's correspondents suggested that he should continue to chase lions until after the elections of 1910, he wrote in a sarcastic letter to Editor Abbott of the *Outlook* a cryptic message in January 1910 indicating that he was coming home to take a hand in the campaigns preceding those elections. "As much as I should hate for the White House to see Cannon, Tawney, et al. defeated," he said, "I fear I will be unable to delay my return on that account." Aldrich attracted him, but Cannon, whom he had urged Taft not to cross, he described after the tariff fight as a "strong, hard, narrow old Boeotian," who had "a much greater personal following [than Aldrich] but . . . excites even more hostility." Once back in America in early summer 1910, Roosevelt, in dramatizing the gulf between himself and the Cannon-haunted Taft, mingled with the progressives, publicly requested the election of progressives to Congress, and enunciated progressives' ideas. The leading student of Roosevelt's progressivism, George E. Mowry, concludes that the former President was inspired in 1910 more by determination to mend the split in the party, which portended loss of control of the presidency and of Congress, than by the leaders' emphasis on conservatism itself. Whereas two years earlier Roosevelt refrained from attacking Cannon out of fear that he would thereby break up the party, now to attack Cannon seemed the only way to hold the party together. Roosevelt's scheme for removing the wedge which Cannon had driven between the factions with his talk of Lucifers was to deliver the party to the progressives.

But neither the progressive nor the conservative faction was strong enough to swallow the other. It grew apparent to Cannon's followers that continuation of the party battle would perpetuate the division and disgust the voters with Republicans. Cannon spoke his mind indiscreetly. "When I cross over," he said on the floor of the House in June 1910, "I would rather go keeping my self-respect than have the plaudits of all the uplifters and all the press that thunders for a purpose from false pretenses." Such frankness agitated the conservatives even more violently than in 1909. Even Sherman asked Cannon in July to say no more, but instead he went to Kansas to assault the progressives with speeches on their home grounds. By each word and action the Speaker drove the progressives further along the path toward novelty. They could not halt their ideological advance as long as Cannon goaded them. Tawney grew alarmed. When the new Congressional election campaign was beginning in August, he wrote to Mc-Kinley that the progressive newspapers and candidates for elective office realized that the "success of insurgency depends primarily on keeping Cannonism before the people as an issue in this campaign." Tawney recommended that Cannon soft-pedal any interest which he might have in election to the Speakership of the House that was to be chosen in 1910. From other parts of the country standpat candidates for Congress beseeched him in letters for permission to tell their constituents that he would refuse to be Speaker again; otherwise "Cannonism" would defeat them. Nick Longworth, Roosevelt's son-in-law, joined the pell-mell retreat from Cannon and announced that he would try to persuade the Republican caucus not to re-elect him Speaker.

Cannon's abandonment by conservatives and progressives alike only made him more stubborn. "The question arises whether or not a course is open to you that will be beneficial to the party as well as to yourself," Representative Denby wrote to him from Detroit in October. "I think it would be better for you and better for the party if you should announce that, for whatever reason you choose to give, you do not care to be a candidate for Speaker again, . . . I am afraid there are districts in which your earnest friends are suffering loss of strength, and may suffer defeat, because of their friendship for you." Cannon replied:

Many times during the last session of Congress I should have been very glad to be on the floor of the House addressing, "Mr. Speaker," rather than be in the Speaker's chair, where necessarily I was prevented from defending myself and the party as I should have been glad to do. I could not resign, for that would have brought chaos; but I sincerely hoped when Representative Burleson offered his resolution declaring a vacancy in the Speakership that it would be agreed to. Then the responsibility would have been upon the majority that declared the vacancy, and, in my opinion, the political situation would be better than it is now. . . . God hates a coward, and for one I will not play that part. I will at least, come what may, retain my own self-respect, for I must associate with myself during the remainder of my life.

A few days after Cannon explained himself to Denby, Roosevelt spoke briefly in Danville from the rear platform of a train and omitted mention of Cannon. "There is something that is even more important than political differences," he said in an oblique reference to the Chicago tariff plank of 1908 and the tariff of 1909, "and that is the question of absolute honesty in public life." The more bilious he grew over Cannon, the more original became his political science. "The man who wrongly holds that every human right is secondary to his profit must now give way to the advocate of human *welfare*, who rightly maintains that every man holds his property subject to the general right of the community to regulate its use to whatever degree the public welfare may require it," said Roosevelt in Osawatomie, Kansas. That thesis is the foundation for the going concern known as the "welfare state."

The campaigning of Roosevelt, however, did not save the Republicans from the consequences of reaction against Cannon's influence in the party. The elections proved that Champ Clark had been sound in anticipating Republican defeat at the polls if Cannon could be kept in his prominent office. The insurgents paid dearly for not turning Uncle Joe out of the chair. The Democrats won control of the House (with the help of the votes of some conservative men of property who voted against Republican candidates because progressive Republican doctrine repelled them). The Republicans carried the Senate, but the election of eleven progressive Republicans (including LaFollette for his second term) gave them the opportunity to create an anti-standpat majority whenever they wanted to vote in league with the Democrats. Tawney fell in Winona. The loss of the House to the Democrats meant that Cannon would not be elected Speaker again, but his own constituents gave him a vote of confidence. "If you want tariff for revenue only," he told them, "don't vote for me. If you want someone to continue tariff agitation in Congress, don't vote for me." They re-elected him by a larger plurality than he had received in 1908.

Soon afterwards a dark fate overtook heroes and villains alike, as the Republican temple, its pillars weakened by Cannon, fell crashing about their heads. Many completed the disaster which Cannon had begun. Instead of unifying his party, Roosevelt cleaved it anew by dividing the progressives in two after the progressives had been split away from the conservatives. LaFollette wanted to run for the presidency in 1912 as the Republican nominee on the progressive platform which the Chicago convention had hooted down in 1912, and Roosevelt wanted to run for the same prize on a less radical but still progressive platform. In that mélange of ambition and jealousy, the conservative Republicans, who kept possession of the party machinery, nominated Taft; and Roosevelt became the candidate of the new Progressive Party. LaFollette, once more thrust into solitude, left alone by conservatives and progressives, too, supported a newcomer in the drama of government, Woodrow Wilson, the Democratic rival of Taft and Roosevelt. A conservative historian, Wilson had caught the discontented temper of the times in 1911, when, as governor of New Jersey, he used the authority of the state government to restrict the influence of property-holders over public and private economy. He campaigned for the presidency in 1912 with progressive arguments for the extension of federal power in order to cope with national economic and social problems. He neither went so far toward novelty as LaFollette nor stated his case with such exhilaration as Roosevelt. But the incubus of Cannon, hopelessly severing the Republicans, and the unabated momentum of progressivism carried him into the presidency in 1913. Roosevelt previously had sought election to three offices and won them all (Governor of New York, Vice President of the United States, and President of the United States); but the voters crushed him and Taft and Cannon, whose constituents chose another for the first time since 1890. Champ Clark attributed the Democratic victory to his party's shrewd exploitation of Cannonism. "Our revolution [through the Norris resolution] gave the Democrats the election of 1910, and then the House, Senate and presidency in 1912," he wrote in his memoirs.

The breaking of the conservative dam by Wilson's election flooded the country with the reform legislation which Cannon had used his powers to hold back. The income tax amendment became part of the Constitution a week before Taft completed his presidential term. The amendment made possible the modern expansion of the authority of the federal government, because federal power rests on federal funds. Wilson's Federal Reserve Act inaugurated the central control over banking and currency against which Cannon had fought through Vreeland. Postal savings were authorized by law. Congress revised the tariff downward in the Underwood Act, and the permanent tariff commission became a fact. Wilson's Federal Trade Commission Act established the federal government as the mentor of business ethics and gave it the authority to publicize tendencies toward monopoly in business. The temperance crusaders persuaded Congress to forbid the sale of alcoholic beverages anywhere in the United States. In ensuing years Congress imposed the literacy test on immigrants, and designated the Appalachian and White Mountain reserves as national forests. Wilson's Clayton Act, buttressing the application of the anti-trust laws to industry, slightly improved the standing of labor unions in their appearances before judges in injunction proceedings. But it was a meager boon that Gompers received from Wilson. Labor was the last faction in American society which benefited noticeably from the new conception of government. Except in Wisconsin the control of the reform movement that swept Cannon aside belonged to men who intended to save capitalism by benefiting the owners of capital. Norris successfully sponsored a bill in 1930 that at last freed the unions from the restraints of injunction, but more than twenty years passed after Wilson's inauguration before the federal government, under the aegis of another Democratic President, Franklin Roosevelt, carrying forward the concepts of progress developed between 1910 and 1913, became the protector of the labor unions.

Is Cannon to be praised or censured for his long-continued effort to hold back the waters that, when released, water-logged the notion of human inequality which imaginative political scientists once had drawn from the writings of Darwin? The elevation of government has not brought unalloyed blessings. It has given us physical security in the present, but it has made us insecure of mind about the future. Application of Theodore Roosevelt's speech at Osawatomie enables people whose counterparts in 1910 lived in misery to enjoy many material comforts today. An American corporal receives the pay of a Hungarian general. Cadillacs are as common as polished walking sticks were half a century ago. We inhabit the real paradise of the proletariat, and business thrives, too. However, the optimism that brightened Cannon's view of the world is dying. When Edward Bellamy seventy-five years ago examined the future in *Looking Backward,* he foresaw continuous betterment and progress in mortal existence. When George Orwell recently examined the future in *Nineteen Eighty-Four,* he foresaw disaster. Each book sold well because it reflected accurately its particular time. Bellamy and Orwell both described regimented civilizations; Bellamy, who had never seen regimentation, praised it, while Orwell, who had barely tasted it, predicted an existence of nausea.

The struggle over the question whether the government ought to have some authority over private lives has given way to an oppressive world-wide controversy to determine whether there is a boundary beyond which the powers of government shall not extend. Nobody can predict whether the survival of our tradition of representative self-government, which long since recovered from the strain of Cannonism, will enable Americans to fix the point where the authority of government and the freedom of individuals reach their nicest balance; or whether we are traveling in comfort to some rude, Soviet-like destination. The controversy has become world-wide, and it obscures the future because it is punctuated by war. Cannon thought that the trend toward great

government actually promoted war. He blamed German socialism [socialism being his generic word for our kind of statism] for
World War I. "All this modern, militant international socialism,
under various names, should bear the familiar trade mark, 'Made
in Germany,'" he wrote in 1919. ". . . . I suspect that the most
destructive propaganda of Germany began years ago when she
sent out to the world this idea of international socialism, which
should unite the workingmen of all countries to direct and control all governments in opposition to 'capitalism as the controlling
factor in fomenting war.'"

Cannon's mistrust of government never faded. He believed to
his death that his course from 1906 to 1910 was correct. While he
lived, the country seemed to bear him out. His constituents returned him to the House in 1914. There he remained, a cheerful
and conscientious member of the Appropriations Committee, until he retired in 1922, at the age of eighty-six, fifty years after the
corn farmers of eastern Illinois first sent him to Congress. As a
simple member of the House, he never bored his colleagues with
boasting tales about his days of glory. "A hundred years from
now," he remarked in House debate, "they will say, 'It does appear
that there was a man from Illinois by the name of Cannon, but I
don't know much about him. There was another man by the name
of Cannon in Congress from Utah, and it was said he had seventeen wives.'"

His villainy faded from public memory, although his colleagues
in Congress refused in 1919 to elect Jim Mann to the Speakership
because he had been the right-hand man of the tyrant from Illinois.
The chair, however, had become a trapping of honor, not a source
of power, as soon as Cannon left it. The House not only removed
the Speaker from the Committee on Rules but also took from him
the privilege of appointing the members of the other Committees.
The friendly quality that Cannon had abused in the chair was
shining forth anew at the time of Mann's disappointment, and
tourists urged their guides at the Capitol and in Danville to give
them a peek at the Old Man. Once more he became a national
character, famous not for despotism but for humor and good-nature
and for his incisive rejection of cant and frumpery.

Not only he but his opinions returned to fashion. Roosevelt and most of the flamboyant moralizers who quit the Republican Party in favor of progressivism in 1912 joined the party again and blessed the standpattism which they had condemned. The Republicans have represented conservatism ever since. The Scandinavians who had stirred the discontent along the Mississippi grew contented, and the other well-springs of radicalism dried up in most of the valley states. Cannon and Norris and LaFollette alone of all the leading characters who have moved through this book stayed to the death utterly true to their own conceptions, without fakery or wavering. LaFollette offered his radicalism to the public as a basis for government when he ran for the presidency as the candidate of a new party in 1924. Cannon remained the antithesis of LaFollette. He rejoiced when the country in 1920 elected Warren G. Harding to the presidency in an Indian Summer resurgence of standpattism, under the label of "normalcy." Fordney wrote a new high-protection tariff bill. Even the Democrats gave up progressivism and turned back in the general direction of John Sharp Williams when they nominated John W. Davis for the presidency in 1924. In the same year the voters elected a good businessman's Republican, Calvin Coolidge, to the White House and rebuffed LaFollette's new appeals for reform. The politician's nineteenth century was coming back for Cannon.

Thus his spirit was comforted in his last years. Once more the U.S.A. was a "hell of a success." The riches that abounded in the country appeared to mean that a new golden age of prosperity had come to stay and that business had forever replaced government as the umpire of society. In 1926, well before later events could destroy those pleasing illusions and bring on America's final rejection of the opinions around which he had built his life as friend and despot, Cannon died in the house on Vermilion Street with his self-respect intact and with an extraordinary number of friends to mourn him.

Bibliography

The unpublished and official materials read in connection with the writing of this book include the papers of John Joseph Gurney Cannon, Illinois State Historical Library, Springfield, Illinois; the papers of James Schoolcraft Sherman, Public Library, New York City; the papers of Theodore Roosevelt, Library of Congress, Washington, D.C.; the papers of William Howard Taft, Library of Congress; the scrapbooks of James R. Mann, Library of Congress; *Congressional Record, Congressional Directory, Rules of the House of Representatives, Hind's Precedents of the House of Representatives.*

The indispensable newspapers are the Boston *Transcript;* Chicago *Inter-Ocean, News, Post, Record-Herald, Tribune;* Cincinnati *Enquirer;* Danville *Commercial-News, Democrat, Morning Press;* Denver *Post, Rocky Mountain News;* Des Moines *Register, Capital;* Kansas City *Star;* Milwaukee *Sentinel, Journal;* New York *Evening Post, Herald, Staats-Zeitung, Times, Tribune, World;* Omaha *Evening Bee, World-Herald;* Philadelphia *North American;* St. Louis *Globe-Democrat, Republic;* St. Paul *Dispatch, Pioneer Press;* Spokane *Spokesman-Review;* Springfield, Illinois, *State Register;* Topeka *State Journal;* Washington, D.C., *Post, Star, Times.*

The magazines and periodical journals include *American Journal of Sociology* 1907; *American Magazine* 1911 and 1912; *Annals of the American Academy of Political and Social Science* 1907 and 1908; *Arena,* 1899, 1906, 1907, and 1908; *Central Christian Advocate* 1908; *Century* 1902, 1903, and 1909; *Collier's Weekly* 1908, 1909, 1910, and 1926; *Cosmopolitan* 1910 and 1912; *Current Literature* 1900, 1906, and 1908; *Educational Review* 1905; *Engineering Magazine* 1907; *Everybody's* 1910; *Forum* 1897 and 1909; *Harper's Monthly Magazine* 1907; *Harper's*

234

Weekly 1903, 1908, and 1909; *Hearst's* 1912; *Independent* 1901 and 1908; *Journal of Political Economy* 1908, 1909, and 1910; *LaFollette's Weekly* 1909 and 1910; *Leslie's Weekly* 1903 and 1904; *Nation* 1906 and 1909; *North American Review* 1889, 1897, 1898, 1906, 1908, and 1909; *Northwestern Christian Advocate* 1908 and 1910; *Outlook* 1908; *Review of Reviews* 1909; *Saturday Evening Post* 1912 and 1919; *Success* 1909 and 1910; *Westminster Review* 1908; *World Today* 1906 and 1909; *World's Work* 1909 and 1911.

Among the books read are:

Abbott, Edith, *Select Documents and Case Records*. Chicago, University of Chicago Press, 1924.

Abbott, Grace, *The Immigrant and Coal Mining Counties of Illinois*. Springfield, Illinois, Immigrants Commission, 1920.

Alexander, De Alva Stanwood, *History and Procedure of the House of Representatives*. Boston, Houghton Mifflin, 1903.

Anti-Saloon League of America, *Anti-Saloon League Yearbook 1908*. Columbus, Ohio, 1908.

Barton, Albert O., *LaFollette's Winning of Wisconsin*. Madison, 1922.

Bateman, Newton, *Historical Encyclopedia of Illinois*, Vol. I. Chicago, Munsell, 1933.

Beckwith, H. W., *History of Vermilion County*. Chicago, H. H. Hill, 1879.

Bell, John T., *Omaha and Omaha Men*. Omaha, 1917.

Briggs, John Ely, *William Peters Hepburn*. Iowa City, Iowa, State Historical Society of Iowa, 1919.

Burford, Cary Clive, and Guy McIlvaine Smith, *The History and Romance of Danville Junction*. Danville, Interstate Printers and Publishers, 1942.

Busbey, Lincoln White, *Uncle Joe Cannon; The Story of a Pioneer American*. New York, Henry Holt, 1927.

Butt, Archibald Willingham, *Taft and Roosevelt: The Intimate Letters of Archie Butt*. New York, Doubleday, 1930.

Carnegie, Andrew, speech on immigration at annual dinner of St. Andrew's Society, New York, November 30, 1891, in *Modern Eloquence*, Vol. I. New York, Collier, 1941.

Chapman Brothers, *Portrait and Biographical Album of Vermilion County, Illinois*. Chicago, 1889.

Church, Charles A., *History of the Republican Party in Illinois*. Rockford, Wilson Brothers, 1912.

Clark, Champ, *My Quarter Century of American Politics*. New York, Harper, 1920.

Cox, James M., *Journey through My Years*. New York, Simon and Schuster, 1946.

Cullom, Shelby M., *Fifty Years of Public Service*. Chicago, McClurg, 1911.

DeWitt, Benjamin Parke, *The Progressive Movement*. New York, Macmillan, 1915.

Doan, Edward Newell, *The LaFollettes and the Wisconsin Idea*. New York, Rinehart, 1947.

Dunn, Arthur Wallace, *From Harrison to Harding*. New York, Putnam's, 1922.

——, *Gridiron Nights*. New York, Stokes, 1915.

Earlham College, *The Earlham Pageant*. Richmond, Indiana, 1937.

Emery, Edwin, *History of the American Newspaper Publishers Association*. Minneapolis, University of Minnesota Press, 1950.

Flom, George T., *Scandinavian Immigration to Iowa*. Iowa City, Iowa, State Historical Society of Iowa, 1906.

Ford, Worthington Chauncy, *Letters of Henry Adams 1892–1918*. Boston, Houghton Mifflin, 1938.

Gardner, Constance, *Letters of Augustus Peabody Gardner*. Boston, Houghton Mifflin, 1920.

Gloversville, New York, Littauer Day Organization, *Littauer Day*. Gloversville, 1927.

Goldman, Eric F., *Charles J. Bonaparte: Patrician Reformer*. Baltimore, Johns Hopkins University, 1943.

Gompers, Samuel, *Seventy Years of Life and Labor*. New York, Dutton, 1925.

Guilford College Trustees, *Guilford: A Quaker College*. Greensboro, North Carolina, Joseph J. Stone, 1937.

Hall, Prescott F., *Immigration*. New York, Henry Holt, 1906.

Hapgood, Norman, *Changing Years*. New York, Farrar and Rinehart, 1930.

Havighurst, Walter, *Upper Mississippi: A Wilderness Saga*. New York, Farrar and Rinehart, 1937.

Haynes, George Henry, *The Senate of the United States*. Boston, Houghton Mifflin, 1938.

Hechler, Kenneth, *Insurgency: Personalities and Politics of the Taft Era*. New York, Columbia University Press, 1940.

Hourwich, Isaac Aaronovich, *Immigration and Labor*. New York, B. W. Huebsch, 1922.

Howe, M. A. De Wolfe, *George von L. Meyer: His Life and Public Services*. New York, Dodd, Mead, 1920.

Jenks, Jeremiah W., and Lauck, W. Jett, *The Immigration Problem*, 5th ed., New York, Funk and Wagnalls, 1922.

Jessup, Philip Caryl, *Elihu Root*. New York, Dodd, Mead, 1938.

Jones, Lottie E., *History of Vermilion County, Illinois*. Chicago, Pioneer, 1911.

Kinsley, Philip, *The Chicago Tribune, Its First 100 Years*. Chicago, 1945.

Kohlsaat, Herman H., *From McKinley to Harding*. New York, Scribner's, 1923.

LaFollette, Robert M., *Autobiography*. Madison, 1913.

Lief, Alfred, *Democracy's Norris: The Biography of a Lonely Crusader*. New York, Stackpole, 1939.

Lodge, Henry Cabot, and Theodore Roosevelt, *Selections from the Correspondence*. New York, Scribner's, 1925.

Longworth, Alice Roosevelt, *Crowded Hours*. New York, Scribner's, 1933.

Lusk, David W., *Eighty Years of Illinois Politics and Politicians*. Springfield, Illinois, 1889.

McCall, Samuel W., *The Business of Congress*. New York, Columbia University Press, 1911.

McCarthy, Charles, *The Wisconsin Idea*. New York, Macmillan, 1912.

McClure, S. S., *Autobiography*. New York, Stokes, 1914.

Moore, J. Hampton, *With Speaker Cannon through the Tropics*. Philadelphia, The Book Print, 1907.

Mowry, George, *Theodore Roosevelt and the Progressive Movement*. Madison, University of Wisconsin Press, 1946.

Munroe, James Phinney, *A Life of Francis Amasa Walker*. New York, Henry Holt, 1923.

Neuberger, Richard L., and Kahn, Stephen B., *Integrity: The Life of George W. Norris*. New York, Vanguard, 1937.

Norris, George W., *Fighting Liberal*. New York, Macmillan, 1945.

Odland, Martin Wendell, *The Life of Knute Nelson*. Minneapolis, Lund Press, 1926.

Ogg, Frederic Austin, *National Progress 1907–1917*. New York, Harper, 1918.

Olcott, Charles S., *The Life of William McKinley*. Boston, Houghton Mifflin, 1916.

Orcutt, William Dana, *Burrows of Michigan and the Republican Party*. New York, Longmans, Green, 1917.

Osborn, George Coleman, *John Sharp Williams: Planter-Statesman of the Deep South*. Baton Rouge, Louisiana State University Press, 1943.

Palmer, George Thomas, *A Conscientious Turncoat: The Story of John M. Palmer 1817–1900*. New Haven, Yale University Press, 1941.

Palmer, John M., *Bench and Bar of Illinois*. Chicago, Lewis Publishing Co., 1899.

Pinchot, Gifford, *Breaking New Ground*. New York, Harcourt Brace, 1947.

Plumb, R. G., *Badger Politics 1836–1930*. Manitowac, Brandt, 1930.

Pringle, Henry Fowles, *Life and Letters of William Howard Taft*. New York, Farrar and Rinehart, 1939.

Redfield, William C., *With Congress and Cabinet*. New York, Doubleday, Page, 1924.

Roosevelt, Theodore, *Autobiography*. New York, Macmillan, 1916.

———, *Gouverneur Morris*. Boston, Houghton Mifflin, 1898.

———, and Henry Cabot Lodge, *Selections from the Correspondence*. New York, Scribner's, 1925.

Russell, John Andrew, *Joseph Warren Fordney, An American Legislator*. Boston, Stratford, 1928.

Seligman, Edwin R. A., *The Currency Problem and the Present Financial Situation*. New York, Columbia University Press, 1908.

Sherman, John, *Recollections of Forty Years in the House, Senate, and Cabinet*. Chicago, Werner, 1896.

Smith, Theodore Clarke, *The Life and Letters of James Abram Garfield*. New Haven, Yale University Press, 1925.

Stealey, O. O., *Twenty Years in the Press Gallery*. New York, Publishers Printing Co., 1906.

Stephenson, Isaac, *Recollections of a Long Life*. Chicago, 1915.

Stephenson, Nathaniel Wright, *Nelson W. Aldrich: A Leader in American Politics*. New York, Scribner's, 1930.

Stirn, Ernest W., *Annotated Bibliography of Robert Marion La-Follette*. Chicago, University of Chicago Press, 1937.

Tarbell, Ida M., *The Nationalizing of Business*. New York, Macmillan, 1910.

———, *The Tariff in Our Times*, New York, Macmillan, 1911.

Upper Mississippi River Improvement Association, *The Permanent Improvement of the Upper Mississippi River*. Dubuque, 1905.

Van Hise, Charles Richard, *The Conservation of Natural Resources in the United States*. New York, Macmillan, 1910.

Virginia Agricultural and Mechanical Society, *Proceedings of the State Immigration Convention 1894*. Richmond, Whittet and Shepperson, 1895.

Watson, James E., *As I Knew Them*. Indianapolis, Bobbs Merrill, 1936.

White, William Allen, *Masks in a Pageant*. New York, Macmillan, 1928.

———, *The Old Order Changeth*. New York, Macmillan, 1910.

William, Charles Richard, *The Life of Rutherford Birchard Hayes*. Boston, Houghton Mifflin, 1914.

Index

239